Immigrants, Brokers, and Literacy as Affinity

Pittsburgh Series in Composition, Literacy, and Culture
Aja Martinez and Stacey Waite, Editors

Immigrants, Brokers, and Literacy as Affinity

Ligia A. Mihuț

University of Pittsburgh Press

Published by the University of Pittsburgh Press, Pittsburgh, Pa., 15260
Copyright © 2025, University of Pittsburgh Press
All rights reserved
Manufactured in the United States of America
Printed on acid-free paper
10 9 8 7 6 5 4 3 2 1

Cataloging-in-Publication data is available from the Library of Congress

Hardcover: 978-0-8229-4863-6
Paperback: 978-0-8229-6771-2

Cover art by Maksym Yemelyanov
Cover design by Melissa Dias-Mandoly

Publisher: University of Pittsburgh Press, 7500 Thomas Blvd., 4th floor, Pittsburgh, PA 15260, United States, www.upittpress.org
EU Authorized Representative: Easy Access System Europe, Mustamäe tee 50, 10621 Tallinn, Estonia, gpsr.requests@easproject.com

To Andreea, for her unwavering support and devoted friendship.
To my father, whose legacy of love and faith propelled me forward.

Contents

Acknowledgments

"The only thing I fear is that you will want to pursue a Ph.D. as well." That was my father's foresight as we said our goodbyes in 2004, twenty-one years ago, when I left Romania to pursue a M.A. degree at the University of Illinois at Urbana-Champaign. My father's predictions proved right. He offered both wisdom and unconditional love that stretched over oceans and countries until the day he passed in November of 2020. Coincidentally, the day he passed I received the great news that my article about literacy brokers' connections to political economies was going to be published in *College Composition and Communication*. A celebratory success on the day when a piece of my heart died. Our last exchange while his lungs were ravaged ruthlessly by COVID-19 was filled with thick emotions knowing that we may never see each other again. Those emotions froze me for the next two years as I processed my father's impact on my life. As a pastor for more than forty years, his influence in deeds and words has been immense. His words of encouragement upon seeing me accomplish more than I initially set to do, his emotionality when he spoke about family and home or about us his children, built me up when I was crumbling and deepened my joy when I was celebrating. As I complete this project, I am grateful for my father's faithful support throughout my life, for his legacy of impact that I hope to carry further. This book is a small step toward that legacy.

Acknowledgments

This project started in the streets of Chicago. As I was visiting friends, driving from place to place, some of the deepest conversation about the immigrant experience emerged. One dear friend trusted me with her life story. As she wrestled to unpack her own immigrant experience heavy with emotions, she became my broker into the Romanian immigrant community in Chicago. To this friend, Andreea Plămadă (now Herholz), I owe my deepest gratitude for her courage to voice her story and her support of this project from the beginning to its completion. Andreea has been my home in Chicago. Andreea introduced me to many key participants in this project. She attended the first conference, Writing Education Across Borders, where I presented my initial results on literacy shaped by the Romanian Communist regime at Penn State. She listened to many stories of my research journey. Supporting it directly or indirectly, from close proximity or from afar, she cared deeply about this project with me, and always sent her encouragement and prayers. I dedicate this book to her.

I am most grateful to all those immigrants whose stories are featured in this book. Your stories are the heartbeat of this project. Your stories kept it alive when the path towards publishing became obscure. Shared in restaurants or coffee shops, in homes around the dinner table or in professional settings, private businesses or religious establishments, these stories have moved the project forward. One of the first welcomes came from Steven Bonica, the owner of the *Romanian Tribune* where several events took place, including the Romanian Heritage Festival. My dear friends, Cristina and Cris Gros hosted me on many research trips to Chicago and offered a home to a broke graduate student in pursuit of her dream to feature these stories. Cristina, like Steven and Andreea, also used her own networks, including their own family, to connect me to others whose immigrant story eventually were included in this project.

I received incredible support from the academic community from the University of Illinois, from advisors, colleagues, and various grants and fellowships. Dr. Catherine Prendergast, my former advisor, guided me with professionalism in starting and shaping this project. Working with Cathy has also built confidence in me, which I needed as I further carried out this project without her direct mentorship in the next decade. Cathy's "So what" questions, our writing group, or her invaluable and consistent feedback helped me clarify murky ideas and refine arguments. Her sharp observations propelled me to become a better scholar of literacy. Other scholars like Drs. Anne Haas Dyson, Keith Hitchins, Rebecca Lorimer Leonard, and Kate Vieira—whose academic rigor, pedagogy, and ultimately, deep humanity I can only hope to attain—have also influenced this project at different times in the last decade. Numerous

Acknowledgments

fellow colleagues—Eileen Lagman, Yuki Kang, and Andrea Olinger—provided support through genuine friendship and often through sharing meals and refreshments, and later, through conference meetups. Other scholars from the History department at Illinois have been a wonderful resource. I am especially grateful for Dr. Diana Georgescu and her assistance with sources and guidance for navigating the Romanian Archives. From Diana, I learned about the amazing work of Eastern European scholars in the History department at Illinois and remained attuned to their scholarship. Additionally, the project has been awarded several grants or fellowships—University of Illinois Summer Fellowship in 2011 and University of Illinois "Cultures of Law in Global Contexts" in 2013–2014—and was generously supported by Barry University sabbatical leave in fall 2022.

I am incredibly appreciative of my editor, Joshua Shanholtzer from University of Pittsburgh Press for his faith and investment in this project; the two anonymous reviewers' sharp observations that made this manuscript stronger; and for the entire team from University of Pittsburgh Press and their labor in making this project a success.

My beloved family—Cristian Mihuț, Mihaela Micicoi, and Florin Micicoi, and Naomi Vlassa, and my mom—their love, grace, and prayers have been the wind in my sail. They listened, inquired, or learned with me about new ways of being in a different culture and life in academia. I got to share and celebrate the final stages of this book project with many others who have come along with me in this journey to the finish line. To you all, my deepest gratitude!

Soli Deo Gloria.

Immigrants, Brokers, and Literacy as Affinity

Introduction

From Warzone to Natural Disasters

In the summer of 2022, I was returning home to the US from a short visit to Eastern Europe. Four days before my flight, the airline had been sending notifications about the unexpected course of hurricane Ian and its potential impact on travel in the southern states of the US. I live in Florida and such messages no longer scare me. As I was carefully packing my carry-on in case I would be stranded for days away from home, I could not shake the thought that I was flying from a warzone (Romania/ Eastern Europe/ Ukraine-Russia war) to a disaster area (Hurricane Ian). Before I left the US, I had bought, among other things, potassium iodine tablets in case a nuclear attack was launched against Romania and other neighboring countries. Perhaps, such measures seem futile, but they may indicate a small amount of control we attempt to exert in a world that has made transnational movement a daring endeavor.

Transnational mobility in the last five years (2020–2025) experienced numerous, dramatic, and rapid changes due to wars, natural disasters, or epidemics. Some of these happened in the span of twenty-four hours.[1] The recent COVID-19 pandemic accelerated our sense of connectedness as we have become incredibly susceptible to health mandates or political and economic directives. Migrants, whether they are refugees, temporary workers, tourists, or immigrants seeking to arrive to a new homeland, are central actors in transnational mobility. Whenever (im)migrants become the center of public discourse, they are often depicted as either heroes or foes. The heroic narrative of the immigrant who left everything behind and pulled themselves up by their bootstraps is a well-known trope. From public figures to ordinary folks, this trope is as pervasive and convincing as its counterpart—the foe. The immigrant becomes vulnerable, particularly in times of political, economic, or societal crises—like the COVID-19 pandemic. It is not only the public sphere that perpetuates this dichotomy. My fieldwork in an immigrant community in the Midwest reveals a similar pattern. The first immigrant I met for my study in this community wanted to introduce me to people who made it: successful businessmen and women, doctors, professors, etc. I, on the other hand, sought to document the literate experience of the plumber, the cabinet maker, the cleaning lady, along with the accounts of outstanding success. These typological narratives of the immigrant experience, divided between success and failure, are not necessarily detrimental to the representation of the immigrant experience unless we neglect the range of different experiences and the diverse and complex lives of these immigrants. Remaining unidimensional, stereotypical depictions of immigrant narratives capture only *the economic* man, through either success or failure. This book aims to change that. While acknowledging the significance of political economies that shape the immigrant life, I account for the economic, political, *and* emotional work that configures the complex lives of immigrants. I use literacy brokers as an analytic to do this. In this ethnographic study of transnational literacies of Romanian immigrants, I show that as literacy brokers move across contexts, they accumulate knowledge, negotiate discourses, and create alliances (co-brokering) to help others with reading and writing. In doing so, these brokers serve more than instrumental ends; they perform literacy as affinity by brokering personal experiences and languages of nation-states and by participating in advocacy for the sake of others.

In the book *Philadelphia: An Open Door for You*, celebrating the fortieth anniversary of the Philadelphia Romanian Church in Niles, IL, Reverend George Galiş narrates fragments about his arrival in the US in the early 1970s. As he boarded on the last leg of his trip to Chicago, emotions ran wild, Galiş writes. He wondered whether anyone would wait for him at the airport, whether he would have a place to live, and what sort of interactions he would forge with the local community of faith. His anxieties were appeased as a group of ten people waited for him. One slender man, who Galiş did not know, approached him, and said, "You, Rev. Galiş, are coming to live with me until your family arrives" (Galiş 2013, 29). The same slender man introduced Galiş to the south side of Chicago and the division of neighborhoods: "From the Onciu family, I learned that we were in the South side of the city of Chicago and that neighborhoods were situated by nationalities as such: In the South, there are the Polish, Yugoslavian, Slovak, African-American, Mexican neighborhood[s]. In the North, there were Scots, Germans, French, Romanians, Hungarians, Italians, and a part of the Spanish" (Galiş 2013, 29–30).

Narratives like this make history. Personal stories—about leaving Romania and arriving in the US but also accounts detailing how the personal intersects certain institutions or social groups such as churches or ethnic communities—document experiences that transcend physical boundaries. From these immigrant narratives that circulate in ethnic communities, I focus on the "slender man," the one who approaches the newly arrived and mediates their process of becoming American. The "slender man" placates the fears of the unknown in a new country, walking with the new immigrant through the steps and aspects of the new life: housing, jobs, enrolling children in school, social security, and so on. Providing a generic map of ethnic neighborhoods, he is the trail guide concerning issues of ethnic divisions, hierarchical structures, and marginalization. Ultimately, the "slender man" functions as a broker— he negotiates boundaries between the old world and the new world, between personal and larger socio-economic and political structures such as immigration and governmental agencies, administrative offices, local communities, schools, and churches. My goal here is to examine how this brokering operates through language, text, and culture.

Deborah Brandt's work on literacy sponsorship and her deep awareness of economic realities has influenced my ethnographic work in the Romanian immigrant community in the Chicago area. Like Brandt, my work on individual literacy development in everyday life is a portal into larger economic systems as they have been discussed, challenged, and reconfigured by individual agents. However, unlike Brandt's work, my analysis shows that, in the economic exchange of information between the sponsor and the sponsored, there is a middle ground occupied by what I call broker and co-broker.

I present here an ethnographic study of transnational literacy histories of Romanian immigrants who immigrated to the US before and after 1989—the year that marks the official overturn of the Communist regime in Romania. Since these immigrants were educated for the most part during Nicolae Ceauşescu's political regime (1965–1989), I was interested in documenting the socio-economic and political conditions that shaped these immigrants' literacy education in their home country (Romania) and what aspects of those literacies they carried with them into the new country (the US). I embarked on this project with a broad question: How do people negotiate textual, cultural, and physical boundaries through literacy? As I progressed in my research and conversations with immigrants, my questions became more focused:

- Given these immigrants' history of censored literacy and a pedagogy focused on the collective rather than the individual, how does one create a space for oneself? How does the individual manage and maneuver larger institutions and to what end?
- As immigrants move, which aspects of literacy education move with them and become recontextualized in the new country? What are the new literate practices emerging in the country of destination and how do people learn to perform them?

The initial data analysis using grounded theory guided me to the middleman, the broker that helps other people with reading and writing in the process of immigration. Hence, subsequent data collection framed the research and the analysis with literacy brokers at the center of this inquiry on immigrant writing. My refined research was informed by these questions:

- Who are the literacy brokers in the context of immigration and what roles do they take?
- What forms of literacy mediation do these brokers perform and under what conditions—socio-economic and political?
- What implications can we derive from their emotional work and how does this impact our view of literacy in transnational contexts?

A focus on Eastern European (im)migrants allows for a few unique perspectives that complement the work of other scholars on immigrant writing.[2] First, due to the Cold War era and the formation of the Communist bloc as a conglomerate of countries that shared similar socialist agendas, political economies are central in the lives of (im)migrants from this region. Certainly, political economies are important in any circumstance, including our day-to-day moments, yet in critical situations like a pandemic, natural disasters, or war, they become incredibly powerful. Immigrant narratives offer a lens that makes political economies conspicuous, allowing our attention to be directed toward and shaped by the mundane and, by extension, our literate lives. Eastern European immigrants have often been treated as a conglomerate, even if each country from this region has its particularities. Romania, for instance, has become known as a Latin island in a Slavic sea, a common self-identification inspired by nineteenth century Romanian historians and linguistics in search of affirming the Romanian national identity (Boia 2001, 36). Romanians speak a Romance language and identify linguistically and culturally with the French, the Italians, the Spanish or the Portuguese. This cultural and linguistic affiliation with Romance languages and cultures becomes significant in the process of migration. It impacts their jobs, professional trajectories, and adaptation.

Second, Eastern European immigrants often are less visible in the US context. Many stories of refugees remain untold because at the time of their departure, Romania continued to be under a dictatorship until 1989. Making their stories known too soon would have posed a risk to their lives. On the other hand, the new immigrants, who came after 1989, also remained largely invisible because the majority were college educated and spoke English well. Many blended smoothly into mainstream America. While their stories remained hidden from public contexts, in other contexts, such as immigrant enclaves, around kitchen tables, or at cultural ethnic events, stories of "escape" have often delighted the ears of the listeners. As a Romanian ethnic, I often heard these stories whispered in small circles even before any research had begun. "How did you escape?" or "How did you cross the border?" Such questions generated many conversations. Such questions have influenced this research.

Finally, the Eastern European experience in the US also provides a window into other immigrant and minority groups' literate and linguistic experience. Due to their historical ties and geographical proximity, immigrants from the southern US border are more likely to be featured in the public or political discourse.[3] Recent immigrant policies to contain or manage immigrant waves are geared more towards immigrants from Mexico, Guatemala, Venezuela, Honduras, and El Salvador and less towards Eastern Europeans. Certainly, the recent war in Ukraine has slightly changed this trend, as it happens with other major global events, but the southern US border continues to be at the center of attention when it comes to immigration. Important to note is that often immigrants develop affiliations with other immigrant groups. As such, stories told by one immigrant group, especially one less visible, can provide insights into trends and problems in other groups and in immigration in general. Eastern European immigrants as a group become that middleman that sees and engages different perspectives. Certainly, immigrant literacy is my main focus. Throughout the book, I will show how Eastern European migrants and refugees use language and literacy bureaucratically and affectively to negotiate political economies across borders. In this process, I also account for how immigrants engage alternative economies that foreground collaborative actions, informal sites, and affinity as energizers for and within discursive formations. Immigrants' connection to political economies is not just engagement, but a transformative experience.

Writing's Impact on Economic Activity, Economic Frames

A quick look at the history of writing shows its strong connection to economic activity. Graham Smart elaborates on how writing has contributed to the flourishing of economic activity, leading not only to the diversification of genres/ types of texts but also to innovation across geographical areas.[4] In seventh century China, documents paved the way for a legal system that would record "commercial disputes" of the Silk Road trade. The innovation of papermaking and printing in the eleventh century helped develop paper currency, thereby connecting the state to business and trade.[5] While writing has helped the expansion of economic activity, this influence has been reciprocal.[6] Smart (2008) explains this through references to new forms of writing that emerged as more complex economies developed through the increased monopoly of the state (e.g., lists, contracts, bookkeeping records and more). On the other hand, in the larger network of economic activity, writing supported information storage and textual mobility. These two processes have thus facilitated the move from simple genres, such as bookkeeping, to more complex genres. Smart (2008) connects the development of new genres to the expansion of international financial markets, the establishment of financial institutions, and new technologies: "New literate practices and textual forms have played an essential role in the development and organization of these financial markets and institutions, which have spawned—and relied on—a vast web of spreadsheets, shareholder newsletters, and myriad other texts" (105). With the help of new technologies—the telegraph, the typewriter, and of course, currently the computer and the internet—writing has sustained thriving capitalist economies and, in turn, these economic developments have contributed to new writing functions, genres, and mobilities.

Taking a step further in analyzing connections between writing and the economy, I build on Smart's critique of political economies to show why it is necessary that we learn from how immigrants have used and reframed economic systems through writing. In this process, we begin to understand how economic activity is linked to knowledge-making, the written word, and alternative economic frames where brokers operate. One of Smart's critiques of economic developments refers to the Keynesian perspective (see Maynard Keynes's *The General Theory of Employment Interest and Money*) and neoclassical discourse in economics and the process of mechanization. Essentially, the critique concerns the fact that economic systems have grown to be overly rational or machine-like rather than a "living organism." Another critique comes from feminist economists, Marianne Ferber and Julie Nelson, for the neglect of poverty and gender as well as disregard of economic activity in the homes. A final critique is directed at global market analysts' skewed policies that protect the developed countries rather than those at the margins of economic activity. All these points of critique—the mechanical over humanistic; neglect of homes and the private sphere as sites of economic activity; and unchecked inequality—shape the economic frame that I propose through the lens of literacy brokers in the context of immigration.

First, the mechanization of economic exchange and writing leads to valuing the rational over personal and emotional discourse. In the context of immigration, rational discourse objectifies personal experience, but brokers compensate for that through emotional work. Literacy brokers reveal that immigrant writing is imbued with personal and affective discourses and networks that help sustain immigrant mobility from one context to another. Second, a neglect of economic activity in the home or domestic spaces is problematic. The economies of writing that I propose in this book will account for this oversight. In chapter 3 and in several other instances, I show how brokers operate in informal sites, away from the official purview of formal institutions. Finally, attention to brokers and political economies will also address inequality in the global mobility of people. Brokers, by definition, are the middleman and intervene to offset inequal power dynamics and, whenever possible, give voice to marginalized people whose experience is censored, silenced, or managed.

Rather than create a stereotypical narrative of the immigrant as vulnerable to neoliberal economies, in this book I show a different account. In addition to the mediation work explained earlier, I also foreground the agency and collaboration that immigrants summon as they engage overpowering economic forces. This agency is captured in the concept of co-brokering as a non-capitalist project, informed by the postcapitalist geographers J. K. Gibson-Graham's notion of diverse economies. Against profit-driven globalism that configures most human activity by market principles (Scott 2016b), Gibson-Graham argue that we need diverse economic frames and with these, new discourses that account for alternative economic activities and subjectivities, ones that have the potential to disrupt, alter, or possibly complement capitalist projects. Expanding on the concept of brokering, co-brokering, conceptualized as the act of mediating texts collectively or with others, is fundamental in the formation of new subjectivities when bureaucracies and standardization erase personal agency. Co-brokering is thus marked by collective action, informal exchanges, and strategies of translating bureaucratic protocols into manageable bits of information through which one can develop a new economic framework and diverse economic discourses.

In doing so, co-brokering not only critiques capitalistic frames, but also helps individuals use bureaucratic literacy to accomplish their goals.

Literacy Brokers and Immigrant Communities

I concentrate on the literacy broker's emotional work in the process of mediating linguistic, cultural, and institutional boundaries. As other scholars have noted (Ahmed 2004; Jacobs and Micciche 2003), emotion comes from the Latin word, *emovere*, which means "to move out, to stir." More importantly, to study emotion in the context of immigration—which implies physical mobility of people, a process of leaving a place and arriving to a new location—entails a study of mobility on multiple levels: social, economic, affective, and certainly, textual and literate. When immigrants travel, their literate repertoire and communicative practices accompany their passage across multiple contexts. They must repurpose their language and literacy inventory and adapt it to new contexts; they also need to compensate for the dispossession that comes with such movement. Loss in the context of literacy includes partially missing one's language, familiar audiences, and a social-cultural context that affords a space for meaning, belonging, and situated knowledge. In this transnational movement, then, the emotional work of literacy brokers intervenes precisely in this gap. Drawing on Sara Ahmed's (2004) work, I approach emotions as an expression of both individual and collective experiences. As such, I envision the emotion work of literacy brokers mobilizing personal stories, language of empathy—which Ann Jurecic (2011) defines as "multidimensional, flawed, and fascinating," attending to both political and the cultural contexts—and an entire socio-economic and political infrastructure connected to situated literacies.[7] With this emotional repertoire—or what I call *literacy as affinity*—literacy brokers intervene in multiple contexts: immigrant communities, churches, schools, governmental agencies, court rooms, libraries—all together co-constructing a multitude of sites that are local, transnational, or anywhere in between. I highlight all these contexts, not because I intentionally sought to address them, but because my participants took me there. In doing so, they confirmed that literacy is much more intricate than we have acknowledged, that personal stories cross over into the public sphere, that filling out immigration forms is indeed a rhetorical act as Ellen Cushman (1998) notes, and it is highly political as well.

In this ethnographic study of Romanian immigrants in the US, I show that literacy brokers intervene with significant emotional work that cultivates deep human understanding through language and literacy. Literacy brokers assume more complex roles and responsibilities than what current scholarship on brokers seems to suggest. While brokers assist people with reading and writing, their role is not just instrumental in accomplishing a literate action. They perform emotional work of mediation by using their own personal experiences, their connections, and language of empathy while also aiding with translations, dealing with legal papers, or compiling the immigration file. They also shift positions, accumulating knowledge from multiple contexts where they broker texts, languages, or cultural gaps. Brokers essentially engage with *literacy as affinity*. Many writing contexts, particularly institutional sites—such as workplaces, governmental agencies, courtrooms, schools, and so on—aim to streamline communication and through this process, to remove the emotional fabric that often supports the literacy practice. Broadly, literacy as affinity is also about sustainability. With its focus on relationality, literacy as affinity provides a framework where the literate experience endures despite gaps of knowledge, unfamiliar texts, or discourse. Literacy as affinity matters for its ability to emerge in spaces of in-betweenness, transitions, and uncertainty, and to thus connect, seemingly disconnected experiences.

Ethnographic and Archival Research

This study combines archival research and ethnographic methods. These methods were informed by the purpose of the study: to understand the relation between personal literacy stories and official literacy education. While ethnographic data allowed me to account for personal narratives, the stories of escape that I mentioned earlier, archival research helped me document the official literacy education and reforms that aimed to subjugate the individual to strong ideological goals. Ethnographic data include literacy history interviews (Bertaux and Kohli 1984) with Romanian immigrants, observation notes of literacy-related events in the Romanian immigrant community located in Chicago, IL, and documents and artifacts functioning as "witnesses" of the immigration experience (e.g., letters from refugee camps, legal documents, etc.). Literacy histories, a qualitative research method used in social sciences, is appropriate for this study because through narratives of daily events of ordinary people, the researcher can explore broader connections to communities, states, or institutions (Bertaux 1981; Duffy 2007). Literacy history interviews focus on the relation between the immigration experience and reading/writing practices in both the country of origin, Romania, and the host country, the United States. I collected thirty-two interviews, each interview lasting between one to three hours, under the University of Illinois IRB approval. The literacy histories come from both old immigrants—those who escaped Romania before 1989, when Romania was still under the Communist rule, and new immigrants—

those who left Romania after 1989 when the borders were relatively open, yet still regulated through visa impositions. Additionally, participants in the study shared personal artifacts, such as correspondence with family/friends, family pictures, blogs, copies of travel documents, refugee certificates, and other documents pertaining to the immigrant experience. I also attended numerous cultural and community events and collected documents related to these events, such as flyers, ethnic newspapers (*The Romanian Tribune, Colorado Beetle, The International Current*), brochures distributed in the community or marketing purposes such as book signings (for instance, Horia Dicher's *Earthly Manuscripts: Baroque Journal*[8]) in March 2012, and the Romanian Heritage Festival in June 2011, 2012, and Romanian Film Festival in July 2012.

In addition, I complement ethnographic work in the immigrant community with historical archival research in Romania. With the support of University of Illinois' Liberal Arts and Sciences summer fellowship in 2011, the archival work in Romania involved collecting primary and secondary sources to retrace the official context of literacy education in the 1970s and 1980s of Communist Romania. Through archival work at Library of the Academy, Central University Library and the National State Archives in Romania, I was able to obtain digital copies of newspapers (*The Spark, The Youth Spark*) and almanacs from the 1970s and 1980s, school magazines (*The Country's Hawks, The Daring*), school curricula, as well as various primary records of the Communist Party documenting its ideological campaign in educational reforms (minutes from the Congress of Political and Cultural Socialist Education, 1982; speeches from the Congress of education and learning, 1973; 1980; 1982, 1987–1988, etc.), numerous brochures of pioneer organizations, including student compositions and literary works.[9] Additional historical documents about Romanian immigrants and Romania-US trade agreements in the 1980s came from archives of daily news in the 1970s and 1980s and Radio Free Europe news broadcasts. All of these helped me review the official literacy education in Romania, the context from where the immigrants left as refugees or as economic immigrants. The immigrant experience, as the participants in this study attest, is marked by numerous forms— certificates, identity cards, affidavits, letters of invitation, and many other documents specific for each category of immigration: humanitarian, family reunification, or employment. Although I had limited access to some of these documents, they were often referenced during the interviews, either by the brokers or by the immigrants who needed the brokers' services.

For data analysis, I used a constructivist approach to grounded theory (Charmaz 2006) that makes the relationship with the participants central to data collection and analysis (130). From the interviews, I obtained and analyzed over 450 pages of transcript using grounded codes; these codes emerged from repeated patterns or key words rather than *a priori* codes.[10] My initial coding categories were informed by the research questions as follows: 1) genres and discourses intertwined in the migration process (e.g., documents, blogs, letters), 2) types of literacies alternative to official literacy education, and 3) literacy and spaces that shape one's learning experience. Informed by grounded theory that takes a comparative approach to data and "emergent categories" (Charmaz 2006, 23), I later developed new categories of analysis taken from a series of interviews already conducted. Among these, significant themes broadly defined surfaced, such as citizenship or cultural identification, that connected to literacy and the immigration experience. Yet, interestingly, higher emphasis was put not on becoming a US citizen, as one might expect in the case of an immigrant, but on processes of losing citizenship and of human rights violations by the country of origin. On the second level of coding, I noticed the repeated reference to an intermediary, mediator, or helper. This code was sufficiently conspicuous that it held my attention. At the same time, in my review of immigrant literature, I found that this mediation relationship has often been coded as "brokering." Hence, this correlation between my initial coding of interview data and review of literature on immigrant literacy led me to focus on the code "broker" and later, develop it as a main analytic.[11] As I analyzed the field where the broker operated, it became clearly connected to political economies and allowed me to develop literacy as affinity as a conceptual frame.

As such, the analyzed data show that literacy brokers in this study serve as significant players in the lives of immigrants, particularly in the process of acquiring US citizenship. I examined their role in mediating and mitigating state powers as immigrants negotiate textual paths through the languages of institutions and nation-states.[12] The Romanian immigrants in this study learned to negotiate both internal and external boundaries during the Cold War period and, after that, visa qualifications imposed on citizens from developing countries. With Romania's history of political and ideological control of its citizens, a mobile identity is both liberating and conflicting in that political freedoms do not necessarily translate directly into economic possibilities of travel, employment, or exchange. The intricate connection between political and economic spheres is highly visible in the context of immigration. The Romanian emigration/immigration in the 1970s and 1980s must be understood in terms of economic benefits and human rights advocacy, as these refugees were permitted, for the most part, to leave the country

Table I.1. Access Brokering

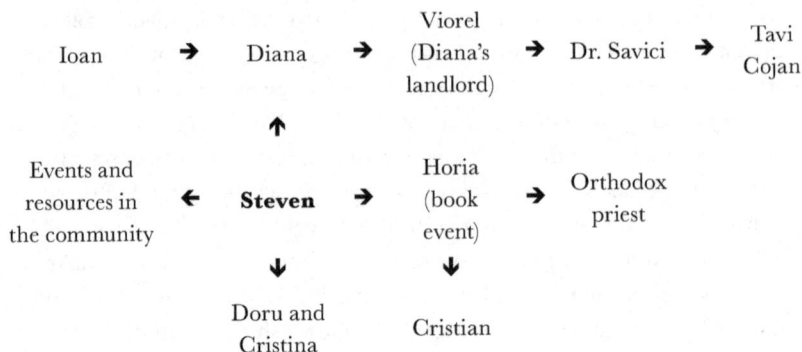

Ioan	➔ Diana	➔ Viorel (Diana's landlord)	➔ Dr. Savici	➔ Tavi Cojan

↑

Events and resources in the community	⬅ **Steven**	➔ Horia (book event)	➔ Orthodox priest

⬇   ⬇

Doru and Cristina	Cristian

on grounds of religious, ethnic, or political persecution; many of them were given a passport and permission to depart only as a result of significant international mediation and trade benefits that Western countries, including the US, initiated with Romania. Although the US and Romania had divergent interests—the US was concerned with lobbying of human rights and probably other interests, while Romania's goal was to extract economic benefits from the US through the Most Favored Nation (MFN) status.[13] Many refugees found themselves navigating both Romanian emigration restrictions and US immigration qualifications. The Romanian emigration/immigration after 1989 is generally framed in terms of economic pursuits and family reunification. Although the conditions of emigration after 1989 are different than those before 1989, particularly in the process of obtaining papers and crossing the border, traveling freely to the Western countries or obtaining a job are challenges that these Romanian immigrants had to face. In chapter 2, I offer a more detailed overview of the immigration conditions before 1989 and their connection to literacy brokering, while chapter 3 focuses mostly on immigrant arrivals after 1989.

Researcher's Access to the Immigrant Community and Individual Profiles

Access to the Romanian immigrant community in Chicago has been quite different than my access to archival materials and libraries in Romania. In 2007, I met my first future-to-be participant, Andreea. I was introduced to her when a few Romanians from Atlanta visited Chicago. My sister was part of the group from Atlanta, and I went to Chicago to meet up with her. Andreea, and then later, Filip—another Romanian international student in Chicago—became my first participants for a small-scale ethnography preceding this current study. From Andreea, I first learned about the *Romanian Tribune,* an ethnic newspaper, and through her I became connected to Steven Bonica, the owner of the *Romanian Tribune,* the founder and organizer of the *Romanian Cultural Heritage* in Niles and also the owner of the Romanian library. Steven, my first participant in this study, has been the key link in establishing contact with other Romanians and with numerous resources and events in the Romanian community. Although arranging an interview with Steven took several weeks and multiple rescheduling, Steven brokered my access as mapped out in Table I.1.

This is just one example showing how access to one person, in this case Steven Bonica, who is centrally positioned in the community, facilitated access to ten different people and multiple other clusters in the community. Although access to the community started with my own personal contact, I was able to branch out of my own networks and gain access to others. Various participants voluntarily made suggestions and mediated access to other people. In fact, almost every participant served as a recruiter for more participants. As such, the model of brokering that works in the community follows the snowball effect. Other recruitment approaches—my announcement in the newspaper or flyers distributed at the *Romanian Heritage Festival* or email to listservs—did not yield any responses. However, connections established through linguistic, ethnic, national, or other type of affinities facilitated access to informants and thus, shaped immensely the recruitment process of this study. A cautionary note is warranted. Being able to speak Romanian was not the sole factor that facilitated my access to the Romanian immigrant community. Immigrant communities are complex, with nuanced relationships and clusters based on numerous variables beyond just speaking the language. Clusters are built based on age, region in the country of origin, religious affiliation/ denomination, education, etc. My access to one cluster of the Romanian community did not necessarily provide access to other clusters, unless a broker intervened to facilitate an entry point.

To provide a better understanding of my participants, I highlight a few profiles of those whose stories are featured in this book. Each immigrant story matters. Each participant offered details and a story of impact. Of the thirty-two participants, I selected a few that would offer a compelling image of this community.

Steven Bonica: Steven Bonica was a central player in my research as illustrated earlier. Both his personal narrative—having to leave Romania when his entire family was persecuted on religious grounds—and his public engagement in the Romania community were crucial to my research and access to the Romanian immigrant community. As the owner of the *Romanian Tribune* and organizer of the *Romanian Heritage Festival*, Steven helped with sharing his story, with materials about the Romanian community, such as newspapers and also books I could not find elsewhere; he also connected me to many other potential participants. Steven comes from Oradea, my birthplace, and this small coincidence did in fact contribute to establishing a good initial rapport. From there on, he became a friend I could trust and call upon for various research related questions.

Octavian Cojan: Mr. Cojan came to the US in 1974. As a member of the Romanian Auto Club, he had the chance to sign up for a tourist trip with the purpose of visiting various Eastern European countries and their capitals: Budapest, Prague, Berlin (in the former German Federal Republic). On that trip, together with his wife, they decided not to return to Romania. Instead, they changed their itinerary and went to a refugee camp in Austria. Mr. Cojan is an important political leader in the Romanian community since his business office in Chicago housed many administrative actions that took place, especially before the establishment of the Romanian Consulate in Chicago. Mr. Cojan has deep knowledge of the Romanian community and has represented the community in various media. For many years, through his business, Mr. Cojan was able to transport literature and newspapers from Romania to Chicago, and thus kept the community informed.

Lucia: Lucia's path to citizenship was facilitated by her husband and father-in-law. She arrived in the US in 1983. After her father-in-law heard on the Radio Free Europe about the MFN status, which provided an open door for Romanian Evangelical Christians to leave the country, he took the initiative to file the papers for the entire family. Lucia, thus, came to the US accompanied by her husband and first child as well as nine additional members of the family—her in-laws and their children. Lucia did not speak English when she came to the US. She remembered the need to learn English when she was sick in the hospital and had to communicate in writing with the hospital staff. The experience was humiliating since while in pain, she did not know how to ask for help for her basic needs. Motivated by this difficulty to communicate, Lucia started to teach herself reading and writing in English by building on previous knowledge of Christian novels. Since she already knew the main plot of some of these books, she would focus on reading in English and using the dictionary for new words.

Dr. Savici: Dr. Savici came to the US in 1981. Because of his Serbian ethnicity, he was able to cross the border into Yugoslavia and sought political asylum at the US embassy. Dr. Savici was a doctor in Romania and managed to further his studies in the US to obtain a job in the medical field. He started a career in neuropathology and currently, owns his own private practice. At Dr. Savici's medical office, I came across many other Romanians. In his office, there were many artifacts that could easily identify him as Romanian, including books in Romanian that he lends out to people. He offered to share some with me.

Sorin: Sorin belongs to the new immigrant wave. He came with a Work and Travel program and made his own path towards US citizenship. His family joined him a few years later; he also enrolled in college to continue his studies. Sorin is one of many "economic immigrants," a cohort of young Romanians who dropped out of college in Romania to pursue their dream of "making it" elsewhere. In Romania, Sorin and many like him "could not dream" of having a decent life free of widespread corruption and pervasive nepotism. Lack of legal papers made Sorin and his friends take jobs they would have never considered in Romania—taxi driving or construction. Sorin and his cohort are generally educated; some have college degrees and most, if not all, speak English well. In fact, those who speak only limited English are often perceived as oddities. For these new immigrants, obtaining legal papers has been their most pressing concern.

Adina: Like Sorin, she is one who came with a solid literacy capital: excellent English and communication skills that she had developed while working for an international non-profit organization in Romania. Having a degree in law and working for a prestigious non-profit organization, Adina nevertheless was discontent. While the organization professed mobility through its presence in Romania, it sought to keep the "local people local," as Adina recalls. She resented this immobility and decided to come to the US. Adina's story highlights her will and determination to accomplish her goals. Adina reads and writes in multiple languages. She has varied reading interests from *The Economist* to fiction and non-fiction novels. Currently she is actively involved in promoting the Romanian culture in the diaspora through various media, in particular multimedia.

Claudiu: Claudiu came to the US through the mediation of a non-profit organization. He got married to a Romanian-American and settled in the Romanian community. He speaks multiple languages and has a degree in English and Romanian; he was able to repurpose his education from Romania quite successfully. Adapting his skills to the US market, Claudiu started his own translation and interpretation business. He often serves as a community interpreter or translator, offering his services benevolently. The fact that Claudiu adopted various roles—such as a community interpreter, a legal translator, or a privately hired interpreter/translator—allowed him to present the issue of language and discourse from multiple perspectives. His viewpoints are all shaped by the contexts where he has been working: the community, legal court settings, and one-on-one translation services.

Diana: Diana's path towards citizenship is unknown. She left a stable university position in Romania because she was disillusioned with a corrupt system that promoted nepotism in all areas of social life. Although her current situation is constrained due to limited job opportunities and her lack of papers, Diana wants to write her story about her refusal to live in Romania. In many ways, Diana represents the new immigrant, dissatisfied with Romania's post-communist situation that curtailed hopes for a better future, particularly for the young generation. Although Diana speaks English well, she prefers to write in Romanian. She also enjoys living amongst Romanians in Chicago, which she sees as both a blessing and curse.

Ema: Ema came to the US because she needed a change. She had visited the US before and decided to apply to a graduate program at the University of Illinois at Chicago. Her college degree obtained in Romania was in Journalism and French. She applied for a MA program in French language and literature. French became her preferred medium of communication, serving as a discursive space of comfort. Although fluent in English and Romanian, her memories of her first years in school are filled with feelings of inadequacy and perceived inability to communicate. The fact that she was alone, without her family, made the entire experience more difficult. She remembers feeling "deficient" in English writing or school-related activities. However, Ema started to write in a different context: for the Romanian newspaper. In a community setting, Ema found a space where she could express herself in freedom.

Ethnicity, Race, and Immigration

The Romanian immigrants whose stories are captured in this book came to the US post-1965 Immigration Act, a period which experienced a rejection of the previous national quota limitations (see the Immigration Act of 1924) and aligned with America's fresh rebranding as a "nation of immigrants" (Foner and Frederickson 2004).[14] For these immigrants, ethnicity more than race became important because, as Lucian Boia (2001a) explains, Romanians followed the German model of nationhood based on ethnicity expressed through culture and language (Boia 2001a), and the Orthodox faith (Shafir 1978). The interview data confirm an emphasis on language, religion, and socioeconomic markers of identity. Race, for this immigrant group, was not central because Romanian immigrants' focus on ethnicity and assimilation allowed them to blend into white middle-class America. Race did not become a category of

18

analysis also because, like other immigrant groups, Romanians tend to maintain their in-group identity, preserve their language and culture through church and schools, other institutions, and various community events. Of thirty-two interviews, only one participant mentioned in passing, "the skin advantage" that he (and other Romanian immigrants) had experienced. This brief mention of skin color as an advantage clearly confirms differentiated hierarchies among immigrant groups, whether such realizations are expressed or not. However, since no other references to race were offered during the interviews, this category of difference was not explored further.

Organization of the Book

In the previous section, I explained how I adopted grounded theory as a method and methodology. The current organization of the book reflects this approach, specifically how I came to understand literacy brokering in this immigrant community. After an overview of transnational literacy in chapter 1, in chapter 2 I offer my initial thinking and work with the figure of the broker in the immigrant community. This is how the broker emerged: from an initial conversation with one immigrant who served as a link to many other community members/future participants in my study. This is how the research started: small, with one individual. This, perhaps, is essential as we consider transnational research and narratives. We start small. We do not start with context or larger sociopolitical frames. We start with one story. Therefore, the broker conceptual frame, begins in chapter 2 with individual accounts of immigrants and how they tell us that one story. The figure of the broker, then, evolved as I examined another group of immigrants—the economic immigrants. As such, chapter 3 focuses on economies of writing and captures the expansion of broker to co-brokering and the larger connections to political economies. It also includes data from undocumented immigrants, an important detail in understanding why certain stories are featured as key narratives while others are not. Additionally, as a researcher I took precaution to acknowledge certain voices and the participants' shared stories but omitted identifiable quotes or references that could negatively impact participants. Sorin, a pseudonym, was a key informant, and unlike other participants, he took a risk in telling me not just his story but the story of several undocumented immigrants with whom he worked and lived. The claims or generalizations are not my own, but Sorin's, who spoke on behalf of the group he voluntarily represented. Chapter 4 reflects the research path further as I went to the archives in Romania to learn more about the official literacy experience of these immigrants. The interviews with immigrants in the community led me to the ar-

Introduction

chives. For the readers who prefer to read first about the context of literacy in Communist Romania to better understand individual narratives, I suggest reading chapter 4 before delving into personal narratives in chapters 2 and 3. For those who want to follow the research path and discover the nuances of transnational literacies and brokering as I have, then I propose you follow the order listed in the table of contents. The book ends with a review of literacy as affinity and some pedagogical possibilities. Ultimately, the book's organization reflects an approach to transnational research—method and data analysis—that I practice and advocate in this book: start small, and from there build up theoretical frames grounded in individual stories; allow the voices on the ground to guide the research path and approach; and then learn about context through the individual story. Not all contexts are the same, as each individual story of escape has been shaped by a constellation of variables.

In the first chapter, "The Transnational Turn in Literacy Studies," I offer an overview of transnational approaches in US rhetoric and composition, giving specific attention to the last ten years 2013–2023. The last decade has witnessed a manifest growth of scholarship focused on transnational literacies. If in the early 2000s, we had occasional articles that served as points of reference or justifications for the transnational turn (see Brandt and Clinton 2002; Donahue 2009; Hesford 2006; Hesford and Schell 2008), the second decade of the twenty-first century exploded with studies of transnational movement. In "Travelling Literacies," Rebecca Lorimer Leonard offers an overview of studies on mobility, including how mobility has been taken up in our field [e.g. Jan Blommaert's (2010) incredibly influential work on the sociolinguistic of mobility; Suresh Canagarajah's "shuttling between languages;" Ilene Crawford's (2010) conception of rhetoric "as the study and practice of movement;" Wendy Hesford's (2010) "discourses of mobility,"] and a compelling discussion of the "paradox" of mobility pointing to borders, stoppages, or obstacles in the project of mobility. Lorimer Leonard, Norquist, Vieira, and other transnational scholars show this need to acknowledge and engage obstacles and borders. Building on this work, I take things a step further in offering an analytic—literacy brokering—to discuss, describe, contest, and understand power dynamics and the mediation needed in studying literacy across borders.

In Chapter 2: "Literacy Brokers and Emotional Work of Mediation: A Bi-Institutional Perspective," I explore how literacy brokers' work of affinity operates transnationally. I report on a data set focused on political refugees at a time when Romanian borders were strictly monitored by the Romanian state. Rather than solely addressing translation or assistance with legal papers and other immigration forms, I show that

20

literacy brokers also use personal stories of oppression to mobilize both personal and public agendas. In this case, personal affinities become a vehicle for impact upon and change of larger political structures. To accomplish this, literacy brokers work within and across institutions, and in so doing, they gain what I call a "bi-institutional" perspective. This perspective presupposes that brokers do not think and act solely from "within" institutions; rather, they think and act "across" institutions. As they move from context to context, literacy brokers accumulate rich language, cultural repertoires, and structures of feelings that are deployed locally and transnationally. The significance of the brokering here resides not in the fact that affinity is reciprocated or treated transactionally; rather, the work of affinity accomplished through personal stories becomes a motivational tool for human rights advocacy, while, at the same time, it humanizes a system that otherwise tends to reduce immigrants to "case studies."

The book's third chapter, "Economies of Writing," addresses the brokering strategies of the new immigrant—the one who can speak and write English and whose mobility is enabled by global economies. Contrary to refugees, new immigrants travel for economic rather than political reasons; they learn to navigate visa restrictions and work qualifications. I advance the notion of affinity by highlighting co-brokering and cumulative agency, created through partnerships within and across one's ethnic group. I show how economic immigrants use co-brokering to negotiate visa regulations, legal papers and procedures, applications and "file selves," a term developed by Julie Chu. In this process, these immigrants learn "to build texts," creating hidden transcripts that mimic the official language of bureaucracy. Here, I show how co-brokering emerges as a by-product of affinities of the marginalized, of those who struggle with socio-economic, legal, or racial disparities.

Chapter 4: "Iron-cast Literacies and the Role of the Authoritarian State as a Literacy Broker" discusses the figure of the literacy broker in the context of mass literacy campaigns. Modeling the Soviet experience, the literacy campaign in Romania—known as "the fight against illiteracy" in the words of President Nicolae Ceaușescu—was central to the constitution of the "new socialist man." This ideology originates with Lenin's own proclamation that "the illiterate person stands outside politics" (Arnove and Graff 1987, 7). Because of literacy's central place in the Communist agenda, I explore the interconnections between literacy, affinity, and politics in the Romanian context. I argue that the Romanian state functioned as the ultimate broker, legitimizing itself as the only author, distributor, subject, and object of literacy. In this capacity, the nation became the sole arbiter of one's affinity. Chapter 5,

"Teachers and Shifting Ideological Positions," shows further how the state used teachers as brokers to expand its reach and control. Teachers' various positionalities operate differently than brokers in a democratic society because their affiliation with the party's line engendered severe consequences. Nevertheless, both chapters show the Romanian state in a central position of brokering, managing, and controlling literacy; it offers a better understanding of the way in which the state managed to incapacitate educational and cultural institutions, teachers, reading, and writing practices.

In the sixth chapter, "Brokering Methods and Methodologies," I approach the notion of literacy broker from the position of the researcher. I envision the researcher as a broker of knowledge, a person who makes use of his or her own affinities with certain groups of power to broker the research path. To this end, I use the notion of particularism and universalism (Mungiu-Pippidi 2005) to further investigate ways in which the researcher's positionality and methodologies are brokered to accomplish research goals. In assessing literacy brokers' work in multiple contexts and roles, *Immigrants, Brokers, and Literacy as Affinity* argues that literacy as affinity and its mediational role is essential for research, methodologies, and pedagogies of impact across languages, cultures, and learning contexts.

Chapter 1

The Transnational Turn in Literacy Studies

We must recognize that global higher education is also infused with discourses and motives that require critique. In other words, we need to reconceive our own global turn not simply as a "turn," but also as hegemonic, agonistic work that critically responds to the visions and programs of global higher education nationally and on our own campuses, even as it responds to critiques, false characterizations, and conspiracy from beyond the walls of the university.

—Christopher Minnix

At the *Symposium for the Study of Writing and Teaching Writing: Transnational Literacies* in 2013 at University of Massachusetts, Amherst, discussions about the "transnational turn" raised the following questions: Can we identify this moment in time as transnational and, if we can, what characteristics define it? Summary notes of that conversation point to some critical moments that are indeed captured by the *trans-* and the *-national* in transnational. That *moment,* as scholars from Amherst symposium suggested, was marked by flexible subjectivities, mobility, and instability of social contexts; the transnational, it was argued then, engages with changes in technologies, mass migration, control of nation-states as well as economic and efficiency models (budget-cuts, restructuring) in higher education. Since 2013, that current moment has changed drastically. Economic and political instability, migration, technological shifts, and more recently, the COVID-19 pandemic have radically transformed our lives in the last couple of years from micro to macro levels. If in 2013, we identified a gentle turn towards transnationalism and global forces, today, in the age of COVID, we all have turned our eyes both inwardly towards city, county, state, and nation-state policies and outwardly towards other nation-states as waves of directives have repeatedly and urgently impacted our lives. It is safe to say that the last ten years reshaped the way in which people communicate and the literacies they craft to engage the world. An examination of this past decade, and the last three years in particular, is thus necessary to understand our historical moment and to find strategies to engage the present and future.

Since the early 2000s, US-based composition scholars have called for and into question the internationalization of US writing education (Donahue 2009; Hesford and Shell 2008), advocated for a translingual approach to reading and writing (Horner, Necamp, and Donahue 2011), or drew attention to mobility across contexts.[1] US scholars have already taken steps towards reassessing historical silences in composition, challenging monolinguistic myths and US-centered research practices (Canagarajah 2006; Matsuda 2010; Trimbur 2006). Building on this scholarship in literacy studies from a global perspective, I propose here an approach to writing and discourse in multiple contexts because this creates a space of inquiry and engagement with basic and complex issues of literacy. It illuminates what literacy means in certain contexts, such as immigration, and how literacy is managed by nation-states—especially since major changes have marked immigration in the last decade. An overview of transnational literacy scholarship in the last decade with gaps, changes, and trends shows that the most significant shift is an emphasis on power dynamics that governs mobility, people, and certainly literacy. In the latter part of the chapter, I show that literacy brokers provide a useful analytic to engage power dynamics as brokers intervene precisely in contexts of inequality and gaps of knowledge in transnational spaces. Overall, the work of literacy brokers introduced in this chapter and developed throughout the book offers a conception of literacy as affinity. Literacy as affinity brings together a language of empathy, personal narratives, and all the relations forged and sustained during the literate activity to accomplish personal, professional, or civic ends.

Before 2019, mobility—signified by the trans- in transnational—captured flexibility and movement through language and literacy or "shuttling" between languages (see Canagarajah 2006); post-2019 global flows have been marked by stoppages. Certainly, many scholars have looked critically at mobility and transnationalism acknowledging which literate and linguistic repertoires are portable, recontextualized, and valued in new contexts. The paradox of mobility has been captured by phrases like: "simultaneous fluidity and fixity" (Lorimer Leonard 2017), "feeling stuck in motion, bound in freedom" or "immobility within movement" (Prendergast 2008, 147), or through metaphoric images of tourists and vagabonds, whose mobility is conditioned and shaped by voluntary or involuntary decisions (Bauman 1998, 93). However, the acceleration and intensification of stoppages and exclusion of entire ethnic groups and nation-states from transnational mobility have increased at a fast-moving pace. For instance, in a discussion of anti-immigrant agendas, Hannah Gilmore (2022) notes that in 2020, nine presidential proclamations were issued that limited immigrant and refugee mobility to the United States. Miller et al. (2020) surveyed immigrant policies and found that "the ACLU alone has filed 90 legal actions regarding COVID-19, including state and city chapters that have filed lawsuits against US Immigration and Customs Enforcement (ICE) detention centers and processing centers in California, Maryland, Massachusetts, Michigan, Ohio, Pennsylvania, Texas, and Washington" (ACLU 2020a; 2020b, 794). Immigration policies in the last three years have changed drastically with the Flores settlement of 1997; the Migration Protection Protocols (MPPs) that provide restrictive guidelines to refugee applicants; CDC orders that in fact overrule immigration law, and many other policies that have limited or restricted mobility across borders (see Miller et al. 2020).

These political and economic transformations are important for us, scholars in rhetoric and composition. We had a moment, and that moment has changed; in fact, it seems that since the COVID-19 pandemic, even more robust changes in immigration have been issued. While early scholarship on the transnational provided lenses and frames to look beyond US-based writing and literacy, the more recent transnational wave centers our attention on the paradox of mobility where borders, stoppages, or obstacles become critical analytics in the project of mobility. In her book *Writing on the Move*, Lorimer Leonard takes a bold stance to describe mobility "in terms of inequality" (10). In the study of transnational literacies, this is a significant shift as scholars have become more aware of differentiated mobility and emplacement. Similar work on mobility proposed by Brice Nordquist (2016) notes how literacy studies intersect several other bodies of scholarship in the study of mobility: "Literacy studies explicitly engaged mobilities in a number of sometimes overlapping, sometimes diverging areas of research. A short list of these includes spatial studies of literacy, studies of transition and transfer, circulation studies, translingual literacy, transnational literacy, studies of access and articulation (including disability studies), and digital literacies" (22). From this list, Nordquist further elaborates on movement as central in translingual approaches and transnational literacy studies without neglecting to point that mobility also involves surveillance and friction. In "What Happens When Texts Fly," Kate Vieira (2019) argues that texts, in the process of movement from one place to another, can contribute to power building (e.g. immigrant laws), can negotiate power, or can reframe it by giving voice to marginalized groups and starting movements from below. Power inequalities manifested through friction, stoppages, surveillance, borders, policies, or language, cultural, or political obstacles emerge across these texts on transnational mobility and literacies. This shift to understand mobility in its complexity is certainly a critical turn in transnational literacy scholarship in the last decade. I take up this angle by exploring how power dynamics is implicated in the work of literacy brokers, the analytic that I propose for exploration and their role in the mediation of power inequalities.

To understand the current moment, we also need to look at this persistent orientation towards transnationalism from a different angle, the gaps to which we have responded, two of which are notable. One gap emerges from the larger field of literacy studies, specifically New Literacy Studies (NLS), and the other from global studies and trends in higher education. The former, unlike rhetoric and composition that is historically grounded in the US, adopts a cross-cultural approach to literacy since many NLS scholars are in fact based outside the US. (e.g., Brian Street, Mike Baynham, David Barton—the United Kingdom; Catherine Kell—New Zealand; Lesley Farrell—Australia; Mastin Prinsloo—South Africa, etc.). The latter comes from labor market changes and the higher education attunement to economic and political shifts. With regard to NLS scholarship and historical changes, Kell (2017) notes that initially NLS was successful in challenging the oral/written divide and advocating for socially-bound ideological models of literacy shaped by the situation or contexts where literacy unfolds. However, critiques of NLS have pointed out a few limitations, including an overemphasis on the local, neglect of power inequalities, and limited engagement with the materiality of contexts and texts (Kell 2017). Whether in alignment with the critique advanced by Kell or informed by other current moments that demand such engagements, our field's turn toward mobility and power dynamics in the social fields has been a powerful reorientation.

The second gap has been identified in scholarship on global or transnational movements. An examination of this scholarship allows us to problematize the nation-state. If in the first part we focused on the trans- in transnational, that is *mobility* across contexts, the latter part of a transnational approach moves us to examine the nation-state's power and the discourses that it manages. Several earlier articles—Hesford (2006) and Donahue (2009)—warned us of nationalist discourses and the danger of an uncritical approach to global forces by maintaining a US-centric paradigm particularly since the disciplinary formation of US composition is deeply entrenched in the US context. Overall, in this second body of scholarship, the transnational turn is invoked by various changes in our field, including global orientations of US higher education, awareness of composition studies' insular history, and perhaps, a more acute awareness of people's actions and mobilities in and outside the classroom. Cautionary messages regarding compositionists' engagement with the transnational turn also abound. Horner and Donahue (2022) for instance perceptively capture the paradox of transnationalism as: the emergence of both global movements of people and texts and "the rising of reactionary forms of nationalism" at a global scale, not just in isolated instances (e.g. UK, France, Germany, and the US). They explain that this type of reactionary nationalism adheres to an ideology of purism, to "racially, linguistically, and culturally pure, stable, and discrete nation-states cleansed of difference and, hence, vehemently opposed to any crossing of borders: a nationalism defined by its opposition to and suspicion of transnationalism of any form" (Horner and Donahue 2022, 10). After a detailed discussion of the internationalization of higher education reflected in mission statements of almost every US college and curricular changes to engage global economic and social forces, Minnix (2017) offers a thorough analysis of the anti-global rhetoric with its contradictions and polarizing strategies. Minnix explains that it is essential "to reconceive our own global turn not simply as a 'turn,' but also as hegemonic, agonistic work that critically responds to the visions and programs of global higher education nationally and on our own campuses, even as it responds to critiques, false characterizations, and conspiracy from beyond the walls of the university" (76). This call to critical work that is deeply political and personal at the same time is crucial; it requires a re-engagement with transnational and global orientations that might have been left unchallenged before. In the current climate of reconfiguration of higher education policies and global orientation, we need to be more attuned to work with the paradox of mobility, engage our critics, including those upholding political discourses that push against individual mobilities, false ideologies, and personal stories—such as immigrant stories—to bring awareness to why mobility matters.

In my study of immigrant literacy, I take a transnational approach to literacy and writing, which I distinguish from global or international perspectives. Many scholars have theorized the distinction between these terms (see Horner and Dohanue 2022; Jordan 2022). In my view, a transnational lens allows a more pertinent discussion of power dynamics because work with immigrant literacy cannot elude differentiated mobility or the nation-state. Michael Kearney's (1995) view of the state as the "guardian of national borders" or Vieira's (2016) exploration of the undocumented or Briggs et al.'s (2008) discussion of the nation as a contradictory—all signal that *the transnational* frame allows for questions about whose interests are advanced and for what purposes. Briggs et al. (2008) focus on the nation as way to show its contradictions and expose the rhetoric around and behind certain nationalistic practices. In their view, nation and nation-centric discourses must be contested, leading to inquiries into elements that are often used to define a nation—"the people, the language, the literature, the history, the culture, the environment" (627). All these attributes of a nation are critical sites of inquiry in my study. The immigrants whose stories I capture in this book go through processes of negotiations, particularly when individuals born in Romania have citizenship revoked by their own country due to their ethnic, religious, or political affiliations. The new immigrants discussed later in the book also push against visa impositions and policies that do not align with their goals. Language, especially knowing the right language at the right time, facilitates movement of some people—those who master English or German with proficiency—while it immobilizes others in low-paying jobs, such as those who learned only Russian and other languages with no exchange value in the US. But, language also directs attention to discourses of institutions, of nation-states or bureaucracies that exert power over those who prove to be less than proficient. Literature, history, culture, and geopolitical spaces are constitutive of the lives of immigrants as they reflect on the literacy education in Romania (see chapter 4) but also on the mentalities—set ways of thinking and being—that immigrants carry with them in the US.

Concerning the relation between the (im)migrant and the state, political scientist James Scott (1988) argues that it has been an ongoing state project to emplace, to "settle these mobile peoples" (1). Surnames or family names, although taken for granted, are significant in the way in which they represent the relationship between the individual and the state's process of legibility, i.e., of transforming its citizens into objectified subjects that can be accounted for. Unsurprisingly, as Scott explains, there is a direct correlation between the introduction of surnames and the development of written, official documents such as tithe records, manorial due rolls, marriage registers, censuses, tax records, and land records. They were necessary to the successful conduct of any administrative exercise involving large numbers of people who had to be individually identified and who were not known *personally* by the authorities. This form of emplacement through documents, as Scott (1998) and others have noted (Vieira 2016), complicates romantic views of travel or mobility. It unveils that mobility or the trans- in transnational is hierarchical (e.g., Lorimer Leonard 2017; Nordquist 2016) and historically connected to regimes of control. Mobility, then, is in reality "differentiated mobility," to use Doreen Massey's (1993) term; it affords an analysis of critical checkpoints, borders, and spaces of access and lack thereof. Mobility as it shapes literacy on the move has to be further explored in its full complexity since most studies of transnational or immigrant literacies have mainly dealt with the "after-effects of movement" where literacy is approached as "durable" rather than in-process (Lorimer Leonard 2017). In my work, I capture both the fixity and the mobility of my participants, which is why narratives of immigration, specifically the immigrants' literacy practices in Romania, are central. Throughout this book, I propose this exploration of literacy brokers throughout the life trajectories of the people they help, not just with discrete literacy events, and I show that these brokers are, at the very core, mobile subjects that deploy literacy resources for and with others. Most importantly, these literacy brokers engage with power inequality since they mediate between the individual and larger discourses of nation-states. Depending on the context and the language resources, this mediation may take place in official and unofficial settings. In each situation, literacy brokers re-orient our attention towards political economies that shape the literate lives of immigrants and thus, from their middle ground offer a critical engagement with both obstacles and stoppages and the policies of nation-states.

Definitions and Implications of Literacy Brokers and Co-brokering

The term *literacy brokers* has gained much traction in New Literacy Studies (NLS), especially in cross-cultural studies of literacy (for example, Baynham 1993; Kalman 1999; Papen 2010). In a rather comprehensive definition, Perry (2009) explains literacy brokering as "a process of seeking and or providing information assistance about some aspects of a given text or literacy practice. Brokers bridge linguistic, cultural, and textual divides for others" (256). While current work on literacy brokers underscores their instrumental roles as translators, scribes, or helpers with texts, I draw attention to literacy brokers' *emotional work* performed in mediating texts locally and transnationally and to the *economic frames* they engage. I call this mediation work *literacy as affinity*—a discursive repertoire comprised of language of empathy and understanding, personal experiences, and social connectivities embedded in the literate experience. I also expand the concept of brokering, with new terminology—co-brokering—conceptualized as the act of mediating texts *collectively* or *with* others, which is fundamental in the formation of new subjectivities, particularly when bureaucracies and standardization erase personal agency. Since brokering is about day-to-day and moment-to-moment operations, in co-brokering, those instances accumulate and formulate more visible actions. Co-brokering is thus marked by collective action, informal exchanges, and the politics of translating bureaucratic protocols into manageable bits of information, strategies through which one can develop a new economic framework and diverse economic discourses. Co-brokering offers a critique of capitalistic frames, but it also helps individuals develop agency by re-orienting bureaucratic literacy toward their goals. In what follows, I will retrace the term literacy broker in current scholarship explaining its roots, distinguishing it from sponsors of literacy, and then expand it further in a discussion of emotions and economic frames.

One particular theoretical concept that connects the individual to larger economic activity is sponsors of literacy, a vastly influential concept advanced by Brandt in 1998. In her article "Sponsors of Literacy," Brandt (1998) explains our field's neglect of larger economic frames that impact individual literacy: "When economic forces are addressed in our work, they appear primarily as generalities: contexts, determinants, motivators, barriers, touchstones. But rarely are they systematically related to the local conditions and embodied moments of literacy learning that occupy so many of us on a daily basis" (166). In other words, literacy sponsorship looks at intimate connections between individual literacy development and larger economic systems that impinge on that activity. Influenced by Brandt's discussion of economic realities and how they shape one's writing, I pay attention to literacy development in the daily lives of immigrants. Their literacy practices open avenues to the local and transnational forces, economic and political systems that configured and were, in turn, reconfigured daily. In this analysis of sponsor and the sponsored and the language practices employed as people crossed borders, I found a variety of economic exchanges and mediation. That middle ground where people help others with reading and writing, I call a space of brokering, and those invisible agents that occupy this space, brokers.

In differentiating broker and sponsor, I seek to extract the former from the broader latter term (Brandt's sponsor), precisely because the broker, through their analytical force, aims to disrupt power dynamics between nation-states and the individual, while sponsor tends to reinforce that dynamic. Earlier in discussing transnational mobility, I explained the need to look more closely at power dynamics. Literacy brokers help us do just that. Unlike the sponsor who want their name acknowledged, literacy brokers remain rather obscure in formal, institutionalized sites of writing, yet their presence is visible in informal encounters: daily conversations, meetings, and contexts where resources are limited. In the economic exchange of information between the sponsor and the sponsored, the broker brings an affective dimension through language, ties, and a host of identification resources. Significantly, the broker and the act of co-brokering reveal the agency of those at the margins that remain rather invisible in the context of sponsorship and other market-driven economic frames in composition studies.

When we examine the term sponsor in the context of US Immigration and Citizenship Services (USCIS), we learn new meanings that also help frame the broker concept.[2] The pursuit of legal papers creates a discursive market, entangling individuals and state powers in complex ways. This market of legal papers regulated through forms, applications, or affidavits allows little room for the individual to negotiate his or her interaction with the state. In the context of US immigration, the notion of sponsorship implicates mobility, national identities, and access through one's mediating role. Specifically, a sponsor in the immigration discourse means to bring to the US or "petition for" (United States "Our History"). A sponsor supports the action and the process of moving from one place to another, in this case, a foreign national's mobility to the US. Whether the petition supports a family member, employment, or an asylum case, a sponsor is often framed in economic terms and is crucial in the pursuit of legal papers. Without a sponsor and an affidavit of support from the sponsor, the incomplete application cannot be processed. Despite the indispensable presence of sponsors in the context of immigration, in my study literacy brokers emerged as significant players on day-to-day interactions. Based on my participants' accounts, there was always someone different from the official sponsor who helped with reading and writing and participated in the moment-by-moment interactions of brokering texts, such as applications, declarations, documentation, and knowledge gaps between the immigrant and state rhetorics. In immigration papers, the sponsor often remains a formal inscription on a document, responding to governmental constraints but in reality, achieves no significant impact on the petitioner. Framed by the US immigration policies, the official sponsor has to be a US citizen and must show evidence of economic stability to support the applicant. On the other hand, literacy brokers, almost invisible in formal papers, help with processing of legal papers in significant ways and offer discursive, emotional, social, and economic support. Unlike the sponsors who want their name acknowledged, as in the case of commercials that inspired Brandt's choice of the sponsor metaphor, literacy brokers remain rather obscured in formal or institutionalized sites of writing. They do, however, permeate everyday practices of literacy, particularly the mediation of the textual immigration paths of immigrants. Their affective work is deeply intertwined in the process of migration and by extension, in other institutionalized contexts of writing.

In addition to understanding the term sponsor by looking at the US immigration context, several other scholars have attempted to extend, complement, and develop the term; these scholars' work proposed a host of alternatives to the sponsor figure, such as literacy emissaries with a focus on the sponsored rather than the sponsor (MacDonald 2015); literacy mediators as translators (Baynham and Masing 2001), literacy mediator and intermediaries (Webber 2012), and literacy stewardship (Frost 2021). In her cogent conceptualization of stewardship, Frost (2011) shows both the limitations and the complexities of the term sponsor, remarking that "such measurement allows for comprehensive understanding of the parameters of literacy sponsors but limits descriptions of the sponsored and his or her community's literacies bound in their own time and place—particularly in the case of Native North Americans whose own sociohistoric communicative tools have so often predated their sponsors' goals for their literacy" (59). In her critical observation, Frost notes that literacy sponsors center our attention onto those in power, in possession of literacy, while neglecting the tools and the strategies of the marginalized, of those stewards who engage diverse forms of literacy.

In this discussion of literacy sponsorship terminology, there is a recurrent move to add, complement, change, or reconfigure the sponsorship analytic as well as to acknowledge that economies of writing are complex. It is evident that the term literacy sponsor—albeit extremely valuable and still relevant—cannot capture a variety of economic relationships. In fact, even Brandt herself acknowledges on numerous occasions the presence of different economies and inequality shaping individual literacy: "I do not wish to overlook the very different economic, political, and educational systems within which US literacy has developed" (169). Surveying the different terms and uptakes of sponsorship, I found a preference for *sponsor* in US-based scholarship. However, in international or cross-cultural studies (see New Literacy Studies), scholarship on refugees (Duffy 2007; MacDonald 2015), international non-for-profit (Webber 2012), immigrant literacy (Mihuţ 2014; Viera 2016), the term literacy broker—which encompasses such nuances as mediators or intermediaries—has been dominant, presenting a significant analytical distinction from sponsors of literacy. Thus, while the sponsorship frame is valuable, it captures only one type of economic imaginary, one driven by profit and capitalist interests. Here and throughout the book, I argue that we need a varied terminology to describe the diverse economic practices that shape writing and rhetorical action. The terms broker and co-brokering offer this new terminology. Literacy brokers take us to formal and informal sites (e.g., homes, coffee shops, cabs, kitchen tables, etc.), not just the classroom, and help us account for varied market and nonmarket activities and allow for the formation of different economic subjectivities.

Literacy as Affinity

In sum, literacy brokers are those who assist others with reading and writing, mediating language, culture, and discourses of power while also developing alliances (co-brokering). The act of brokering involves emotional work through language, personal stories, and networks of affinity based on various connections. To account for all this work, I use *affinity* as a capacious term comprising empathetic language, emotional and personal narratives, as well as those relations that create the infrastructure of texts, people, and communities. The study of emotion is certainly complex, precisely because it has been historically defined and studied as a dichotomous category in contrast to rationality. Catherine A. Lutz (1990) explains the problematic ways to see emotions in this way: "something natural rather than cultural, irrational rather than rational, chaotic rather than ordered, subjective rather than universal, physical rather than mental or intellectual" (69). However, research on emotions has come a long way. In this study, I conceptualize emotion by drawing on Laura Micciche's (2007) explanation of "emotion as a valuable rhetorical resource" (1). Rather than just expressions of personal feelings, emotions have rhetorical force intersecting and shaping personal and interpersonal, social and political realities. The social and political frames that brokers mediate are particularly important in this study. Julie Lindquist (2004) also contends that "emotions are situated and constructed" connected to all aspects of the social (201). On the other hand, Lynn Worsham (1998) contributes a rich depiction of emotions as "the tight braid of affect and judgment, socially and historically constructed and bodily lived, through which the symbolic takes hold of and binds the individual, in complex and contradictory ways, to the social order" (216). Based on these definitions, emotions are integral components in the fabric of everyday life, entangled in how people think, speak, and act socially and historically, politically, and economically.

Building on this work, three essential dimensions of emotions need to be highlighted, and they are all embedded in this conception of literacy as affinity. First, emotions should not be understood solely as an expression of one's personal experience. Emotions can be both collective and connected to issues of political power. In *The Cultural Politics of Emotion*, Ahmed (2004) expands on the circulation of the phrase "soft touch" to refer to the UK as a nation that has been too "emotional," allowing its borders to be assaulted by the presence of foreigners, the immigrants. She further argues that such images of "softness" conceive emotions as "attributes of collectives," and as in the case of the nation, of those who belong within a particular jurisdiction and those who seek to trespass it (2). Collective emotions, particularly those that relate to the nation, constitute the grounds for antithetical subjectivities—us against them—potentially forming boundaries difficult to transgress or challenge. In chapter 4, I offer details about the ways in which the Communist regime sought to regiment and manufacture certain types of emotions to create a national Romanian subjectivity. Similarly, immigrants that come to the US are socialized through discourse in what it means to be American. I discuss this in chapter 3 in terms of expectations to comply with a certain *image* of socio-economic stability and respectability.

Second, emotions are more than ways to stir or provoke certain effects. Ahmed (2004), for instance, describes emotions as attachments and connections established between things. While I assent to this relationality of emotion, I make a subtle distinction between affinity and connections or alliances. Whether I call them alliances, partnerships, or connections, I understand them as relations based on certain affinities, such as ethnic affinity, professional affinity, and so on. As such, affinities provide *the motive* for creating partnerships. However, literacy as affinity, as I envision it, refers to the comprehensive emotional work that comes from sharing personal stories, language of empathy, and various partnerships created for or in the context of a literacy practice. Both aspects, the emotional and the attachments established through affinities of various sorts, are essential, and both are captured in the brokers and co-brokering concepts.

The third observation relates to the fact that emotions constitute an easy target for manipulation, constraint, or falsification. Studies on affect and emotion show that emotions are also tied, managed, or regimented, particularly in the context of institutions; or, to use Megan Boler's (1999) words, "Emotions are a primary site of social control; they are also a site for political resistance and can mobilize social movements of liberation" (xii).[3] Studying the connection between emotions and racism, Jennifer Trainor (2008) argues that schools as educational institutions represent a critical site where various affective experiences are being constructed. She further shows how "emotional regulation" occurs through institutional and language practices (85). Similarly, Lindquist (2004) contends that institutions must acknowledge the "emotional labor" of writing teachers and emotional formations that emerge in the writing classroom.

In this study of immigrant literacy, the institutional constraint operates through immigration agencies and bureaucratic practices or policies of nation-states. What state agents and bureaucrats value is procedural knowledge rather than emotions: what forms to use for what purpose and how to fill out a given form in the most efficient way. For these types of tasks—filling out forms, translating, writing a document, and other—literacy brokers have been conceived as tools serving such specific literate ends. Similar to Lindquist's example of the writing classroom, emotional work in these bureaucratic writing contexts including immigration applications has been regulated and managed. The immigrant stories I present here show that literacy brokers recover emotional work lost in the context of immigration and humanize the system. Since literacy brokers hold multiple positions and develop bi-institutional perspectives, as shown in chapter 2, they perform the emotional work in the following ways: 1) through their own experiences of migration, they are able to tap into these personal narratives when they assist others with their literate immigration experience; 2) when institutions prescribe ways of being, reading and writing, literacy brokers are attuned to emotional regimentation and regulations, since they function "across" institutions. Their mobility across institutions allows them to develop a critical stance of institutional language and to recover the loss of affective language experiences. When literacy brokers function within the boundaries of the nation-state, particularly in situations when the state positions itself as a broker of knowledge and literacy such in the case of literacy education in Romania discussed in chapter 4, they manage and control personal experiences, language, and the relations and institutions that produce and distribute literacy education. While literacy brokers in the context of immigration and transnationalism can facilitate mobility, recontextualization, and adaptation to new contexts, they can also emplace subjects within certain discursive spaces, as in the case of the Romanian authoritarian state who emplaced its citizens through language and literacy. Various institutions, local or transnational, as well as non-profit organizations or nation-states operating through visa regulations, can manage, restrict, or facilitate the mobility of individuals and their affinities.

Literacy as affinity should be understood as an emotional repertoire and the process of establishing a series of connections: personal, national, ethnic, or professional. Although literacy as affinity originates in the public sphere, as I examined immigrant literacy outside of formal education, it has potential to be adopted in other contexts, including schools. In creating varied affinities, literacy builds sustainability. I elaborate more on alliances and connections built to create the immigration file in chapter 3. In a literacy-as-affinity model, writing and learning does not stop the moment the writer finishes their task whether that took place in formal or informal sites, in or out of class. Rather, literacy as affinity has potential for transfer and motivation to write beyond institutional walls. Literacy as affinity sprawls to all aspects of the learner's life, across contexts vertically and horizontally. This means that it can build connections with current social spheres but also with past and future rhetorical contexts. A disregard of the role of emotion in writing makes the learning experience limiting in terms of the subjectivities involved—it engages a truncated self—and in terms of social contexts. As a further implication, from this study of immigrant writing, we can envision literacy as affinity's potential for transferability: writing developed in one context becoming a resource and platform for new projects and new initiatives in other contexts. In studying the transnational literate experience of people, Hawisher et al. (2006) introduce a similar concept *guanxi*, defined as "a complex set of social networks operating through personal connections" (620). Similarly, to guanxi, literacy as affinity expands to communities, families, and other contexts in order to connect and support personal literacy experiences.

Literacy as affinity has the power to bridge gaps. In this study of immigrant literacy, writing unfolds mostly in non-traditional sites of education, operating in response to real-world exigencies. While it is regulated and sanctioned by various institutions, it is sustained precisely because those involved conceive it as a series of affinities. People's mobility brings forth gaps of knowledge, experience, or language. Yet, the brokers' work of affinity intervenes in these spaces. As such, literacy as affinity is also about creating connections where loss, disconnect, or change happens. Recent research in neuroscience and cognitive psychology underscores the significance of emotion. Discussing the role of emotional processes in civic discourse, Sharon Crowley (2006) draws on neurobiologist Antonio Damasio's work on brain injury. Damasio found that reason and emotion must work in tandem. Similarly, in cases of cultural and geopolitical shifts, literacy's emotion work becomes even more potent. Learners in and outside the classroom always have to transition in and out of academia, from one workplace to another, or from one culture to another. Given the pervasiveness of mobility, literacy as affinity mediates these in-between spaces.

The following chapter shows how literacy as affinity functions in the context of an immigrant community focusing on refugees. In the context of immigration, their stories provided evidence for the application for asylum. The stories were crafted by literacy brokers in the community who used their own experience to advocate for and advance the cause of others like them.

Chapter 2

Literacy Brokers in the Community

We pleaded our case. I read a few stories. I read a few letters that I received from people in the refugee camps. And I said, "Look, these are stories from our people. They escaped from Communist Romania. If we do not do the papers for them to come to the United States, they'll be sent back to Romania, and they'll be imprisoned."

—Eugen, an American of Romanian heritage

Eugen, a former political refugee from Romania, now a US citizen is aware of the power of writing, of writing a personal story. Eugen learned to write in a rather unexpected way—through drafting of immigration documents for other people, including their stories of persecution. With these stories, he also appealed to non-profit organizations advocating for the cause of many other asylum seekers stranded in refugee camps in Europe. Different from a typical writing classroom, Eugen would write in the high-stakes context of US immigration, where his literate actions generated life-long consequences for many immigrants. Eugen is what we might call a "literacy broker," a go-to person in the community who helped others with immigration papers, mediating between refugees, local churches and non-governmental organizations, and Immigration and Naturalization Service (INS). Often taken for granted, those who facilitate, manage, and connect different agents in the communicative process remain largely invisible despite their crucial role in drafting or helping with immigration files and documents, court proceedings, etc. In the case of assisting Romanian refugees in the 1970–1980s, the last two decades of Communist rule in Romania, the literacy brokers' emotional work is important; it resides in the use of personal experiences and empathetic language in contexts where emotions are highly censored and regulated, such as immigration documents and legal institutions.[1] Based on this work, these brokers develop a bi-institutional perspective and employ personal stories as a form of advocacy.

In the context of transnationalism, which foregrounds ties and attachments to more than one state, the dynamic position and disposition of literacy brokers in relation to multiple nation-states and stakeholders results in what I call a "bi-institutional perspective."[2] A bi-institutional perspective presupposes not just thinking and acting from "within" institutions; rather, it also means to think and act "across" institutions. In his book, *On Institutional Thinking*, Hugh Heclo (2008) defines institutional thinking by providing this example: "It is one thing to think about a sport. . . . It is another thing to honor a sport by entering into its institutional tradition, thinking from inside its thinking, living it from the inside out" (4). To say it more directly, thinking institutionally means "'thinking within' institutions." Through this bi-institutional perspective, literacy brokers accumulate rich language and cultural repertoires in the process of mediating texts locally and transnationally. Assuming this position of mediation, these literacy brokers perform significant emotional work that humanizes the process of immigration. Rather than treat people like "cases," literacy brokers use an emotional discursive repertoire—language of affinity, personal stories, and empathetic work—to recapture and partially reconstitute familiar contexts, literate practices, and audiences that may be lost when people and texts travel from place to place. "The cases" of refugees is similar to the "file self" of economic immigrants discussed in chapter 3; in both situations, bureaucratic contexts seek to reduce people's lived experiences to manageable categories and regulation of personal or emotional discourses.

In addition to the bi-institutional perspective, the personal story is central in the case of refugees; the personal story provides the main account based on which the motive for requesting asylum is established. While literacy brokers operate as mediators on the personal level, they also interact with larger institutions and discourses of nation-states. This type of interaction often positions them to become agents of change, and some do so when they decide to use brokered texts and stories, as the epigraph at the beginning of the chapter shows; as such, they move into roles that advance the cause of other disenfranchised groups. Through a series of literacy events, literacy brokers become engines of public advocacy and change. Although the use of personal stories for advocacy of human rights may seem to reinforce the very instrumental role that I have critiqued in other studies of brokers, this use of personal stories is different. First, there is no pay-off for the broker or for the person whose story is being "used." The actual purpose—intended to produce a change—concerns a similar issue: the need to humanize or personalize an institutional context where decisions are made about transactions and trades with little regard to people's lives. Rather than instrumental, the role of the broker with its emotional work is persuasive and as such, it transforms the rationality of institutions and bureaucratic writing, often deprived of personal and emotional touch.

While I draw on the immigration narratives of nine Romanian refugees, I foreground the brokering experience and practice of four key participants: Eugen, Manuela, Claudiu, and George. The section on the brokers' profiles and background offers details about each one of them (see Table 2.1 and Table 2.2). The first key informant was Eugen. His work as a paralegal, community translator, and interpreter was the first account in which the notion of brokering emerged clearly and convincingly. Interviews with the other participants were conducted later in the data collection process, as informed by emergent themes in the initial sampling.[3] In addition to the interview data, I examined supplemental copies of travel documents, refugee certificates, and documents pertaining to the refugee's immigrant experience shared during our interviews. I also used historical documents, particularly newspaper clippings about Romanian emigrants and Romania-US relationships in the 1980s; all these primary documents originated from the daily press of 1970s–1980s and Radio Free Europe news broadcasts, the main source of uncensored information for many Romanians before 1989.[4]

Situated at the juncture of the individual and rhetorics of nation-states, the broker leverages his or her knowledge to mediate, facilitate, and even advocate a particular course of action. Because mediation in the case of political refugees and human rights rhetoric takes place in larger international contexts, understanding foreign relations between Romania and the US in the 1970s and 1980s is crucial. During this period, the economic agreements between the US and Romania had a direct impact on Romanian emigration/immigration. Having knowledge of these agreements, brokers employed their multiple positions in the community to help with translations, legal papers, and other immigration-related issues. In doing so, these brokers developed a bi-institutional perspective and advocacy work.

Importing American Goods, Exporting Romanian "Political Traitors"

On June 3, 1986, *The New York Times* announced, "Romania to Allow More Than 1,000 to Emigrate" (Gwertzman 1986). This news made its way to Washington in the context of President Reagan's deliberation concerning the extension of Romania's trade benefits through the Most Favored Nation (MFN) status. The benefits emerging from this special status ensured preferential trade rates, allowing Romania to export goods of almost one billion dollar worth and importing about $300 million of American goods (Gwertzman 1986). The Romanian president, Nicolae Ceaușescu, was particularly enamored with the Most Favored Nation title as it carried a certain rhetoric of excellence, Romania's excellence in the world—a status that Ceaușescu often used as a point of pride—of personal achievement; on the domestic front, it served as a powerful argument that the Romanian economy under Communism was thriving. He sought earnestly to secure it even if he openly resented the US's demands for compliance with human rights in exchange for the MFN status and its provisions.

On the immigration front, the US indeed used the MFN status as a leverage to constrain Romania to release its non-desirable people. In different news reports, Richard Schifter, Assistant Secretary of State for human rights and humanitarian affairs, spoke of the MFN's status for Romania in terms of accumulated human benefits; although an economic transaction, it directly affected Romanian emigration since, over the course of twelve years, more than 170,000 Romanians were permitted to emigrate. Schifter also offered specific numbers for the year 1986 when 12,000 ethnic Germans went to West Germany; about 2,000 Romanians went to the United States; and 1,000 to Israel ("US Official Says Trade Favor Improved Romanian Emigration"). In all these news announcements in the 70s and 80s, Romania's MFN status had been framed in economic terms: "losing benefits," being in "jeopardy to lose the MFN status," or in danger of missing "agreements" and "contracts;" these economic transactions effected a significant impact on Romanian emigration. In exchange for the MFN, this highly prized status, Romania agreed to facilitate the departure of several types of citizens: Romanian Evangelicals (who did not align with the official Eastern Orthodox faith practiced by the majority of Romanians) and ethnic minorities who failed to absorb into the national Romanian identity project (German, Jewish, etc.). Eventually the US suspended Romania for its violation of human rights and revoked the MFN status. However, while it lasted, particularly during the negotiation phases, it forced Romania to release some of those "problem" citizens.

Knowledge about such transactions, like the MFN status and economic negotiations between Romania and the US, affected thousands of lives particularly the status of many petitioners for emigration. Literacy brokers had to familiarize themselves with these transactions, specifically with the resulting policies because these facilitated or stalled processes of emigration/immigration. In one of his news reports, Emil Hurezeanu (1987), a journalist and former reporter for Radio Free Europe, offered a descriptive textual path of the emigration which included approximately 20 different petitions, applications, and documents, each of these requiring an intricate process that an applicant had to go through before departing Romania. As such, literacy brokers had to be attuned to both economic negotiations or information gleaned from Radio Free Europe, because the MFN directly impacted the passage or blockage of passport petitions for Romanian émigrés. At the other end—in the US, the deliberation process concerning the MFN trade status was equally textual. In the review session in the House of Representatives on July 30, 1987, Congressman Christopher Smith presented abundant textual evidence of various human rights reports, newspaper articles, and even personal testimonies, for example: a July 1987 Report on Romania from *Amnesty International*, USA; "The Romania Problem," a July 16, 1987 *Wall Street* editorial; Dr. Juliana Pilon's testimonies from the Heritage Foundation, D.C.; Mihai Botez, a Romanian mathematician and human rights advocate; and many others (United States Congress, 1987).

In the 1980s, the "problem" citizens were well monitored not only from within the country through close surveillance but also in the international press (for instance, Radio Free Europe news reports). Radio news in particular reached Romania fast, thus allowing many Romanians to seek ways to petition to leave the country. Although in the country they were cast as enemies of the state, these personae non grata reached out to international forums, strengthening transnational ties. Given this local and transnational context, there was little suspicion concerning political asylum cases from Eastern Europe. Established as a distinct category for immigration to the US, the US Citizenship and Immigration Services (USCIS) uses the classification of "refugee" based on an earlier definition provided by 1951 United Nations Convention Relating to the Status of Refugees. According to section 101(a)(42) of the Immigration and Nationality Act (INA) of 1952, a refugee is "any person who is outside any country of such person's nationality or, in the case of a person having no nationality, is outside any country in which such person last habitually resided, and who is unable or unwilling to return to, and is unable or unwilling to avail himself or herself of the protection of that country because of persecution or a well-founded fear of persecution on account of race, religion, nationality, membership in a particular social group, or political opinion."

Based on this definition, a refugee is framed within the bounds of human rights rhetoric, with special attention to persecution because of one's ethnic or national standing, political, religious affiliation, or racial identification. An examination of the language used by a nation-state or human rights organizations to define those eligible for this category shows that certain aspects of these qualifications are omitted. In chapter 3, I discuss more extensively the fact that, although official immigration classifications and categories for refugees are distinct and clear-cut, in real life contexts the boundaries between a political refugee and an economic immigrant are often rather fuzzy. To put it simply, while many Romanian refugees had been treated abysmally by the Romanian government and human rights were violated on a regularly basis, it also happened that some did not suffer persecution—rather, they left the country because of terrible economic conditions of austerity; yet, the larger political frame created the right context for their petition to leave the country. The official definition of a refugee represents one piece of information that the literacy broker in this context had to master since this knowledge helped connect the immigrant's story to the larger discourses of nation-states.

In pre-1989 Romania, the highest number of those under persecution were German and Jewish minorities who, on the basis of their ethnic heritage and identification, were inevitably potential threats to the national identity project instituted by Ceausescu's regime. Most of these minorities, as shown in the statistics presented by Radio Free Europe, repatriated to West Germany and Israel. The second major category of Romanian refugees, classified as such on the grounds of their religious identification, were directed to seek asylum in the US. Most of these refugees were Christian Evangelicals, including the Pentecostal and Baptist denominations; there were other non-Evangelicals, such as Jehovah's Witnesses, whose religious activity, unlike the Evangelicals,' was decreed unlawful under Ceausescu's regime. Both these alternative identities, framed through the lens of ethnicity and religion, disrupted the national Romanian model of citizenship advanced by the Communist regime in Romania. At that time, the Romanian Communist party's goal was to build the national ethos with an emphasis on common language, heritage, and a common religion (Boia 2001a). Under the Communist regime, this ideal national project was conveniently reinforced by the Orthodox Church, which through its hierarchical structure and national reach, surrendered to "the local Caesar" (Shafir 1978, 23–4).

Many of my participants were refugees persecuted on the basis of their religious beliefs. In exchange for the travel papers, the Romanian state misappropriated everything these people owned and revoked all legal rights: the right to medical health care, to employment, education, and most outrageously, it stripped them of Romanian citizenship. While this practice seems strongly punitive, one must remember that if the Romanian state sought to function as a family (as shown in chapter 4), disobedient "children" had to be ostracized and forced to sever their affinities with the fatherland. Many participants remembered with great difficulty leaving the country without the possibility of going back. One of my participants explained the humiliation and pain experienced in the process of leaving the country: "What was really weird about that is that all the passports were either blue or green. Blue for people who were allowed to leave the country in good terms. Green for people who were allowed to visit. And brown [passports], were for people with non-citizenship. And there was a terminology associated with that, căcănari, you know, shitheads." The brown passports marked these people as non-citizens, a way to signal that their right to Romanian citizenship and identification was suspended not only within the country but outside of its boundaries as well. In exchange for a brown passport, a mark of a persona non grata, the Romanian state tried to repossess these expatriates' property and thus make a profit. Others who left with green or blue passports confessed that they too renounced their Romanian citizenship in fear that the Romanian secret police would extend their reach overseas.

These various paths of leaving the country determined in turn the process towards a new citizenship status for each immigrant. Whether one followed the religious or the political path, each story of oppression was influential in the way the United Nations directed an asylum seeker towards a particular country. The next stage was then determined by the application procedure in the receiving country and their process of becoming a full citizen. Immigration categories determined the type of brokering that took place and the chain of brokers that would support the mobility of the applicant. For instance, Mr. Doru, a Romanian political refugee, left the country carrying abundant textual evidence: court hearings and sentences of his brother and written accounts of instances of persecution; all these documents compiled a case used to request political asylum for his family. Of all the interviewees, he is the only one that presented me with his Romanian secret police file (a file containing more than 400 pages). For some, like Mr. Doru, the process of brokering started in Romania, in the country of origin, but it was highly dependent on the larger transactions between nation-states, as shown in the MFN status debate.

Background and Profiles

What happened in the refugee camp? Just like other networks of communication, Romanians found each other in these camps. One informant told me that certain names and their phone numbers were shared. "You have to call Eugen. He knows how to help." The most valuable information concerned not only knowledge of sponsoring agencies—the World Council of Churches, Interfaith, and other organizations—but also connecting with the right people, those brokers that could facilitate access to information outside the refugee camps in Austria or Italy. These brokers helped with immigration texts such as legal documents, applications, and stories of immigration that were modified into legal accounts; for refugees, this story was essential as it constituted the basis for requesting asylum. They also helped refugees with finding a sponsor—a non-governmental organization that, together with local ethnic churches, offered to officially petition for legal status. Once the papers were processed, the refugees would need help with starting anew in the US, including airport pickup, finding an apartment, furniture, assistance with job search, and various similar needs. Often this assistance was offered by a "go-in-between" person, generally a church representative delegated to help with the adaptation of the newly arrived immigrants. Other than daily provision, there was another component in this brokering process: textual and language assistance, such as advice concerning legal documents, obtaining a social security card, driver's license, and additional paperwork.

Literacy brokers in this immigrant community were not known because they were many; rather, they were known by their *reputation*. A large number of immigrants called on these brokers' services and then, based on their experience, they would further recommend them to others. Eugen and a few others like him were central in my process of learning about this community. As someone who has occupied various brokering positions from volunteering in the community to becoming a church representative in legal affairs and working as paralegal, Eugen offered the most details about literacy brokering relative to legal papers. Given that his brokering role of legal documents had ended, he was the most open to relating practices and events as he remembered them. He also connected me to many other influential brokers. The other brokers' experiences complemented details that Eugen either missed or did not recall during our interview. Although George, a different broker, agreed to participate in the study, he seemed unexpectedly hermetic in his answers. For this reason, I reference him the least. In Table 2.1, I list various roles these brokers held in the community. I also organized

Table 2.1. Literacy Brokers

Literacy Brokers	Education	Education and Training	Languages	Multiple Roles in Literacy Brokering
Eugen	High school degree (Romania) Associate Degree (US)	Volunteer, Training on the Job	Romanian, English, Italian	Former green card applicant Volunteer
Manuela	High School degree (Romania)	Trained on the job; feedback from supervisor	Romanian, English	Legal representative Consultant
Claudiu	College Degree (RO) Certificates (US)	Certificates, Training, Translation conferences; Training on the Job	Romanian, English, French, Hungarian	Legal representative Translator Official interpreter Unofficial reporter
George	College Degree (RO) College Degree (US)	Training in School, and as a community member.	Romanian English (information about knowledge of additional languages was not provided)	Paralegal Legal consultant Community interpreter

Note: I used pseudonyms to protect the identities of my participants.

the brokering activities in Table 2.2 to offer a better understanding of the range of activities that took place in the community. The table also shows the type of documents or the purpose of the brokering activity.

The language that surrounds the mediation process in the case of Romanian refugees includes phrases such as "helped sponsor," "helped these people come to the US," "helped them bring their families," "church representative, legal representative," "doing translations," "[do-ing] all kinds of legal paperwork," "advice on immigration," "we pleaded our case." These activities denote the broker as an assistant, consultant, advocate, or translator, suggesting flexibility of roles and perspectives.

Table 2.2. Types of Brokering Activities

Types of Documents or Purpose of the Brokering Activity	Brokering Activities
Forms	Filling out: Green card applications Citizenship application Biographical forms
Legal Documents	Filling out or writing: Affidavits, declarations Documenting and/or writing personal stories of persecution (asylum seekers) Researching and writing briefs
Consulting	Applicants: Giving legal advice; giving advice concerning particular forms Other entities: Consulting senators and other government officials in regards to an immigration issue Researching and writing briefs
Advocacy and Research	Interviewing people Recording and collecting stories of oppression Compiling reports Preparing briefs
The Immigration File[1]	Compiling and organizing various forms into a coherent "file self:"[2] applications, certificates of birth, marriage, divorce papers, evidence of mailing addresses of applicants, etc.

Notes:

1. The immigration file includes a series of documents and immigration forms that can be considered individually but also as an independent unit. Individual files need a particular rhetorical arrangement to make up the immigration file as single unit.

2. The "file self" is Julie Chu's (2010) term in reference to immigration documents that Chinese applicants compiled to build their case at the US Consulate (132).

Building on these multiple identities, the literacy broker materializes as a malleable construct, permitting the creation of new meanings based on context and roles. Acknowledging this flexibility of positions and contexts, I draw attention to the dynamic nature of literacy brokering and the multiplicity of social contexts embedded in the brokering process.

Accumulating Roles and Points of Affinity in Literacy Brokering

Accumulating Knowledge, Accumulating Roles

A closer examination of the literacy broker in more than one context and with more than one role reveals the complexity of knowledge gleaned from multiple social contexts where the brokers operate. In 1987, Eugen and his family arrived in the US at the intervention of an American congressman. Three years later, Eugen became himself a broker for several other political refugees from Romania. As a broker or, more precisely, "the go-to" person—the actual term Eugen used to refer to his brokering activity in the Romanian immigrant community—he negotiated and mediated the mobility of religiously persecuted Evangelical Romanians in various capacities. He started as a volunteer for the World Council of Churches, for Interchurch Refugee Ministries, and for Immigration Ministries. His role became more official as the Romanian Church of which he was a member delegated Eugen as a legal representative to the Immigration and Naturalization Service (INS). Eventually, Eugen started ed working as a paralegal for various immigration attorneys.

This shift of positions—from being a volunteer with non-profit organizations to being a church legal representative and then a paralegal—marks, on the one hand, the process of institutionalization of the broker's profile; on the other hand, it signals a shift in the roles of mediation. In previous studies of language brokering, the broker seems to be situated between institutions (Orellana, Meza, and Pietsch, 2002; Perry 2009), but the relation between the broker and other constituents, particularly institutions, is somewhat unclear. While sometimes brokers are viewed as having specialized knowledge and representing an institutional perspective, they are often perceived informally as offering assistance (Perry 2009). From my analysis of the broker's work, the broker almost always assumes collaboration with or works under the patronage of some type of institutional authority: as a volunteer working with human rights organizations, a legal representative working with local churches, or a paralegal functioning under legal institutions such as immigration law firms. Certainly, some of these institutions are more or less hierarchical or structured, yet even when brokering takes place in rather flexible contexts, a logic of power and representation is still in place, even in settings such as an immigrant community. Since religious or ethnic persecution was the main reason invoked by Romanian refugees in leaving Romania and requesting asylum, non-profit and religious organizations and institutions, such as Romanian churches in the US, became central sites of support for families arriving from Romania. Various leaders in the immigrant community—Steven Bonica, the owner of the Romanian newspaper, the *Romanian Tribune*; Octavian Cojan, founding member of the Illinois Romanian-American Community organization; and Reverend Valentin Popovici, pastor at a Romanian Baptist Church—offered multiple examples of ways in which churches were actively involved in supporting immigrants, including airport pick-up, help with finding an apartment/job, or help with enrolling children in school. Whenever brokers work with institutions, they receive additional support that endorses the broker's authority to fulfill his or her purpose of mediation. This collaboration of the broker with other institutions—humanitarian organizations and churches—points to good models of civic and public engagement. This means that brokering takes place through collaboration and joined actions. As Judy Kalman (1999) writes, writing practices that are situated locally and culturally often point to larger spaces of communication and knowledge. As brokers partner with others, they create webs of support often based on commonality of experience and quite frequently on ethnic ties. In their position of mediation, brokers harness various types of affiliations—civic, ethnic, local, or global—and channel them to accomplish goals for those individuals who need their assistance.

When Eugen and his family left Romania, his citizenship was revoked; prior to departure, he had been expelled from school and all family possessions seized by the Romanian state. Yet through these changes and shifts of identity, Eugen learned new roles and perspectives. His success in accumulating knowledge, adapting his literate skills, and establishing partnerships came from personal interactions with bureaucratic structures. His knowledge started small. It started with his personal experience and knowledge of institutions familiar to him, which at the beginning included his family, the local ethnic community, and the church; all of these were tied together to the Romanian state that controlled all these social groups before his departure. But from being an expatriate, Eugen became a middleman. In the refugee camp in Italy, Eugen started to translate for his family and for other Romanian refugees. After his arrival in the US, despite limited English, Eugen gradually accumulated useful knowledge and brokered partnerships with multiple stakeholders for other asylum seekers. People would ask for his advice on immigration issues at church and then inquire about his business office—which he did not have at the time—to further solicit his assistance.

In "Accumulating Literacy," Brandt (1995) explains that with changes of literacy expectations and conditions, past literate practices may resurface in current sites of literacy learning (659–60). Although Brandt's analysis refers to transformations and changes in literacy between generations, Eugen's case shows an ability to adapt his past literacy to new contexts. In addition to accumulating various literacies, such as the learning of new languages—Italian in a refugee camp in Rome or English in the US—Eugen also acquired knowledge about the languages of nation-states, about governing state powers, and about mediation. This accumulated knowledge from various roles as a literacy broker enabled Eugen to assist others with writing their own stories of persecution, to help people with documents, and to work with various organizations on behalf of the refugees themselves: "I would sit with clients just like you're sitting with me now and I would ask, I had a form, and I would ask all the questions pertaining to their situations and . . . then I would translate it in English. . . . I've become an expert in writing umm . . . writing people's stories and writing . . . umm affidavits, declarations, statements, whatever you wanna call it." Because of his own personal experience and interactions with larger socio-political structures, Eugen has gained credibility in the Romanian community. People entrusted him with their personal stories in hope of obtaining legal papers, just like Eugen had. His accumulated knowledge built his credentials, but it also connected him to people, to their stories of oppression. Through this accumulation of experiences, webs of knowledge were shared and used in the service of others.

Shifting Roles and Increased Institutional Constraints

As the broker accumulates knowledge from multiple contexts, interactions between brokers and institutions change, and so does the nature of these interactions. This shift is more noticeable when the same literacy broker conducts similar text-related practices—translating/interpreting, filling out forms, researching information, interviewing people, and documenting stories—in various contexts, such as in the immigrant community (less structured, less bureaucratic) and in court settings or an immigration agency (highly controlled). In previous studies on literacy brokers, translators and interpreters have been consistently identified as important language brokers (Martinez et al., 2009; Morales et al., 2012; Tse, 1996). Yet few studies have explored how these translators may operate in multiple settings. From the beginning of my interview with Claudiu, he explained that a community interpreter is very different from an official translator/interpreter. Claudiu, a Romanian-American citizen, owns his own translation and interpretation business, but he also serves regularly as an official translator/interpreter in court settings as well as an informal community translator/interpreter. In a nutshell, he clarifies that while the official job "pay[s] the bills," the other one, in the community, is "the most rewarding." The reward comes, as Claudiu explains, from the ability to help. In a case implicating a community response to elderly abuse, Claudiu volunteered his service as a language interpreter because he too wanted to support this initiative as a member of the community: "I went in voluntarily and in the end, and all the way at the very end, I was offered money. I had a hard time accepting it, but I did. But that was one of those cases when I went in voluntarily, and I went in helping other people help people."

By emphasizing the constraints of the official job—the translation and interpreting in the contexts of institutions such as court settings—Claudiu also managed to capture the shifting position from working in the community to working in the confinements of an institution. In reference to his work in institutional settings, he repeatedly described his role as a "tool" and as an "instrument." Claudiu accepts his role as a "tool," although it may seem deprived of any personal or emotional dimension. The person is there to fulfill a clearly established function—in the case of interpreting in a court setting, to transmit the message exactly as is from one interlocutor to another. Based on Claudiu's account, the position of a translator or interpreter is limited to the mere rendition of the interaction "to the best of his abilities." Claudiu explained that "helping" a defendant in official interactions such as court proceedings is neither possible nor his "job." Since the broker has been framed as the one who assists, who mediates partnerships, the "help" offered by the translator/interpreter is constrained when situated in a regulated setting such as a court, particularly in immigration cases. Conceiving the literacy broker as an instrument or tool at first glance shifts agency from the broker to a model of agency embedded in systemic structures. Yet given the assumed multi-positionality of a broker, if agency is limited in one context, it can be potentially exerted in other settings. For instance, even if Claudiu cannot help someone in the context of a court setting, his knowledge of this institutional discourse can be transferred easily to his role as a community translator. This type of brokering has not been possible in studies of brokering performed by children of immigrants, since they were studied only in the language mediation between their parents and school officials, parents and bank representatives, and others. In these studies, attention has been placed on the type of brokering occurring, rather than on a possible transfer of accumulated knowledge from one setting to another. While speaking multiple languages is crucial in such cross-cultural interactions, in this mobility of positions I emphasize the formation of what I call a bi-institutional perspective. Earlier in the chapter, I explained that a bi-institutional perspective involves thinking and acting in two ways: from "within" and "across" institutions. I use the term "bi-institutional" rather than multi-institutional perspective because I prefer to steer away from the idea that multiple perspectives, or additive processes, would increase the value of this work. Rather, the goal is to suggest that a bi-institutional perspective adds depth and mobility rather than range. Learning and knowing the discourse of institutions—with its procedures, specialized languages, and practices—contributes to an agentic literacy broker who can manage multiple languages and specialized discourses of bureaucratic structures. Since this learning and knowing includes more than one institution, the literacy broker gains multiple perspectives visible not only in actual texts, but implicit in practices and ways of thinking across institutions. In the example mentioned earlier when Claudiu participated as a community member in the elderly abuse case, he shifted his role to that of an interpreter and translator. He says, "I was there as both [community member and interpreter]. That's another very unique thing about the work that I do, that I can have multiple hats depending on the circumstances."

Taking on "multiple hats" allows the broker to adopt multiple roles even though they may involve unequal responsibility or degree of flexibility. Within the institution, procedures take priority over individual actions. Institutional constraint is built into these procedures, operating on multiple levels. First, the translator/interpreter must take an oath. The oath in itself is a formal verbal circumscription of one's identity into the institutional context where s/he operates. To ensure accuracy of translation/interpretation, a security measure is in place when the court, especially in immigration cases, provides a second remote translator selected only from approved language service providers. In such situations, the dynamics between various parties is evidently different. The hierarchy of control is well established, and the interaction is scripted. Claudiu likened this scripted procedure to "a train, once it starts, it goes at a certain pace and unless something major happens, the train keeps rolling." This analogy with train tracks is quite potent, especially that it is language and linguistic procedures that keeps the "train" going. Set on their tracks, institutions shape language and discourses precisely since their role is to "keep going" and to stop only at established points of destination. Inevitably, these prescribed discursive practices constrain individual choice and action.

In the case of the paralegal who works in an immigration office, institutional constraints are similar. At the beginning of my interview with Manuela, she described her job in terms of dos and don'ts, what is allowed and what is not: "A paralegal cannot give legal advice; you are allowed to fill out papers, but you cannot give legal advice . . . [A paralegal] can write letters to immigration, can call to ask about cases that are represented by the attorney. Basically, preparing many legal documents, but not any document." When I asked whether there is flexibility in certain cases or multiple approaches, Manuela answered, "the law is the law." As a literacy broker dealing with scripted texts, particularly working with documents and official applications for immigration, Manuela confirms that the process of filling out papers is a highly regulated practice. In dealing with institutional constraints, both Claudiu and Manuela adopt the perspective of the institution that they represent. To be more specific, they adopt an institutional voice—a concept that Brandt (2005) identified in her study of workplace writers. The institutional voice is not reflected solely in the production of a document, but also in how these brokers speak about their jobs. Manuela is clearly emphasizing that "the law is the law" and that there is little or no room for changes or additions. Claudiu apparently functions as a tool, as one piece in the larger machinery that follows established moves and structures. However, despite the brokers' assumed institutional identity within the institution, they act as more than tools, and their mediation is more than instrumental.

Language of Affinity and Empathetic Work

In both situations, that of a translator/interpreter and that of a paralegal, the issue lies, as Claudiu explained, with who hires you and under whose authority you work. Institutional control, particularly in the case of immigration, leaves little to no room for mediation as help, as was the case with the translator/interpreter in the community. However, even in these cases of rigid or prescriptive mediation, the emotional work of mediation comes to surface. After Claudiu explained the constraints that were part of his job as a legal translator and that "help" and "assistance" had to be within the legal proceedings, he elaborated further: "Sometimes, you feel bad for someone . . . and it's actually not my job [to help]. And sometimes, I see people, they spend two hours building a case and then they say something in like 3 seconds, and they . . . tsss ruin everything. But it's not my job to censor anything. I'm there actually as an instrument." Besides the fact that Claudiu sees himself as a mere instrument who solely reports on the language exchange in a court setting, his follow-up comment—"Sometimes you *feel bad*" (emphasis mine)—reveals his affective involvement. I see this as a moment of interruption; it is not marked by an external gesture or an actual intervention of help, yet it represents a significant point of institutional critique. Generally, and most of the time, there is no room for "help" in a court proceeding. But sometimes there are moments of empathy similar to Claudiu feeling (bad) for and with his clients. While these moments do not dismantle the institutional structure, they do offer points of critique. They also profess that brokers are more than instruments, even in an institutional context that regiments people's discursive practices through patterns of communication.

Like Claudiu's empathetic regret, Manuela shared a moment of empathetic joy based on commonality of experience. In response to my question about the reasons for liking her job, she replied: "Every case is specific . . . very individualized and you see the result right away. And when we receive the approval for a green card, I feel as I did when I received my own green card. Seriously, that's how I feel." One can only assume that the moment when she got her own green card was an exhilarating experience, and thus she relives that joy through the experience of her clients. Even George, the literacy broker who offered the fewest details about his interaction with his clients, used language of affinity during the interview. In reference to his clients and immigration procedures, George repeatedly used the phrase "*our* Romanian" (italics mine). When discussing immigration categories based on profession, George explained that "our Romanian" can apply for this or that type of visa only if there are no US citizens or residents qualified for this position. If Manuela's moment of affinity is based on personal experience, George's affective language "our Romanian" indexes an affinity based on ethnic and community connectedness. Instead of referring to his clients as applicants or immigrants, George adds the possessive "our" to denote shared ethnic ties with his clients. Although a possessive adjectival phrase could be used with a neutral connotation or with sarcasm or derision, in this case the context and the experience of the utterance indicate the affective underlining layer. George is, after all, an immigrant himself, mingling with community members while also working formally as an attorney of immigration. It is precisely in this context of immigration discourse that he uses a language of identification and empathy with his fellow Romanians. In performing this language of affinity, literacy brokers re-instill a lost sense of belonging in the process of immigration. They perform emotional work that matters even if it is not always highly perceptible.

These moments of identification established on the basis of personal experience, community ties, or simply human understanding shape the profile of a broker as someone who has knowledge and experience both within systems and across institutional structures. As brokers, even those working within state or bureaucratic institutions, show affinity with the disadvantaged, with those outside of the system, they manage to human-ize and soften rigid boundaries for those whose interests they represent. Although unexpressed in action, these affinities count as interruptions of the system. Bureaucratic systems of control are not restrictive only to the extent that they manifest in action. They are also controlling in the way they regiment structures of feeling and ways of thinking. One may suggest that by choosing to work in these institutions, these individuals are in reality doing the feeling work—even if it is repressed emotions—for the institutional structures. I argue that while brokers do this work from "within institutions," following institutional rules of practices, their ability to think and act *across* institutions unlocks them from one partic-ular role. If structures of feelings are regimented in one context, they are redistributed in other contexts, institutional or non-institutional. For instance, even if Claudiu cannot help in one particular case such as in a court setting, when he is privately hired by a community member, he can use his experience and feelings of affiliation to engender a better outcome for that person.

One relevant example about regimented structures of feeling comes from another participant in my study, Horea, as he witnessed lack of mediation, of literacy brokering. As Horea interacted with the US bank clerks, he shared his frustrations. He explained that he was not upset that his application for opening a bank account was denied. Rather, he was outraged that several bank clerks could not understand or conceive that a man in his mid-thirties like him had not previously owned a bank account. This inability to envision a different alternative to the rules or regulations that operate in one system shows dogmatic thinking and rigid structures that suppress identification of any sort. It creates a gap between those in the system and those outside of the system or those familiar with a different system, reinforcing the fact that those margin-alized must be kept outside. Brokers often come in and bridge these gaps. Depending on setting, they can build bridges of understanding that un-lock perceptions of rigid social structures. Points of affinity are construct-ed through an accumulation of knowledge from multiple viewpoints, in-cluding from institutional communication and interactions.

These points of affinity, which I conceive as moments of identifi-cation, afford an understanding of language brokering as more than just action. Language and literacy, if conceptualized as sociocultural constructs deeply involved in the lives of people, must engage the entire personhood, not just discrete elements. This means that people do not just participate in language and literacy interactions with knowledge or particular languages but bring with them feelings, attitudes, thoughts, and often preconceptions about a particular literacy, a language event, or specific literacy contexts, such as courtrooms, banks, government agencies, and so on. In *A Rhetoric of Motives*, Kenneth Burke explains the formative effect rhetoric can have on one's attitude in situations when one's action is conscribed. Burke (1950) gives the example of a criminal who might be moved into repentance by a priest's sermon (rhetoric) even if he cannot take any particular action (50). Making this fine distinction between action and attitude, wherein attitude is defined as "an incipient act, a leaning" or predisposition, illuminates more cogently the role of attitudes, feelings, and predispositions in literacy events. Even if action may be limited or constrained by various social structures or bureaucratic formations as seen with Claudiu's train analogy, literacy brokers can effect change through attitudes of empathy and identification, albeit momentarily.

To sum up, developing a bi-institutional perspective entails mobility through various social spaces, which present themselves as somewhat rigid structures. As literacy brokers shift through various roles as volunteers or members of the community, as Eugen's examples show, they take on more institutionally-defined roles, and in doing so they accumulate experiences, languages, cultures along the way. But they also gain different perspectives depending on the context of their work. For example, Claudiu as a language broker and certified translator in an immigration court accumulates particular knowledge, such as familiarity with the legal system, glossary of legal terms, and knowledge of procedures. Since Claudiu is also a member of the Romanian ethnic community, people from the community sometimes ask for language assistance with papers and with various other documents. And, importantly he also has experience as an immigrant himself, having gone through the naturalization process. All these multiple roles enable Claudiu to position himself as a powerful agent of mediation among multiple stakeholders. Literacy brokers also learn to sift through these perspectives, to select rhetorically useful literacy practices and repurpose them in new contexts for themselves or for others in similar circumstances. Through this mobility across contexts, literacy brokers develop a bi-institutional perspective that involves ways of thinking across institutions and ways of feeling across institutions. This bi-institutional perspective allows one to detach from a particular institution and to adopt a critical stance. In doing so, literacy brokers learn various institutional discourses and ways of thinking, but they can also offer an institutional critique. Although this critique is not explicit, it becomes visible in the emotional work that these brokers provide in addition to their typical mediation tasks—assistance with papers, legal advice, consulting. Through moments of affinity and language of empathy, the brokers intervene between the individual and larger bureaucratic structures, precisely because they have adopted bi-institutional perspectives.

Literacy Brokering and Personal Stories as Advocacy

The work of literacy brokers expands beyond local or transnational communities to occasions for advocacy. From being the "go-to" person in the immigrant community, Eugen often moved on to being a "go-between." In his interactions with INS and human rights organizations such as the World Council of Churches and the International Rescue Committee, Eugen was the voice of the larger immigrant community and even of those who were still in refugee camps. In this middle position, Eugen became an advocate for the cause of refugees, pleading with non-profit organizations to extend their sponsorship to other soliciting asylum seekers. After signing for the fiftieth person, Eugen remembers being called for a special interview with the leadership of the non-profit organizations that acted as official sponsors. "You already have fifty people. You got to stop," was their message. But Eugen did not give in. As exemplified at the beginning of the chapter, Eugen took action and advocated for more sponsorship with the help of written stories and letters from the refugees themselves: "And we pleaded our case. And I read a few stories, I read a few letters that I received from people in the refugee camps. And I said, 'Look, these are stories from our people from the refugee camps. They escaped from Communist Romania. If we do not do the papers for them to come to the United States, they'll be sent back to Romania and they'll be imprisoned.'" In this situation, literacy brokers like Eugen employed personal stories to evoke emotions for the cause of marginalized groups, asylees in this case. Although not in a courtroom, Eugen takes on the task of "pleading a case," and in doing so he identifies with those for whom he advocates; in Eugen's appeal, asylees become "our people," and their plight in turn becomes "our case." In the Romanian language, the word for attorney, *avocat*, has the same root as the English word, advocate. The Latin root for both Romanian and English terms is advocatus (Latin), "one called to aid" ("Advocate"). In his position as an advocate, Eugen indeed was aiding other organizations in understanding the cause of Romanian asylum seekers he was representing.

In another situation, serving as a liaison for the INS, Eugen took on the advocate's role again, but this time it involved documenting and doing research abroad. His task was to document ongoing religious persecution in Romania in 1992, after the official fall of the Communist regime, which took place in 1989. Eugen's research and documentation took the shape of a report for the US Department of Justice as a way to provide evidence for certain political asylum requests on the roll and help determine if they were valid cases for asylum. The legitimacy of these cases was established based on evidence of religious oppression that was still taking place in Romania, even after the official socialist regime had been overthrown. In preparation for this report, Eugen went back to Romania and talked to people. Concealing the real purpose of his visit, Eugen interacted with people in the streets, videotaping and audiotaping their stories: "I documented everything, all my stories, and even while walking in the streets, we were videotaping and we were audiotaping and all the stories were documented and then, when I came home, I wrote each individual story . . . and I published a booklet about 160 pages . . . [of] stories of persecution that went on in Romania even in '92." Such a document is similar to various other texts that were presented in the House of Representatives when the MFN trade status was frequently negotiated or under review.[5] As in Eugen's report for the INS, several House representatives made use of personal stories to demonstrate Romania's need for the MFN status, which was directly tied to emigration from Romania (United States Congress 1987). It was not just in the discourse of human rights organizations but also in governmental branches that the emotional work of personal stories represented an intervention with powerful economic and political implications. While the MFN affected trade benefits between Romania and the US, it also pressured the Romanian government to release thousands of religious and ethnic minorities. This interconnected relationship between immigrants' personal stories of persecution and larger governmental agencies demonstrates the need for and the centrality of literacy brokers in bridging communication between individuals and larger structures. It also shows that emotional work and the personal can be tied intimately to issues of economics and politics.

This latter example of Eugen's work of advocacy marks a change in scale and audience. It involved a larger process of documentation, including audio and video evidence to support the case for Romanian families seeking asylum in the US. Since Eugen did not have any special training either in writing or research, one might ask what has been his motivation for doing this work. There is no apparent gain unless we speak of emotional benefits. At first glance, this rhetoric of "help" inside and outside of the community through advocacy seemingly contradicts the economic frame of a broker. Help, particularly in ethnic communities, is rarely conceived in financial terms and often means doing a service, giving a ride, assisting with documents and papers, or aiding someone in finding a job. Yet this "help" is not necessarily without payoff. Indeed, if the broker is positioned in a reciprocal relationship with different parties at the same time, the payoff is invisible. However, if this brokering activity comes in exchange for having been helped in the past, for having experienced it, then the exchange happens diachronically. In doing so, the broker can certainly mediate current transactions, but often the motivation comes from identification with his or her past experiences.

In many ways, the broker embodies a Bakhtinian discursive identity, oriented both towards future actions and past experiences, and always carrying traces of the sociohistorical contexts s/he has inhabited. Eugen has certainly oriented his resources towards future actions, brokering not only local immigrants' legal papers, but advocating for future engagement concerning unresolved cases of refugees. In discussing social knowledge that surrounds the texts drafted by scribes in the plaza, Kalman (1999) shows that these texts are connected to knowledge about future consequences of these texts and their circulation to various audiences. Similarly, Eugen is aware of the power of brokered texts. These texts serve multiple functions as stories of persecution of asylum seekers whose immediate purpose was to obtain legal passage into the US; they also address a larger purpose—to bring awareness about the refugee situation and human rights violation in Romania.

To be engaged in such actions of advocacy requires more than knowledge of macrodiscourses, that is, languages of countries and institutions; it requires intimate knowledge of those whose interests the literacy brokers represent. Brokers then hold a strategic position combining knowledge of small, particular details with larger discourses and structures. In this position, brokers can potentially leverage their experience, their emotional investments, and sometimes their official roles to compensate for unequal power relations, particularly in transnational settings. A literacy broker in the context of immigration must have knowledge of larger discourses, the languages of religious institutions and political ideologies exercised by nation-states, and must learn to use this knowledge strategically. Such accumulated knowledge implicates the personal, the national, and the transnational.

The personal, particularly in the case of refugees, is crucial since one's own personal story of oppression constitutes the grounds for seeking asylum in the first place. But the personal must be framed relative to the national and transnational. Eugen, for instance, left Romania with great difficulty after going through a painstaking process to obtain a passport to leave the country. The first step—filling out the application to request a passport—was in itself considered a subversive act. As we learned earlier, many had citizenship revoked and left the country with a brown passport—"for shitheads," as Eugen relates in the interview; the Romanian state issued brown passports, passports of "no citizenship," to people with whom it sought to sever all relations. In such situations, the personal intersects the national and transnational, and it is not only understood to be an expression of one's individual experience. Rather, it becomes political and inherently rhetorical. Micciche (2002) suggests that "the political turn in composition . . . has been slow to address the emotional contexts of teaching and learning" (435). In immigrant literacy, the intersection of the political and the emotional become evident not only in the broker's engagement in advocacy but also in work with immigration forms and immigration agencies as well as advocacy for human rights.

Textual Brokering and the Document Event

The inclusion of a personal narrative in the bureaucratic writing context, especially immigration papers, is rather rare. Only in the case of asylum seekers does the application form permit a discursive insertion that involves a personalized and flexible genre. Generally, immigration forms are inherently formulaic and prescriptive, with this notable exception of the narrative of asylum-seeking applicants. It is this supplementary form that I would like to discuss further since it creates space for the individual narrative to unfold. Clarifications, disclosures, details, and descriptions included in this narrative, altogether build a case that qualifies or disqualifies one for asylum. Based on Eugen's account, the story of persecution was central in the brokering activity of Romanian immigrants.

Conceptually, the document event has been defined as interaction between two or more interlocutors participating in the drafting of a written document (Kalman 1999). Besides various rhetorical decisions about the audience (the addressee), content (what to include), Kalman (1999) explains that a document event engages a series of other activities: "dictating, note taking, copying or consulting ancillary texts" (35). In examining Eugen's assistance with a document event, I will follow similar conceptual guidelines, although decisions concerning audience for instance are unnecessary. The audience in the context of immigration papers is evidently decided by the rhetorical context: immigration agencies and respectively, immigration officers.

The document event, as explained by Eugen, serves as a pattern for his interaction with community members. Rather than focus on a particular story, Eugen's account provided a window into his activity as a broker and the process of learning to write for legal purposes:

> I would sit with clients just like you're sitting with me now, and I would ask, I had a form, and I would ask all the questions pertaining to their situa-

tions, and I would record it on tape, and then I would take their statement and type it, then I make it literate. I would make it so that it sounds like a nice story, and it's fluid, right? I mean it flows. . . . Then, I would read it back to them, or have them read it, and acknowledge that nothing has been twisted or changed, . . . then I would translate it in English. So basically I've become an expert in writing, umm . . . writing people's stories, and writing . . . umm affidavits, declarations, statements, whatever you wanna call it.

First, we notice a linguistic shift from a neutral interaction between community members to an exchange controlled and structured by a formal document and its bureaucratic language: community members become "clients," a personal story turns into a typed "literate" statement. The moment the community member becomes a client, their story gets molded in the discursive space of the immigration form. In this process, the personal story is translated into a "nice story" which perhaps alludes to both an emotional and coherent story as Eugen explains; it is then typed, revised and approved as a truthful statement, and finally, it is translated into English. All these steps turn a story of escape like many that I have heard shared around kitchen tables into a legal account; it is a project that turns individuals into legible citizens (Scott 1998).

References to "flow" or "fluid" reveal that some of these stories might have been quite difficult to share. These were, after all, stories of persecution, and people may have provided fragments of experience, incomplete accounts, or partial memories not necessarily produced in a chronological, coherent, or logical manner. It is this latter part—the logic of the argument—that interested me further. As such, in my conversation with Eugen, I solicited additional details about the refugee narrative, for instance I asked whether the story had to advance an argument:

L: I assume it's a story that has to put forth an argument, a case right?
E: not . . . yeah. It has to bring the, it has to bring the . . . the problem, in such a view as to show it is a problem, that it occurred more than once, that it occurred to a very, very few number of people, not to a lot, that you were singled out for whatever reason, that it caused persecution, or that it was part of mistreatment and harassment.

I asked the question about whether the story had to make an argument because writing argument is at the core of writing instruction in in the US higher education. I was interested whether argument-focused writing permeates other rhetorical contexts beyond the writing classroom. I raised the same issue in my conversation with Manuela the paralegal, who explained that with documents and document files, it is all about qualifications rather than arguments:[6] "You never have to convince the state. Just show them you qualify. You see in immigration the rules are very clear; nothing is with a double-meaning or tricky.[7] You qualify or you don't; it's black on white." Whether rules are as clear as Manuela suggests is debatable. The phrase "it's black *on* white"—a word-for-word translation of a Romanian expression—means that a message is clearly visible and permanent, as black ink gets imprinted on a white sheet of paper; The technology of writing gives durability to the meaning through the very act of inscribing a message on a paper; a similar operation works in legal accounts. The rule of law, the written law is associated with permanence. The qualifications for citizenship, as Manuela suggests, seem immovable because they are written law.

Returning back to Eugen's explanation about the political asylum story, the argument in this case is reflected in a list of specific criteria that create a credible story of persecution: the story had to identify the problem, establish a unique situation, and demonstrate its repetitive occurrence. Ultimately, this process of drafting political asylum cases was more than "just a nice, flowing story." The story had to be a fairly sophisticated narrative that involved a skillful transformation of a personal experience into a compelling legal account.

As such, the most significant actions in brokering a refugee story concerns the use of rhetorical strategies to point to and describe what constitutes a problem. Generally, exigence is often framed in local or national contexts. However, showing that a "problem" is still exigent in transnational contexts, especially in relation to two or more nation-states, requires more refined rhetorical knowledge. In a news report from Free Europe Radio from 1983, Tamara Jones explains the distressful situation of several Romanians who, against all odds, received passports, gave up Romanian citizenship, and were awaiting on approval from US immigration. In response to this situation, a Western diplomat explained that these Romanians did not understand the necessarily qualifications of US immigration. These Romanians apparently mistakenly thought that "freedom to emigration should also mean freedom to immigrate" (Jones 1983). A year later, in 1984, a similar problem—that of catching people in between the Romanian emigration restrictions and the US immigration rules—occurred when Romanians with a "non-citizenship" status were rejected entrance in the US because their cases exceeded the US immigration quota of 1,000 ("US Praised and Warned on Human Rights Policy in Romania" 1984). This illustrates the challenge to pose a problem rhetorically in the context of transnationalism. While for Romanians under Communism, freedom to leave was exigent and was often obtained at high costs, symbolizing an act of defiance and refusal to endorse a repressive political regime, for the American counterpart this freedom meant a form of trespassing, or at least a presumptuous act showing lack of knowledge of the US immigration system.

A problem framed rhetorically at the national and transnational levels is indeed challenging. Freedom to travel, for instance, is regulated and differentiated across nation-states. For Romanians, before and after Communism, freedom to move, work, or pursue an education continued to be restricted through visa requirements in many Western countries. These restrictions imposed on people and texts limiting mobility and knowledge unmask layers of inequality based on national origin, ethnicity, or socioeconomic background. This facet of globalization and knowledge economy shows that only certain knowledge can be exchanged, and the value of that knowledge is often determined based on national identification. In chapter 4, I discuss in more depth how visa regulations operate as forms of control being generally imposed on many nations-states that have already been socio-economically or politically marginalized.

Setting up a problem in a transnational context also depends on specific political agendas of the respective countries at a particular time. In other words, the immigrant problem could be a priority in one administration but not in successor administrations. While several participants in my study had knowledge about various special agreements between the US and Romania, *when* they applied for papers changed everything. Lucia, for instance, who immigrated to the US in 1983 with her entire extended family of thirteen (her husband and one baby, parents-in-law and their six children, brother-in-law and his wife) remembered that her father-in-law learned about President Jimmy Carter's agreement (probably the MFN) with Romania, in exchange for money, that involved releasing Romanian religious minorities. In 1978, one of Lucia's family members reacted fast, filed for a passport, and within one year left the country. However, by the time the rest of the family applied to emigrate, the US administration had changed and so did policies and attitudes towards immigration; as such, the family had to wait for papers until 1983, when they were finally able to leave Romania.

Besides establishing "a problem" that is conceived transnationally, the broker also had to show that the refugee's story of persecution happened to only a few people. This was particularly difficult because under Ceauşescu's oppressive regime, the entire Romanian population suffered—with a few exceptions—from basic human rights deprivation. The challenge in crafting the written legal account for immigration purposes was to frame the narrative within the context of oppression that was internationally well known, while also to particularize each case and thus, demonstrate an immediate need for intervention. As such, the US immigration context asked for a demonstration of particularism in the refugee's story while Romania's socialist agenda was entirely focused on reducing the individual to a member of a social class. The mismatch between two countries' political projects and their impact on the individual merge in the mediating experience of the literacy brokers. Only knowledge of both systems could lead to adequate literacy brokering that transformed a personal story of oppression into a unique narrative befitting the immigration project. The brokering of asylum stories reveals that the literacy broker's knowledge must be situated dialogically and strategically, adapting to political economies across contexts.

Understanding literacy brokers in more than one context provides a complex view of their dynamic roles and accumulated literacy practices. As such, literacy brokers act not just in local communities, but in transnational communities, communicating within and across larger institutions, organizations, and nation-states. In doing so, the personal matters as much as the national and transnational in shaping the literate experience. As various personal accounts show, including Eugen's retelling of the document event, real-world genres intersect multiple layers of personal and institutional contexts.

An important take-away point is that literacy brokers acquire a bi-institutional perspective when they move from context to context. It is this bi-institutional perspective that enables brokers to bridge literacy gaps through emotional work. This emotional work, or literacy as affinity, in the context of immigrant communities encompasses personal narratives and language of empathy, even when institutional constraints limit individual expression or feelings. Literacy brokers' work of affinity shows that emotions have social and political dimensions, and most certainly, economic purchase as well. Thus, the brokers' emotional work permeates all aspects of the social context, including the economic and political, altogether challenging us to pay closer attention to larger socio-economic and political formations and to how individuals mold their lives to respond to current exigencies while also maintaining a sense of purpose and agency. When institutions and political agendas are strong, literacy brokers can potentially alleviate or restore the loss of individual agency through their work with literacy as affinity.

Chapter 3

Economies
of Writing

To find someone to offer you a job, you know how hard it is to get it, to show that you are somehow more special than a million other Americans, who probably do similar work. Someone must want you badly.

—A Romanian immigrant

Recent engagements with economic frames in rhetoric and composition (e.g., Edwards 2014; Horner et al. 2016 *CCC* special issue, Welch and Scott 2016) show that our field is just beginning to grapple with economies of writing and the exigence for interrogating the economic as an ascendant force.[1] Although this work connects individuals, writing labor, and ideologies to material conditions, the general tendency is to adopt economic frames that are deterministic—in other words, that neglect human agency. In a rigorous review of economic scholarship in composition, Edwards (2014) found that compositionists tend to adopt a "market-based capitalist economy [that] relies on an ideology of individual choice while at the same time refusing the possibility of human intervention" (247). This deterministic model overlooks the marginalized, ignores their capacity for self-empowerment and, if unreservedly embraced, leaves our field bereft of a body of significant literacies. Co-brokering, a critical-theoretical term I am proposing, addresses this limitation by capturing the agency, affinities, and experiences of those at the margins of society—immigrants, low SES groups, etc.[2]

Framed in the context of informal economies and networks, co-brokering involves textual mediation, translation of texts and bureaucratic practices, and circulation of information; it also aims to unveil how writing at the margins is being produced and distributed through various strategies involving both market and nonmarket interactions. Most narratives envision immigrants as vulnerable to neoliberal economies, often framed in crises or managing to get by. The accounts presented here foreground the agency and collaboration the immigrants summon as they resist and recast overpowering economic forces. Further, I complement existing frames by proposing co-brokering as a noncapitalist project, informed by the post-capitalist geographers J. K. Gibson-Graham's notion of diverse economies. Against profit-driven globalism that configures most human activity by market principles (Scott 2016b), Gibson-Graham argue that we need *diverse* economic frames and with these, new discourses that account for alternative economic activities and subjectivities, ones that have the potential to disrupt, alter, or even complement capitalist projects. To create such a terminology, we need to look elsewhere to different, possibly informal sites (e.g., homes, coffee shops, cabs, kitchen tables), not just the classroom, to account for varied market and nonmarket activities and to allow for the formation of different economic subjectivities. A discursive practice emerging in unofficial sites, co-brokering involves mediation, translation of texts or of bureaucratic language into lay terms, and circulation of information that act as a bridge between formal (visible) and informal (invisible) economies; co-brokering also foregrounds particular sites and infrastructures as units of analysis (e.g., homes, intimate spaces) where immigrants can develop their own discursive practices, hidden transcripts that mimic official bureaucratic protocols.[3] Unlike formal markets that rigorously and precisely document all work following established protocols, diverse economies allow for varied types of activities to flourish; they are flexible in nature and tend to be enacted on the basis of social ties or contexts different from or complementary to the marketplace: barter, cooperative enterprises, alternative currencies, state allowance, household chores, gifts, favors, and even unpaid labor.[4] Most importantly, in the neoliberal economy logic, people can develop agency to reconfigure their economic, political, and legal identities. Immigrants and migrants are not mere laborers in a market-driven engine. They craft agency. They develop discourses. They build alliances and break down market monopoly and bureaucratic practices to serve their own ends.

In developing the term co-brokering and the formation of diverse economies, I rely on the discursive tactics of seven Romanian migrants who were enrolled in a Work and Travel summer program designated for college students. This group of migrants are different from the refugees discussed in chapter 2. As seasonal workers, they embraced an economic and agentic subjectivity in the neoliberal market and in doing so, they simultaneously resisted and refashioned their status as disposal laborers.[5] Through co-brokering, these migrants reconfigured their marginality and undocumented status as they built affinity-based relationships and exchanged immigration experiences and affective labor (Hardt 1999). In the process of obtaining US citizenship, they developed hidden transcripts—clandestine knowledge and discourses that allowed them to understand and navigate official bureaucratic practices and diverse sites of economic and discursive actions (e.g., qualifications for a summer job, visa regulations, identification documents, personal networks, and households).

The seven respondents, mostly economic immigrants, who arrived in the US through the US Department of State Work and Travel program, are representative of the new immigrant, who is mobile and moved by capitalist flows. The Work and Travel program offers college students temporary employment, yet many repurpose their stay; once in the US, they craft a plan and path toward citizenship. Functioning under the auspices of the US Dept. of State, the Work and Travel program is managed by a transnational company, Council on International Educational Exchange (CIEE), that takes care of the applicants' legal procedures, such as visas, job placement, and additional work details. Situated in the larger global mobility and economic frame, the Work and Travel program follows a neoliberal market logic as it advances the interest of global businesses facilitating the mobility of migrants in exchange for cheap labor. Although global capitalism values these migrants' skills—their mastery of multiple languages, college education, and a global-oriented mind—they remain seasonal workers, disposable and dependent on transnational corporations' economic interest. Despite such limitations, this generation of new immigrants formulate their agency as they navigate formal paths toward citizenship as well as informal economies—that is, networks of affiliation and rhetorical strategies brokering each other's path to obtain legal papers. Having been marginalized in Europe and elsewhere through visa impositions and elaborated criteria of mobility control, these immigrants forge their own alliances as agentic selves disrupting the imposition of nation-states and border control.

When studying documentality, the method of investigation can be challenging, requiring varied approaches. While interview data come from seven key respondents, not all shared the same amount of data or the same kind of information regarding legal papers, documentation, or the path to citizenship. Some were fairly open about their status, while others alluded to their undocumented status by the nature of their emplacement and lack of mobility, and yet others avoided references to legal papers altogether. One account in particular, Sorin's, is central as his narrative constitutes the backbone frame of my thinking of informal economies and marginal economic subjects. His account provided the most comprehensive, step-by-step rendition of migrants' entire process from obtaining papers to full citizenship status. In using third person reporting, Sorin reconstructed the full narrative of the migrant experience, not as an individual story, but as a collective experience of migrants with similar background: college students from Eastern Europe taking a seasonal job in the US. Additional respondents reported on their experience and that of their compatriots. One migrant, for instance, mentioned that at his first job as a taxi driver, about 40% were Romanians who he had met at the taxi driving school. Several other respondents offered detailed information about the immigrant file (Julie Chu calls it "paper trail" or "the file self"[6]) where they documented their bona fide marriage and the economic ties with their spouses; they also mentioned marriage for legal papers as a routine practice. The accounts of these migrants—along with references and ties to other similar experiences—were used to ensure the validity of my research methods and analysis. Sorin's narrative remains central in my discussion of informal economies because he helped reconstruct the other migrants' stories that were partial, fragmented, or unrecorded depending on their legal status. Interview data reveal that although informal economies are ubiquitous, they are difficult to document. Overall, my methodology—fine grained qualitative research documenting migrants' discursive strategies—is significant in that these stories are easily missed in political economic analyses that are only looking at relations around capital and monetarization. Attention to personal, fragmented narratives, and navigation of formal and informal economies, have allowed a theorization of co-brokering as a rhetorical practice that captures agency and action even in contexts where such agency is routinely denied.

Diverse Economies

Understanding co-brokering as an agentic rhetorical tactic is organically tied to the economic frames where it emerges, diverse economies, and intimate sites. Informed by feminist geographers and local activists, J. K. Gibson-Graham remarked that a large number of economic activities include nonmarket transactions, informal economies, and alternative paid and nonpaid labor. For instance, economists have shown that care services and unpaid household labor may account for 30% to 50% of economic activity (Ironmonger 1996) while others demonstrate the complex link between the paid and unpaid economies when gender is taken into consideration (Himmelweit 2002). In "Diverse Economies," Gibson-Graham (2008) expand their earlier work with concrete examples of various alternative economic activities, such as movements to care for landscapes and the environment; diversified local and complementary currencies; social economies like cooperatives, voluntary organizations, nonprofits; informal financial networks of migrant remittances, and a host of other economic endeavors: "landless and co-housing movements, the global eco-village movement, fair trade, economic self-determination, the relocalization movement, community-based resource management, and others" (617–18). Most of this new activity, as Cameron (2020) explains in a discussion of new enterprises, involves a "social mission" in which people's wellbeing is highlighted. It is within this diverse economic framework that I situate co-brokering as a discursive practice emerging in undetermined or intimate, personal spaces straddling formal and informal economies.

Understanding the difference between formal and informal economies—also called diverse or alternative to capitalist economies—is essential in developing a new language and terminologies different from market-driven practices.[7] This difference is established based on the type of economic activity, setting, and the subjectivities involved in economic processes. In formal economies, human activity and discourses unfold through a series of set procedures, clearly established. Formal economies are marked by visible, tangible actions wherein official roles such as formal aides, attorneys, paralegals—as in the case of migrant workers—take on the responsibility of bureaucratic literacy. Written discourse follows the protocols, genres, and conventions dictated by the respective institutions. As an example, which was discussed previously, a formal legal institution such as a courthouse shapes the tasks and discourses of interpreters as brokers. As such, the "institutional constraint" imposed on the interpreter is also reflected in pre-established legal procedures in a US court proceeding. First of all, the translator/interpreter must take an oath: "The very very first thing that I do when I walk in there, is I take an oath, and that is common in any proceeding, whether it's a deposition, court proceeding, even the simplest one, I take an oath that I will translate to the best of my ability" (Interview with a translator/interpreter). The oath in itself is a formal verbal circumscription of one's identity into the institutional context where s/he operates. To ensure accuracy of translation/interpretation, a security measure is in place when the court, especially in immigration cases, provides a second remote translator selected only from approved language service providers. The hierarchy of control is well established, and the interaction is scripted, with distinct pre-established roles and practices. The translator/interpreter's actions, as shown earlier, follow the court's (a formal institution) entire process, which proceed like a train "set on their tracks" with little to no possibility for intervention: "With immigration, it's different. It's not like with a trial, when they can drag a case for years even in the case of murderers . . . There's no trial and, you know, error. There's no trial or a jury to decide. It's decided by one person, very easy, very fast. If you didn't, if you didn't convince the guy, that's it" (Interview with a migrant). In comparing a murder trial with the case of an undocumented migrant, this participant basically explains that the former, a murderer, seemingly has higher chances to be acquitted than an undocumented immigrant. The murderer, even if punished by the legal system, functions within a legal structure rather than outside of it. The undocumented migrant, on the other hand, is almost always in dispossession; the undocumented migrant has no right because most rights function under the umbrella of state powers or formal institutions, often perceived as "the guy," as one person who has the power to decide one's destiny.

By contrast, informal economies rely less on official roles and settings. Rather, they foreground the work of friends, acquaintances, or community members who put their experiences and knowledge of bureaucracies and systems at others' disposal. Economic activity in these contexts unfolds through flexible enactments, and while they may parallel official discourses, they are often imbued with personal intentions. The sites for this economic activity are less visible or determined. Straddling oral and written discourses, these negotiations co-construct a hidden transcript that is less formal and often changeable with each interaction.

Informal economies are flexible in their roles and the sites where the discourse is crafted. Notably, they are marked by two traits: 1) *locality*: information and discursive exchange occur in intimate, unofficial sites; and 2) *informal* or *underground transactions* that may involve various types of currencies: unpaid or affective labor, reciprocal services, or monetary exchanges. Informal, intimate localities allow immigrants to formulate their own discursive practices, that is, discursive agency, which at times involves mimicking official bureaucracies. Navigating the labyrinths of legal and bureaucratic literacies, migrants built an informal economy through the brokering of friends and acquaintances as guides. As I will show later, in these spaces, migrants are not mere victims of political economies and immigration bureaucracies; instead, they learn how to obtain legal papers, "their bread and butter" as one participant explained, and thereby co-construct their own economic system of sustenance and livelihood. Although the migrants' economic mobility for their summer job through the Work and Travel program is facilitated by neoliberal markets of cheap labor, their intimate exchanges about papers and attainment of a new documented status involve nonmarket, affective transactions. It is the "friend of a friend" or an acquaintance with one's parents or other community members who provide information and/ or address questions about social security cards, an ID, a cheap place to live, etc. Alanna Frost's work illustrates a similar practice in Native American communities that have formed "trade routes" inspired by belief systems and practices that were distinct from the modern marketplace. Resorting to the term literacy stewards, Frost explains their roles as "less akin to Western economies and more connected to grassroots development of noncommodified resources" (61). Similarly, in "*Ayni* in the Global Village," Porter and Monard (2001) explain the meaning of ayni, "an indigenous Andean concept of reciprocity" as a foundational principle in various types of relationships, including economic exchanges. In this economic frame, transactions are grounded in relationships and commonalities of experience which turn out to be closer to a "covenant than a contract" (Porter and Monard 2001, 6). This work then proposes alternative economic exchanges that do not necessarily demand paid labor or monetary transactions as expected in a traditional Western economic system. Rather, their economic routes are determined by day-to-day interactions and exchange of knowledge. As migration has led to the formation of a new global class of diasporic selves, commonality of experience, at times based on ethnicity, age, background or the experience of being a migrant, engenders the formation of new alliances and subjectivities that reshape those institutions seeking to regulate mobility (border patrols, visa regulations, etc.). These new subjectivities are essential because in diverse economic frameworks, migrants seek to escape impositions based on territoriality, nation-state identification, or socio-economic status. As a result, they attempt to formulate their own agency through networks of information and, eventually, secure formal citizenship of their own choice.

An important aspect about informal economies, and in fact, alternative economies broadly defined, concerns the issue of scale. The danger, Stephen Healy (2020) explains, is to see alternative economies as localized actions, marginal and perhaps less valuable than global impact economies. In a hierarchical spatial ontology where local is always incorporated in larger frames (regional, national, or global), alternative economies will routinely be relegated as insignificant despite their potential to transform global markets. For this reason, Healy (2020) and other postcapitalist geographers like Gibson-Graham, propose a "geography of ubiquity" that dislodges a hierarchical spatiality in favor of a "flat spatial ontology" where power comes from the connectivity between seemingly distinct actions, practices, or people. Extending Healy's example of the geography of women who can, by their mere ubiquitous presence, engage transformative global forces, I suggest that migrants too create a geography of presence that can transform geopolitical spatialities, specifically discursive categories of emplacement (e.g., immigrant/native-born; documented/undocumented, economic/political/affective, etc.).

Drawing on these strands of scholarship on political economy, co-brokering thus functions as an agentic, discursive practice of diverse economies. In this economic framework, experiences, affinity, relationships of reciprocity, and associated discourses are central to both market and nonmarket transactions. Bureaucratic literacy, such as filling out applications, procuring documents, gathering evidence for legal status, compiling immigration files, and the affinities built through the interactions between various stakeholders according to flexible conventions, constitute the hidden transcript that departs from official protocols, but it is always in dialog with them, sometimes to critique or complement official practices. To break down seemingly impenetrable bureaucratic discourses, immigrants develop their own systems through legal papers and connectedness in which co-brokering is both a cohesive force and a means of expressing agency despite political economies that obliterate individual action. Agency, or more exactly, cumulative agency—named as such since it develops through the *collective* and *aggregated* efforts of individuals forming alliances and exchanging information among groups of people—emerges from a flow of information between mobile bodies, experiences, and exchanges. [8] Immigrants learn to pull together various documentation experiences involving papers, legal procedures, or knowledge of immigration interviews, and to collectively share them. As such, migrants invite other subjects, who have been "othered" by the nation-state as illegal or precluded from becoming part of a nation of immigrants, to join them in solidarity in their own citizenship project. Co-brokering in this case is constituted essentially by affinities of the disadvantaged, of those who are marginalized on the basis socio-economic status or ethnic and racial identity.

Informal Economies, Visa Impositions, and Regulated Travel

In the case of these Romanian immigrants, the Work and Travel program seems to have presented them with an attractive package—to travel and have a summer job in the US, a country which otherwise has rigorous restrictions for visitors from Eastern Europe. In Western Europe and in the US, visa impositions function as "remote control" systems through which a visa requirement can regulate mobility and access to a country from afar (Zolberg 1999). Before undesired immigrants approach their desired destination, they are subject to numerous checks, verifications, and thorough scrutiny. When documentation criteria and regulations are set in place, they are meant to ensure that Eastern European travelers have sufficient ties to their country of origin. Often these immigrants are asked to document and demonstrate robust financial and familial ties to their country before a visa is issued. The paradox of global mobility comes full circle when evidently these migrants—college students from Eastern Europe enrolled in a Work and Travel program in the US—desire to participate in the global market for financial reasons, yet they are asked to demonstrate precisely that which they lack: a stable economic status measured by Western criteria.

A host of immigrant accounts point to dysfunctional economies in the country of origin and implicit connections to political corruption and systemic injustice. Sorin left Romania because of corruption and a lost hope of any economic betterment: "I felt that, during that time, in those years, that I . . . I don't know if there was anything left to steal in Romania. People, everyone, I don't know, was trying all sort of illegal ways to make [money]." He further explained that there were "unnatural distances" between the haves and have nots; he also described his economic shortcomings as a life with no future: "This is not a life. You can't, you can't dream of anything, you can't accumulate" (Personal Interview 2012). Sorin clearly shares this discontent with the social-economic disparities in Romania, but not in the US, unlike a different participant, Cristina, who remarks on a different disparity. Specifically, Cristina mentioned that although she considered herself part of the middle-class in Romania, when she arrived in the US to pursue a college degree, the newly ascribed social status was quite different: "When I came here, I was [pauses and puffs] . . . (laughing) in the lowest bracket." "The lowest bracket" is where Cristina located herself as she acknowledged the visible socio-economic distance between her status and that of her peers whose "parents pay for everything." As an international student, highly dependent on scholarships and with her family residing in Romania, Cristina had a different status. The socio-economic differences became more evident for her at the private college where students' parents were visibly rich "wearing the pearls and everything," as Cristina relates.

Adina justified her decision to leave Romania by pointing to global organization's unfair treatment of local hires. Having worked for an international non-profit in Romania, she unveiled the double standard applied to Eastern Europeans who were never hired as employees with benefits but only as part-timers. In the neoliberal market, locals represent disposal labor that is valued for its cost effectiveness, allowing maximum corporate profit. Hiring part-timers allows transnational corporations to evade paying taxes in the country where they establish their business. Following its own economic pursuits, corporations want to keep local people local. Adina explains, "They kept saying . . . local people are good where they are at. So I was like: F— off." Local people and local knowledge can be *emplaced* through strategies that serve only one end in global partnerships, the partner who has financial mobility and a national identity that leverages flexible global positioning and mobility.

Another immigrant, Diana, explained her mobility as fueled by a desire to break off with her country of origin. Her goal is to write a manifesto entitled "Refusal to Live in Romania" to express her disapproval of Romania's systemic corruption. Diana came to the US looking for "another way of life" where "there isn't such evident corruption," a place where success should not be achieved primarily through favors and personal connections.

These accounts demonstrate a global market governed by visa regulation and travel impositions on marginalized global subjects (Eastern Europeans) while also inviting them to join the project of globalism. In *Writing on the Move*, Lorimer Leonard described global mobility as marked by fluidity, fixity, and often, by friction. For Eastern Europeans, this differentiated mobility has been impacted not only by various political, institutional, and historical developments, but also by unjust and corrupt systems. Sometimes, fixity comes from Western countries' long histories of exclusion of Eastern Europeans through visa impositions and other measures. Other times, unequal access to globalism is the result of a country's own political system, such as in the case of Romania. A totalitarian regime, as the one in Romania, permitted the development of an economic system in which informal economies flourished. Political anthropologist Verdery (1996) clarifies that these informal economies developed under Communist Romania as a series of practices expanding from "the quasi-legal to the definitely illegal" (27). One such example is carpentry, Verdery explains, which was not against the law when done at home for extra cash, except that people would illicitly use tools from the workplace. As Verdery (1996) suggests, with secondary (or informal) economies there is a "range" of practices, rather than a clear-cut distinction between legal and illegal. Similarly, in the case of immigration, it would be difficult to set a clear boundary between legitimate and illicit practices. For instance, many of the participants in my study, if not all, had legal entry into the US, but some crossed over into illegality when they overstayed their visa.

It is in this political economic landscape that co-brokering operates. In the case of immigration, this mediation may at times occur at the margins of legality in order to bring one back into lawful presence of the US jurisdiction. It is essential that we understand co-brokering and alterative economies both in light of local and personal trajectories (Adina's disenchantment with global organizations; Diana's disappointment with Romania; or Sorin's discontent with unjust economic and political systems) and in view of macro-level events (histories of Eastern European marginalization; familiarity with local informal economies formed under a totalitarian regime; global markets like the Work and Travel program; the formation of a Romanian diaspora that develops a community of experience; and many more). Although these Romanian (im)migrants may operate under the purview of political economies that seem to curtail their agency, they resist emplacement. Designed for college students, the Work and Travel program allows for a way out of their emplacement and their country's history of oppressive political structures and a move towards a sense of agency.

Your Papers, Your System, "Your Bread and Butter"

One textual location where brokering emerges is bureaucratic literacy, specifically immigration papers. This is where the individual and the state meet, and their encounter demands sustained negotiations of social, economic, and political structures (e.g., Cintron 1993; Chu 2010; Lorimer Leonard 2015; Vieira 2016). The market for legal papers and writing in legal contexts in general is a high-stakes enterprise. Legal papers have the power to create discursive legal categories such as "immigrant," "alien," "illegal" or "legal," "documented" or "undocumented," and the move from one category to another can be extremely burdensome. Notably, errors in immigration—filling out forms, inadequate evidence, or inconsistencies in immigration cases—are extremely consequential, leading to separation of family members, loss of income, deportation, and various other problems. To facilitate the path to citizenship, co-brokering begins at the most basic level of legal papers, and it unfolds in intimate homes through the mediation of friends away from official institutions. In intimate settings, migrants learn to understand the basic vocabulary of documentality: social security card, driver's license, permanent address, and how to secure these as respectable citizens. Through co-brokering, migrants build hidden transcripts—ways of learning what to do, say, or write in the intimacy of homes—to turn bureaucracies into their own system. In these informal economies, where information is exchanged for the benefit of the other person as affective labor (Hardt), hidden transcripts, unlike the formal protocols of official institutions, ensure that immigrants can ask questions and populate intimate spaces with their own intentions.

Essentially, two levels of documentality emerged for this group of migrants: the basic one of legal papers (an ID, the driver's license, the social security card, etc.) and a more advanced level—one marked by status and the citizenship process discussed in the following section. For those that have them, legal papers are taken for granted; yet for others, as Vieira (2016) notes, "Everything you want to do . . . you depend on a document you don't have" (1). For Adina, a Romanian migrant, and many like her, securing official papers is necessary, "getting the ducks in a row" as she called it. It basically meant obtaining the papers first, then going back to school or accumulating work experience. For Sorin, papers are a survival kit; they are nourishment or a staple: "[Papers] are your bread and butter, [they are] your system." In this sense, the economic metaphor of an immigrant's existence is directly tied to a material economic reality, that of obtaining a job only with papers in hand. Like "bread and butter," legal papers function as an intimate system of survival—the social security card, driver's license, utility bills, and others. But, papers simultaneously provide economic sustenance since without legal papers, one's work is not visible, valued, or rewarded. Co-brokering starts through the mediation of a friend or an acquaintance and, to a certain extent, follows a prescriptive process already established by formal institutions and bureaucracies:

> The friend of my friend, with whom I came in contact, he knew the routine beforehand, from . . . just like that. Again, where exactly he knew it from? I don't know but he knew the steps: that you have to have an address; to have your name on the mailbox, and you self-address an envelope. At that time, a utility bill was not required . . . .. It was a letter or a postcard written by to yourself, to pass through the mail stream; basically, it arrived, it meant that you have an address. You take it with you, you're good. You're valid. Once you have that, they can send you [stuff].

Securing a valid address through a self-addressed letter/postcard constitutes a form of writing determined by bureaucratic expectations. In "Writing Through Bureaucracy," Lorimer Leonard (2015) explains the loss of the communicative function of correspondence in bureaucratic contexts as letters are turned into "symbolic texts" whose ultimate goal is to mobilize family members. Indeed, this form of communication mimicking bureaucratic practices but deprived of content captures the interplay between formal and informal economies, between complying with the tools of official institutions and repurposing them to serve one's goal. In developing a more dynamic agency when individuals and communities are positioned between the "herculean and minuscule," Frost (2011) shows the limitations of sponsorship by introducing Gerald Vizenor's critical term, *survivance* (survival plus resistance). "Survivance," Frost explains, "gets at the dynamism of the forces" (56). In other words, it uncouples oppressive forces or discourses from their seemingly strict positionality. Similarly, in the case of Romanian immigrants, agency manifests in brokering processes connected to the letter writing event, the brainstorming stage, production of the letter, and its circulation through hidden transcripts. James Scott (1990) explains that the hidden transcript "takes place 'offstage,' beyond direct observation by powerholders" (4). While public transcript involves the circulation of a postcard or letter through the post office, the hidden transcript consists of the entire process of intimate information exchanges that support and, at the same time, subvert official communication.

In the process of ensuring legal papers, the immigrant, as Sorin noted, builds *their* "own system," one that can ensure economic stability. Mimicking official bureaucracy, the personal system is constructed through various processes of mediation and translation of specialized terms into laymen's terms, through personal ties and an interplay of roles, scripts, and documents. A friend or family member brokers an immigrant's access to basic identification and work documents in unofficial settings, probably personal homes, away from the public eye. Such alliances facilitated by a common ethnic identity and language can generally thrive in informal economies. The exchange of information, the mediation of a friend or a friend of a friend is based on reciprocity and affinity rather than economic profit. This meditation translates bureaucratic discourses, which at first seem unintelligible, into distinct actionable steps. Similar to a traveler or merchant who needs a local guide to make foreign cities and spaces "legible" (Scott 1998), Romanian economic immigrants learned the practice and language of bureaucracies around them. They write letters without an actual message solely to provide proof of an address and to be recorded as "official" citizens with a permanent address. This brokered action transforms a relatively unknown system into a familiar space through the mediation of others.

In the hidden transcript taking place in homes, intimate places or among friends and acquaintances, questions are permissible, which otherwise would be unacceptable or mark one with an outlier status if present in formal protocols. In the hidden transcript, the path through textual labyrinths is brokered through dialog and a series of questions that can only be discussed in the privacy of a familiar context. In the following sequence, Sorin reconstructs an interactive dialog with his friend as a performative act, alternating between his voice and that of his friend (his impersonation of his friend's voice is marked in italics):

> Ligia: How did you know where to go?
> Sorin: I think I found out from a person the weekend when I was in Detroit that I need to go to . . . what is called . . . social security administration.
> "What is that?" [S. asked his friend]
> *"Well, you go there with your passport, you show you have a visa, they make a copy, you fill out a form, and then you wait."*
> "How long?"
> *"About 3 weeks."*
> "And what does this do?"
> *"Well, that . . . it gives you the right to get an ID and driver's license."*
> "Really?"
> *"Yes."*
> "Very good, I need this for sure."

Information questions ("What is social security?" or "How long [should I wait]?") or questions about the purpose of documents and forms ("What does this do?") are coupled with a series of specific steps that delineate expectations of official institutions: "You go there with your passport, you show you have a visa, they make a copy, you fill out a form, and then you wait." While information about applications, waiting time, etc. are easily found on websites, certain types of questions are only permissible in contexts of privacy. This preparation on how to answer and what to do happening outside the purview of the public eye equips one in anticipating a particular discursive interaction. As illustrated in Sorin's rendition of the exchange, the hidden transcript creates a flexible space where the delineation of roles and purposes is clarified. Sorin explains that *you go* there with *your* passport, *you show* you have a visa, *you wait; they make* a copy. While in most bureaucratic contexts, writers have little to no space for individual expression or authentic questions—in other words, for agency—in the hidden transcript where the brokering occurs, the individual takes over the space with questions, their experiences, and their way of building a personal bureaucratic system that is manageable and easy to navigate through the guidance of friends. If forms and bureaucratic literacy stifle the personal, in formulating hidden transcripts, one recuperates their agentic subjectivity.

Making a Case

Cumulative Agency

While legal papers constitute the most basic foundation for the economic life of migrants, and a system of survivance (Frost), co-brokering also involves broader information networks and alliances as migrants advance in their process of securing not only a survival system through papers but a legitimate identity through the immigration file application in pursuit of citizenship. Co-brokering at this level is accomplished when immigrants come together to discuss, unpack, and exchange information about specific immigration cases of friends and acquaintances with a similar socio-economic status. In doing so, immigrants accumulate information, bits of experiences, and nonmarket exchanges about bureaucracies, and this assemblage helps migrants formulate what I call "cumulative agency," which is discussed in this section. Through cumulative agency, migrants build a credible "file self" or "bureaucratic paper trail" (Chu) as they attempt to translate their individual lives, including marriage arrangements, into economic and bureaucratic discourses.

To assemble all the paperwork for the "file self"—forms and documents that constitute the application for immigration—one must develop a deep understanding of the qualifications for a particular path to citizenship and associated obstacles. In the rhetorical assemblage of the immigrant file, much labor and varied sources of information are harnessed from formal and informal sites such as the Internet, neighbors, apartment mates, co-workers, and members of various immigrant communities. From Sorin, and several other informants, I learned about the economic lives of these migrants: men start working as taxi drivers or construction workers while women work as nannies or babysitters. Ion, for instance, estimated that about 40% of taxi drivers in this metropolis were Romanian, perhaps also because in a class of twenty trainees, four or five were Romanian. Another informant, Leo, said he refused to work in construction since taxi and limo driving were better choices. Of all informants, Sorin was willing to offer a detailed account of how these undocumented migrants obtain their information and manage to find a niche in the immigration system: "There is a sort of *collective consciousness* [this is the exact phrase Sorin used in English], a sort of collective information flow that streams away. I don't know where from. But it comes from the congregations or get-togethers that take place ad-hoc, most of the times with people who see each other for the first time." This exchange of information concerns details related to paperwork—the type and number of documents to be used as evidence—as well as specifics about interviews with immigration officers. Below is a more detailed description of how this alliance operates in action:

> The stereotype [with taxi drivers] is that they all have earphones; that is great medium. It was. There . . . cases were dissected . . . were being discussed. While picking up clients, "Hi, how are you?" and whatever. "Do you mind if I use the phone?" "No, I don't mind." And you started in Romanian, not loud, discreetly. But there, [cases] were dissected. That guy did so and so, another one had the interview as such. I call a guy, this guy calls another guy, I connect to him, and it was a branching out, like a conference call, of almost eight participants sometimes . . . and all those were discussing [immigration cases].

The connection between these immigrants is first established by their economic condition—most of them college graduates, having had a summer job through Work and Travel program, and now working as taxi drivers in a large metropolitan Midwestern city. Using technology as they navigate new geographic routes, they also connect to deliberate on cases of immigration. In this exchange, co-brokering operates through relationships that bind a socio-economic group together.

Due to its perceived impenetrability, bureaucratic literacy is broken down into manageable bits and negotiated through language and rhetorical practices in daily encounters. This is possible by the fact that co-brokering operates in informal economies, in unofficial spaces like taxi cabs and through networks of affinity. In this process of exchanging information, migrants "dissect cases" in order to assemble bits of knowledge and discursive practices like pieces of a puzzle to understand the state and its requirements. In this brokering of texts, applications, and documented evidence, the power resides in the pieces of information that each individual brings to the conversation. As participants analyze various cases, there is a moment-by-moment engagement with the information received. In the process, the origin of information dissolves in the interaction. Although each migrant's interaction with social structures is unique and the path to citizenship is particularized, their subjectivity is built through underground collective action, thereby disrupting sedimented bureaucratic practices. In *The Struggle and the Tools*, Ellen Cushman maintains that critical consciousness does not necessarily need to implicate collective action; rather, the individual and the day-to-day interactions with power structures can significantly alter the perception of social structures and their impact on the individual. While that holds true, in this study, the immigrants' collective action matters. Through *cumulative agency*—a strategy through which one recovers their agency—migrants are able to break down impenetrable bureaucratic structures.

Cumulative agency results from alliances of those at the margins who make use of their experiences and discursive repertoires as they assist others in their pursuits. In other words, cumulative agency is accomplished through co-brokering. Because of this expressed agency, co-brokering is significant in 1) making informal economies visible; 2) allowing for varied discourses to thrive; and 3) disrupting the belief that capitalist economies and discourses are the only viable exchanges.

Brokering Immigration Categories, Brokering the File Self

Although immigration-related discourses employ distinct categories for immigration—political (for refugees), economic (for entrepreneurs and work-related visas), and family reunification paths to citizenship—these classifications in practice are more fluid and complex than anticipated. Political anthropologist Karolina Follis (2012) argues that the "blurring" between the political and the economic classification is more and more evident, as there are increasingly more refugees due to natural calamities, poverty, or ongoing war zones. Although immigration regulates people's mobility and classifies their access to citizenship based on distinct categories (e.g., asylum, family reunification, employment), the complexity of human experience reveals fuzzy spots, in-betweenness, or ambiguous contexts where fluidity and the circulation of information trumps fixity. Co-brokering emerges precisely in these spaces of indefinity when people collaborate and bridge those categories through a shared sense of belonging—Eastern Europeans, Latino/a in the US, seasonal workers, DREAMers, the undocumented, and others. When people are excluded from one category, they find paths to rhetorically inscribe themselves under classifications that allow them to pursue their goals.

Although this cohort of Romanian immigrants ensured entrance through temporary employment—the Work and Travel program—they soon became aware that to secure a job in the US through a legal path would be almost impossible despite their college training, excellent writing and literacy skills, and multilingual capital: "To find someone to offer you a job, you know how hard it is to get it, to show that you are somehow more special than a million other Americans, who probably do similar work. Someone must want you badly" (Personal interview). Faced with the impossibility of qualifying for the economic path toward citizenship through employment, many immigrants formed different alliances through marriage. In so doing, they initiated a transaction implicating a seemingly non-economic relation—one of intimacy and marriage—in pursuit of legal papers and citizenship status.

Explaining the increased number of circumstantial marriages, especially between Romanians and Puerto Ricans, Sorin further comments that "at the beginning, the system was unprepared here, and they didn't see this. So, some people passed easily; it gave courage to others" (Personal interview). However, when each week a Romanian and a Puerto Rican were about to get married, certainly the "system" reassessed its blind spots and demanded more evidence from the applicants. In response, couples prepared more and more documents to support their claims of a bona fide marital union. While the system seems "blind" and "unprepared" for both individual and collective actions that subvert its control, the system simultaneously adapts and responds to attempts to break through its control. Rather than view bureaucratic system as utterly strong and the marginalized as completely overtaken by power structures, this dialogic interaction reveals how power is co-constructed and less determined in noncapitalist economic spaces. Individual action changes as the system responds to instances of transgressions.

While immigrants' personal experience and their bureaucratic literacy activity disrupt economic determinism, nation-state ideologies shape the contexts of intimate relationships. Ironically, when the economic immigrants in my study resorted to marriage alliances to obtain legal papers, this path to citizenship continued to be driven by the nation-state's market ideology that holds economic ties as guarantor for intimate bonds. In creating the documentation file for citizenship as a proof of their union, a married couple must first and foremost provide economic documentation that connects the two together, thereby validating and securing their emotional union. Solid evidence for a marriage, as my respondents explained, comes in the form of bank statements of joined accounts, documentation of residential lease, proof of car loans in both names, and if available, mortgage documentation, to strengthen a couple's case of a bona fide marriage. All of these represent economic evidence of one's emotional bond. Even more, this economic documentation needs to be prioritized first at the top of the immigration file while additional soft evidence—pictures from family events, emails between partners, testimonials from friends and family attesting to the relationship—gets inserted at the bottom of the application dossier.

As the state seeks to develop legible citizens through documentality, personal ties are commodified and measured in economic terms. Marriage becomes a transaction, and at one end of this transaction, we find the most vulnerable economic citizens. On the one hand, there is the economic immigrant who cannot secure their path toward citizenship through other means but through marriage to a US citizen. On the other hand, we find the US citizen, who due to a market-driven economy, makes an alliance in a circumstantial marriage in pursuit of financial gain. These alliances, however, are never an equal exchange. An astute observer, Sorin explains: "For them, it's about money. And then you ask yourself: Who does this for money? And when you answer: *Not the best persons, not the nicest*" [words in italics are Sorin's exact phrasing in English, not my own translation]. Sorin's comment points to a socio-economic discrepancy in this alliance that he further explains, "These are people that are desperate to pay a loan that's hanging over the head, or maybe a drug addiction. Or maybe they have 7 kids at home or a so-called divorced husband." Loans, drug addiction, or a large family, these are all aspects that propel the other side of the alliance—an alliance wherein a US citizen with the right papers establishes a transaction in exchange for money. In Vieira's (2016) study, the connection between assimilation and literacy is established as two immigrant groups, the Azoreans and the Brazilians, use language resources and legal status to facilitate access to legal papers of the undocumented; although occasionally they foster unequal relationships, they manage to assimilate partially to each other's groups. In this study, the language describing immigrant partnership between different ethnic groups evades notions of assimilation. It is a transactional language, an economic exchange that involves bodies, papers, and agreements, all contracted temporarily. Each party pursues their purpose and leaves the partnership once their goals have been attained. Although I report here from only one side of the transaction, of the person with the money but without papers, it seems that those with economic power guide the transaction more than those with papers and no economic leverage. The cohort described here is a particular group of Romanians with money who worked hard for every penny. They are, after all, economic immigrants. Although they arrive poor, they find jobs and work hard, but they also possess a rich social and cultural capital. It is this combination of socio-cultural and multilingual assets coupled with economic power that gives them a strong leverage. Although they start at the bottom of the socio-economic ladder with blue-collar jobs, their linguistic and educational status due to their knowledge of English and some college education is acknowledged even by their employers, and as a result, they advance faster on the socio-economic ladder. When Sorin first met his future employer at a coffee shop, the latter was surprised to hear him use English effortlessly with a barista as he asked for a pen and paper to jot down the employer's phone number. "You speak English? What are you doing here?" asked the employer, and then followed apologetically: "I still have to put you to work." The implicit assumption is that physical hard labor—such as in construction, where Sorin and many Romanians work—is designated for those with limited or no English literacy knowledge.

The importance of a socio-cultural and multiliterate capital has been emphasized by another participant. Although Adina acknowledged the role of financial power in the pursuit of legal papers, she underscored that such transactions require a lot more: being smart, being street-smart. "Being street smart," Adina explained to me, meant the following: 1) "very good command of English" 2) "seeking legal advice" whenever that is necessary 3) "conversation with successful people." In other words, all these "extras" are connected to aspects of language and literacy. First, knowing English is a necessity, or it is perceived as such in this group of young Romanian immigrants. In fact, those who do not master English stand out. Cristian related a conversation with a taxi driving instructor about Romanian taxi drivers. Based on the instructor's observation, the "good" stereotype was that Romanian taxi drivers speak very good English. While Cristian confirmed this stereotype, he also added jokingly that Romanians do speak English except for one guy, a friend of his whom everyone apparently picked on for his limited English. Certainly, there are many other Romanians who do not speak English, yet the general expectation of Romanians for Romanians is that they would speak English well. This in-group affinity defines the types of literacies that are valued: speaking English is one of them. A multilingual ability affords flexibility of communication that positions the individual at an advantage in various professional and non-professional interactions. The second aspect concerns specialized knowledge from a particular field and accessing it through the mediation of experts; in this case, if an immigrant seeks legal papers, it is important to request legal advice from someone who has knowledge of immigrant institutions and discourses. Finally, accessing brokered information and developing one's social capital ensures a more powerful leverage in establishing partnerships, as Adina explained. Ultimately, even as minority ethnic groups broker each other's way through legal papers and information, unequal partnerships are forged, driven by economic leverage and mastery of languages and specialized discourses.

In addition to economic leverage, emotional discourses also shape these alliances. His story and her story must match *their* story, which in turn must match the narrative of the documents already submitted. In preparing their stories, the couple must learn to portray the correct emotions. Those emotions, of course, must have been first documented through written evidence and then performed in person. To achieve coherence between the two stories, Sorin explains that the couple must "build texts" together and then practice. As each person involved "build[s] texts," they create a hidden transcript that should meet the expectations of those in power. In the oral interaction, the couple must put forth a marriage performance unfolding through role-play. We have a husband and a wife, and they must play their part; they learn about each other, what they like, what they don't like, where was their first date, and they act out their script. These scripted emotions must be performed to perfection to avoid raising any doubts. Practicing and acting out the emotioned script ultimately means learning the language of a nation-state, with its hidden ideologies:[9]

> There's an application you give them, and another draft that you use to practice with her. . . . You practice. You give papers with information about you. You ask her and you memorize like in biology. Like for an exam. You memorize important dates, names of the parents, names of aunts if they show up somehow. You must consult . . . how did we meet, why did we take each other. When is our anniversary? Where was . . . the first kiss. It's like a game. Where is the first dinner? What is your favorite food? (Personal interview).

These "texts" about the personal selves are built in such a way to prove to the immigration officer that they are a bona fide couple. Thus, they must demonstrate knowledge of anniversaries, favorite foods, and other personal details. "It's like a game," says Sorin, but ultimately it is about putting on a role and acting it out for an audience that has laid out the guidelines for these roles. The game involves memorization, learning, and acting out a particular part. It is a performance of a scripted identity, a scripted citizen that must follow a screenplay. This performance and the process of "building texts together" are highly brokered through in-group alliances but also through partnerships with other ethnic groups.

This scripted path of emotional performance through texts seems significant, but in reality, it matters only to the extent that the bond is solidified through economic ties. This alliance in marriage between the socio-economically marginalized reveals the nation-state's impulse to define its citizens primarily in economic terms pushing one as far as to transform the covenant of marriage, an intimate bond, into a transacted contract documented through legal papers and financial bonds. This study substantiates similar findings articulated in Vieira's (2016) study of undocumented Brazilians making alliances with Azorean Americans. As Vieira (2016) suggests marriage alliances produce a more certain path to citizenship than education. The nation-state's and other governmentalities' tendency to see individual identities in economic terms and exchanges as transactions raises a deep challenge for rhetoricians and compositionists. While scholars have certainly exposed the perils of *homo economicus*, a subjectivity resulting from neoliberal and entrepreneurial mentality (Scott 2006a), their approach remains focused on the limits of this subjectivity and thus, neglect the possibility for agentic expression. More attention needs to be given to discourses of resistance and those agentic selves who strive to develop alternatives to market-based practices.

"Seeing Like an Immigrant"

Approaching the participants in this study through the perspective of illicit brokering and their pursuit of documents is important, because at certain points in life, documents determine the course of every aspect of their lives: their jobs, their relationships, education, etc. As I followed the documentary path of this cohort—starting with the Work and Travel program, creating "their system of papers" to making alliances so as to obtain legal papers—I drew on information shared with me by several participants. My goal was to show these immigrants' perspectives, and the strategies employed to understand state powers and state rhetorics. As such, focusing on their documentary/non-documentary status depicts what "seeing like a state" or "seeing like a guard" means. This "seeing" is a narrow vision. It approaches the individual only through established categories or selective features that matter in the bureaucratic system of various institutions. In *Seeing like a State*, Scott (1998) documents the gradual imposition of state control through spatial organization but also through the use of documents and last names as tools to manage the population. Alternatively, in "Seeing like a Border Guard," an analysis of reconfiguring Eastern borders in Europe, Follis (2012) relates that one of the most essential pieces of equipment of border guards is their eyes. Their enhanced vision, through the aid of thermal cameras and other surveillance devices, complements what the naked eye cannot perceive. It is also their "sense," albeit subjective, of something suspicious that shapes the vision of a border guard. But there are many aspects that these visions and languages of nation-states cannot capture—deep motives, the entire personhood, regrets, and other complex issues that immigrants face. Although I sought to give voice to these economic immigrants, I faced some obstacles because several informants avoided any reference to legal status. Others simply said, "It was hard. And it was expensive. That's all I want to say;" while a few expressed regret about their condition but refused to offer further details. The literate experience of these immigrants should be conceived in all its complexity. The fact that all these economic immigrants shared a wealth of other literate practices—besides illicit brokering of documents and papers—is worth further attention.

Implications and Contradictions

To sum up, co-brokering emerges as a discursive tactic in the context of informal economies and is developed and sustained through alliances established for the purpose of writing and communicating in a bureaucratic system. Based on this research of young, globally minded immigrants, I learned that these alliances are built on shared experiences and affinities of those at the margins of official discourses and practices, and thereby they defy the market-based identities that a capitalist system valorizes.

In co-brokering, there is a dynamic interaction between rigid rules and individual approaches to these regulations. Co-brokering may engage with informal, alternative economies and in-between spaces of legitimacy, locations that are otherwise filled with insecurity, indeterminacy, and often, flexibility; this means that writing practices emergent in these sites must become attuned to change and exhibit adaptability. In the context of co-brokering, power relationships are interrogated, debated, and whenever possible, reformulated. This is accomplished in intimate sites, homes, local neighborhoods, personal cars or taxi cabs, through daily encounters and conversations, creating a hidden transcript that mimics the discourses and rhetorical moves of the official world of bureaucratic writing. Most importantly, co-brokering challenges capitalist-based economic relationships as the sole measure of economic exchanges. As demonstrated earlier, immigrants are often cast as economic subjects in the global economy and allowed to enter the US only if proven to be an asset to the US economy. However, they resist this categorization; through co-brokering, they reconfigure economic positionalities from profit-driven subjectivities to affinity and nonmarket alliances. Co-brokering encapsulates the philosophy of shared responsibility through exchange of information, a piece of advice, or an experience that would assist one with writing, documents, or bureaucratic literacy. Co-brokering is, thus, a form of resistance to institutional control and a discursive strategy of building relationships with those at the margins. In this conception, any one of us, immigrant, citizen, green card holder, foreign national or occupant of any position from the center to the margins, can join in solidarity through words, discourses, and action. If economic realities push us to reconfigure our writing courses, departments, or our academic and non academic identities, we must find ways to consider the role of affinity, exchanges and reciprocity among diverse stakeholders with any type of power or knowledge involved in the rhetorical situation.

A final observation on the perils of co-brokering is warranted. When the information is exchanged in the form of a "flow" whose source is often unclear, unreliable data are a high probability. However, since co-brokering involves sharing of personal experiences, it reduces substantially the risk of exchanging untrustworthy information. Personal experience is variable and contingent, and those involved in co-brokering practices are aware of this. Co-brokering at its core relies on partnerships built on trust, mutual help, and a history of relations developed over time. In such trusted relationship, both reliable information and problems circulate fast. This means that unreliable brokers are known and exposed fairly quickly. It also means that those involved will constantly verify the source of their information. An understanding of co-brokering and diverse economies affords a deeper grasp of intimate discourses, documentality, and bureaucratic literacy as being shaped by and influencing economic, political, and global forces. It also encourages compositionists to explore a range of discourses in formal and informal political economies since by limiting ourselves to capitalocentric frames, even if only to critique them, we continue to render alternative frames as inexistent and agency as impossible to develop. Co-brokering and immigrants' agency as highlighted here prove otherwise.

Chapter 4

Iron-Cast Literacies and the Role of the Authoritarian State as a Literacy Broker

The illiterate person stands outside politics. First it is necessary to teach the alphabet. Without it, there are only rumors, fairy tales, prejudice, but no politics.

—Robert F. Arnove and Harvey J. Graff

A third grade *Reading* textbook published in 1987 starts with the lyrics of a famous Romanian song "The Union." Underneath the lyrics, the following acknowledgment has been inserted: "[Excerpt] from comrade Nicolae Ceaușescu's speech at the grand assembly of December 5, 1981, dedicated to disarmament and peace." A student, most likely a third grader, had crossed out "comrade Nicolae Ceaușescu," leaving the rest of the text intact. This textual alteration, small as it is, achieves a remarkable task. It removes precisely the center of ideological control, Nicolae Ceaușescu, a metonymic representation of the Communist Party. Whether visually or textually in the public sphere, Ceaușescu was the image and the embodiment of the Party.[1] This blending of identities has often been achieved particularly through slogans but also through songs and poems dedicated to Ceaușescu. Ceaușescu was the Party and the Party was Ceaușescu. As this example shows, in Communist Romania, literacy—whether in the form of textbooks, reading magazines, pioneer magazines (*The Daring*), or pioneer writing—became the main vehicle to distribute the Party's ideology.

A distinct approach of literacy brokering comes through the image of the authoritarian state, which, I argue, functioned as the ultimate broker of literacy as affinity. I examine how the state—and its extended presence in everyday lives via teachers, pioneer organizations, and numerous ideological magazines—sought to socialize students in how to *feel* for Romania and for the Romanian *patria* (Engl. homeland or motherland/ fatherland[2]). In this analysis, I focus on the latter decade of Communist rule, the 1980s, and follow the extension of the Communist Party's presence and control over school literacy and all domains pertaining to everyday literate lives of teens and children. A look at this decade also provides ideological and political context for the Romanian refugees' literacies discussed in chapter 2. As the ultimate broker, the Romanian state sought to use literacy as tool for manipulating people's affinity for the country. This was accomplished through limiting literacy's purpose to proclaim "the Party, Ceaușescu, and Romania"—a slogan that even today may resonate with many Romanians. In many ways, we could consider the Romanian state a sponsor of literacy. Viewed from the broker's perspective, however, the State as a mediator but also as an annihilator of alternative literacies emerges more forcefully, thereby allowing and legitimizing solely the Party-line literacy. In Perry's definition, brokers are defined as "bridg[ing] linguistic, cultural and textual divides for others," (256); based on this definition, at the core of the broker's identity is their middle position. In this sense, seeing the State in this central position of brokering, managing, and controlling literacy affords a better understanding of the way in which the Romanian state managed to incapacitate educational and cultural institutions, teachers, and literacy practices.

The state, as the ultimate literacy broker of one's affinity, expanded its presence through various agents of mediation—schools, teachers, pioneer organizations, etc.—thus reaching into the lives of teens and children. It encroached on small, everyday activities—weekends filled with patriotic work, summer camps, pioneer circles as extracurricular activities—including people's free time, their emotional attachments, and their social relations. As such, the state used education and schools to create an infrastructure, to use Trainor's (2008) term, that would facilitate the formation of particular discursive practices. Students, for instance, were required to cover long reading lists during their vacations and, when returning to school, write eulogies to the Communist life and the Party's achievements. They were encouraged to develop "feelings" for the patria and to then perform them through poems, songs, or readings of various texts. Through literate genres, such as the pioneer report and the poem, the state brokered its ideological presence and managed to recruit children and teens as brokers of the Party's image. The state's ideological impact ultimately came from its capacity to position itself as a broker of literacy, managing the distribution and production of literate products and subjects. Literacy, thus, was refashioned to produce a citizen who would feel for the patria through everyday reading and writing.

The resurgence of nationalist discourses has been noted by many as an expanding phenomenon both on a global scale and in the US. Here in the US, whether driven by fears, economic insecurity, or political agenda, media and the public discourse tend to polarize communities into "us vs. them" camps—American vs. immigrant, Black vs. White, the East vs. the West—all to such a degree that we must find new ways to re-engage dialogs with responsibility, diligence, and careful contextualization. With regard to global trends, Donahue and Horner (2022), Martins (2023), and Gilyard (2023) identify the rise of anti-globalist and nationalist tendencies, whether political or economic in nature (e.g., the reelection of prime minister Viktor Orbán in Hungary, Narendra Modi, Brexit, etc.), and propose strategies to cultivate transnational orientations in the composition classroom. Historicizing, contextualizing, and problematizing current national ideologies and discourses, as Gilyard (2023) proposes, are effective strategies in exposing such perils.[3]

I situate the current discussion of brokering in this context of mass literacy and the role of the nation-state in shaping individual literacies. With recent shifts in transnational mobility, a global pandemic, and the surge of right-leaning political rhetoric in several countries, we need more awareness of historical mistakes regarding how literacy can be manipulated in the service of particular ideological agendas, frequently framed through false binaries of us vs. them rhetorics. Romania serves as a notable example of a destructive nationalist discourse that shattered a country and its citizens. Given the importance of advancing a socialist doctrine in schools, textbooks, and literacy education in the 1980s in Romania, the Romanian state functioned as a broker of literacy and affinity in two ways:

1) First, in the case of educational institutions, the State brokered its ideology through the manipulation of textbooks and teachers. Textbooks as well as school curricula were altered to reflect discursively and visually the image of the Party. Specifically, literacy textbooks circulated selected themes aimed at developing one's affinity for the socialist patria. Since the State found ideological gaps between the lives of the children and teens and those of adults and political citizens, literacy and rhetorical practices in schools were intended to turn children and teens into

"little workers," representatives of a particular social class contributing to the making of the socialist state. If everyone in the socialist state was called to work, so were children and teens. Historian Stephen Kotkin (1995) explains, "In the Soviet context, work was not simply a material necessity, but also a civic obligation. Everyone had the right to work; no one had the right not to work" (202). Similarly, in Romania, everyone, including children and teens, were deemed important workers for patria through their school activities, specifically reading and writing practices. In addition to textbooks, teachers were instrumental in brokering the Party's ideology. As workers for the State, I argue that teachers occupied a series of positions ranging from an inflexible monologic stance where they themselves mirrored the rigid discourse of the official rhetoric, to mixed mono-dialogic discourses, and to truly dialogic discursive positions. This will be discussed in chapter 5.

2) The State also brokered its ideological presence and control through literary magazines and extracurricular activities. To extend its reach beyond educational institutions, the Romanian State positioned itself as a broker of free time. Beside school-related work within formal education institutions, the State's theory of *loisir*, of managing children's free time, developed through the expansion of pioneer organizations and pioneer houses. The pioneer organizations aimed to socialize children (second grade through eighth grade) into the Party's socialist agenda; a particular ethos had to be formed, turning children into political subjects, especially as they were automatically enrolled in student organizations. In all this extracurricular work, patriotic feelings were routinized through a wide range of activities, many of which involved reading and writing. While pioneer organizations intersected with school activities, most of their work extended to summer camps, patriotic work (outside of school), celebrations and festivities for the Party, and most notably, special interests clubs called "circles." *The Daring* was the pioneer organization's magazine, to which each devoted pioneer had to subscribe. Its purpose was to inform, but also to better mobilize little citizens and the patriotic work that defined them. Patriotic work, it was hoped, would better tie one to the nation.

In this extracurricular work promoted by the state, I pay attention to specific genres—the pioneer report and the poem—and their role in carrying more forcefully the Party's ideological themes and images. These two genres contributed to the making of the "everyday socialist life" through language and discourse since they were meant to mirror daily events and the mundane pioneer life. While the pioneer report and the poem were employed as means of producing the socialist man, these genres brokered the socialist life as a *sensorial*, bodily experience rather than mere consciousness raising. This attempt to broker the image of the state through bodily senses, to create images of ideological satisfaction, led to people's rejection of the communist ideals. By regimenting feelings for the patria and seeking to create idealized vision of Romania—images depicting it as the land of prosperity, high technological advancement, the perfect place to live one's childhood—the State subjugated the personal to the interest of the socialist ethos. My participants recall ideological education as a poor attempt to produce patriotic feelings. They reported that most teachers were welcomed with derision whenever there was an attempt to glorify patria.

To understand how the State brokered its ideological presence through textbooks, magazines, and extracurricular activities, the broader context of education must be presented. Notably, three instrumental forces have shaped literacy in Romania in this period: political agendas, socioeconomic contexts, and institutions of control. First, education, specifically literacy education, was a means to advance the Party's political agenda. National campaigns during this time show a deep connection between the socialist regime and literacy and politics. Second, the emergence of informal economies in communist Romania reveals how the State positioned itself as a broker of literacy rather than a sponsor. In the political economies of a totalitarian state, the production of secret files emerged forcefully and with this, informal economies developed as well. Finally, the ideological control of educational institutions operated through institutional structures employed by the Party to broker the Marxist-Leninist ideology. To sum up, national literacy campaigns along with political economies that controlled educational institutions contributed to the formation of the literate subject and the brokering of literacy through top-down approaches that functioned through daily, seemingly small routinized actions.

To advance this line of argument, I draw on archival research conducted in Romania in 2011. I use textbooks, school magazines (e.g. *The Country's Hawks,* and *The During),* school curricula from the 1970s and 1980s, as well as various primary documents of the Communist Party, featuring its ideological campaign in educational reforms (minutes from the Congress of Political Education and Socialist Culture, 1982; speeches from the Congress of Education and Learning, 1973; 1980; 1982; 1987–1988, etc.), brochures and guides of pioneer organizations, including student compositions, and literary works. This research was guided by the following questions: What was the socioeconomic and political context that shaped literacy education of Romanian immigrants before their departure to the US? What were the most pervasive features of the official literacy education in Romania in the 1970s and 1980s?

Literacy Campaigns and Unintended Consequences

In *National Literacy Campaigns*, Arnove and Graff (1987) suggest that "large-scale efforts to provide literacy to the masses have not been tied to the level of wealth, industrialization, urbanization, or democratization of a society nor to a particular type of political regime" (2). Rather, literacy served as a mobilizing engine of the masses in situations when "centralizing authorities" sought to achieve "moral or political consensus." In this sense, the goal of literacy campaigns is primarily the advancement of a particular ideology, whether religious or sociopolitical. In communist Romania, the advancement of the socialist ideology has certainly been the main concern as various educational reforms have been implemented. While the year 1948 in Romania marked a major education reform through a series of laws and decrees, the centralization and censorship of information started to reinforce the State's power over education under Ceauşescu. Under his directive an ideological campaign through literacy was forcefully implemented in the latter part of the Communist regime (1971–1989). Following the Soviet model, the literacy campaign in Romania or the "fight against illiteracy" as Ceauşescu called it, was central in the making of the "new man" and the molding of one's consciousness by the socialist doctrine. Without the ability to read, the political subject was considered outside of the realm of politics, as Lenin explains in the context of the 1917 Russian revolution: "The illiterate person stands outside politics. First it is necessary to teach the alphabet. Without it, there are only rumors, fairy tales, prejudice, but no politics" (Arnove and Graff 1987, 7).

The interconnectedness between literacy and politics is well established here; evidently, through literacy, the Romanian state propagated its political agenda. Nevertheless, in this effort to spread an ideology, the emphasis was on appearance rather than substance. Regarding literacy campaigns or programs, Arnove and Graff (1987) explain the misguided concern with quantitative results over quality of content. Similarly, in the Romanian context, literacy was not measured for one's proficiency in competently using the language of the State, but rather what mattered most was the quantification of literate subjects. The obsessive reporting of the number of graduating students, often with falsified figures, would ensure a self-serving system that perpetuated the Party's existence; numbers represented an objective tool measuring the level of success of the campaign. Generally, the outcomes of literacy campaigns/programs have been difficult to evaluate since they always produce unexpected effects, such as resistance to centralized models or a preoccupation with "undemanding" readings (in the Soviet Union) or with romance and adventure stories rather than how to organize a collective (as in the case of the People's Republic of China) (Arnove and Graff 1987, 26). Nevertheless, examining both the State as a centralized power and its role in brokering literacy reveals intricate relationships between literacy and State control. A vehicle for promoting a particular doctrine, literacy produces powerful shifts even if the end results may be multiple and unexpected, often different from or contradictory to initial goals.

Aiming to use mass regimentation of teachers and students, the State positioned itself as a broker of literate practices, but despite many reforms, its success was limited. The State's literacy campaign fell short of attaining its main goal—creating the prototype of the Communist citizen—precisely because it sought to regiment people's affinity through literacy. As the State advanced the nation as the sole arbiter of affinity, of one's reading and writing experiences, it denied interactions with alternative texts and discourses. The State succeeded, however, in crafting a certain type of literate citizen who has learned the value of mastering multiple languages as well as the value of reading—particularly distinguished authors. All these comprise a cultural capital with which most participants in my study pride themselves. It is a cultural capital that shapes an individual into "a man with culture," an asset that seems disjointed from economic constraints. Most participants with whom I talked rejected the ideological dimension of education in Romania, but paradoxically valued all other aspects. Like the third grader's act of removing the center of ideological control of the textbook, the Romanians learned to value literacy and the "man of culture" descriptor but refused the Party's encroachment on their affinities. In fact, the immigrants in my study placed a high value on the education they received in Romania, which means high regard of texts and readings and their cosmopolitan identity as well as their ability to speak multiple languages and readily embrace diverse cultures. They also denounced the profit-driven American society relative to education and culture but valued the economic advantage they have gained through their jobs in the US.

Informal Economies and Socioeconomic Profiles

Another aspect regarding the State as a broker of literacy concerns the larger socioeconomic context that shaped literacy in communist Romania. As mentioned earlier, children and teens were cast as little workers, and schools can best be regarded as factories where the main activity of these little workers took place. In this context, literacy was manufactured as a product of mass consumption following the Fordist model of learning. Yet, this centralized model of production is quite different from a capitalist economy model, the same one that Deborah Brandt

(1998) used in her discussion of literacy and economic development. Brandt (1998) introduces sponsors of literacy in a frame where literacy participates actively in "engines of profit and competitive advantage" or more specifically, literacy functions as a "lubricant for consumer markets" to "integrate corporate markets," or as "raw material in the mass production of information" (1998, 166). The rhetoric surrounding this conception of literacy includes *profit, competitive advantage, consumer markets,* and *mass production.* This language of economics is very different from the discursive context of communist Romania where the ultimate end was the production of a "new socialist man." Unlike the productive citizen in capitalist systems—marked by competition, initiative, and profit—the profile of a socialist "new man" is comprised of cultural, political, and economic features: work ethic; worker's profile as it fit with patria's economic and technological development; national identity through ties to one's native land, to one's national history, and to national literature; a revolutionary spirit; desire for technological advancement; and a constant cultivation of one's love for nature. All these represent modes of expressing affinity for the patria as they relate to a historical ethos, to literary works, but also to ways of investing one's affinity in the interest of the country. Because these forms of capital are substantially intangible economic products, with little purchase value outside the national context of Romania, the inherent merit of these literacies might appear limited. In this socialist economic model, when the economic capital resides solely in the hands of the State, it would be difficult to use a capitalist vocabulary, such as sponsors of literacy. For this reason, as shown in the previous context of immigrant literacy, the figure of the broker whose emphasis is on mediation and social relations captures more befittingly the type of relations established between the State and its citizens.

Communist Romania focused its energy on control over production rather than promotion of consumption. This explains in part the regime's obsession with work and work productivity. Attention to regimenting production and products led to development of two types of economic systems: 1) the "first" or the "official" economy, where central authorities exercised their control, and 2) the "second" or "informal" economy, which emerged as a strategic process of counteracting the control of the official economy (Verdery 1996). The secondary economy consisted of a variety of strategies and methods, ranging from "quasi-legal to the definitely illegal" (Verdery 1996, 27). In chapter 3, where I introduced the concept of diverse economies, I included a brief reference to secondary economies. In my view, secondary economies are a type of diverse economy, which is why I only briefly mentioned them in chapter 3. Here, I explain in more detail how secondary economies functioned, and the political context where they evolved. Describing secondary economies in Communist Romania, Anthropologist Verdery (1996) explains that while moonlighting for extra money was not illegal, people did various types of work with materials or tools lifted from the workplace. This type of informal economy generated a particular vocabulary, eventually leading to the development of particular mentalities. Two such words, for instance, carry with them particular mentalities: *hatâr* and *bacşiş* and the expressions "to do *a* hatâr [ha-tur]" (Engl. to do/pay one a favor) and "to pay or give bacşiş [buck- shee-sh]" (Engl. to give bribe). Both bacşiş and hatâr carry some nuances of illegality, of operating somewhat at the limits of state regulations. While the first term, hatâr, establishes a relationship of almost mutual service in the informal economy, the latter term bacşiş points to a strategy of subverting the authority of the state by paying a sum of money to break through a closed door. In a 2010 interview, Romanian historian Florin Constantiniu explains Romania's inability to create a viable democracy and sustainable economy by pointing to the legacy of these two mentalities, hatâr and bacşiş (Popescu 2011). They represent a way of thinking and being in the world that evades the state or the official economy, established as a barter system based on preferential relationships.

This mentality underscores a strategic way of acting, being, or speaking that seeks to game the system, particularly a controlling, authoritarian regime. Acknowledging this mentality and secondary economies can further explain how their function extends to other domains of social life, beyond the economic realm. Translating this mentality of second economies to the context of language and literacy, we notice that people learned to develop different registers depending on context. While people learned to speak the official language—the language that historian Stephen Kotkin calls "speaking Bolshevik"—people would also resort to their "secondary" or subversive language, to readings and writings that were not officially approved. In truth, the official economy of language and literacy, the one brokered by the State, was secondary to most of its citizens. Romanians had to *learn* this official language, *practice* it, and *cast* it in particular forms and genres acceptable in the official language of the state. "Speaking Bolshevik," as Kotkin (1995) explains, does not simply mean "speaking" the official language. He contends that this language of self-identification, a language showing affiliation with a particular social role, such as, in his example, the wife of a locomotive worker, did not necessarily mean that the wife wrote, thought, and behaved in this social role. Rather, mere participation or using the language of the Party was sufficient: "We should not interpret her letter to mean she believed in what she likely wrote and signed. It was not necessary to believe. It was necessary, however, to participate as if one believed" (Kotkin 1995, 220). This participation and socialization in the official language of the State was particularly important in regard to children in communist Romania. Children, like all other citizens of the country, became little workers *participating* in the construction of the socialist patria. They did not have to "believe" in the system or "believe" the system. Participation—that is, the rhetoric of bodies and their quantification—constituted sufficient action to gratify the system.

A second important trait of the Romanian economic system under Communism concerns the producing and manufacturing of "personal files." Similar to the production of goods, Romanian political prisoner Herbert Zilber speaks of the "production of files," containing "real and falsified histories;" these files represented a significant form of control as the state sought to create "political subjects:" "This new industry has an army of workers: the informers. It works with ultramodern electronic equipment (microphones, tape recorders, etc.), plus an army of typists with their typewriters. Without all this, socialism could not have survived . . . In the socialist bloc, people and things existed only through their files. All our existence is in the hands of him who possesses files and is constituted by him who constructs them. Real people are but reflections of their files" (Verdery 1996, 24). This industry of secret information implies an industry of writing. Writing became a recorder of the daily life of all who were discontent or seemingly discontent with Ceaușescu's ideal patria and the ideological principles of the "golden age," (Rom. "epoca de aur") as Ceaușescu used to call it. This production of secret files and writing serving as a recorder of everyday life created an atmosphere of suspicion and distrust, changing communication from talk to whisper, even in the privacy of one's home.

Consolidating Institutional Structures

In this socioeconomic context of informal economies and brokers, ideology emerges as a central site of literacy brokering in education. In the 1980s, the latter period of Ceaușescu's regime, the cult of personality of "the most beloved son of the people"—an obsessive refrain on which he built his public image—expanded along with the monopoly of the Romanian Communist Party (RCP) to every aspect of the social life. The domineering discourse of the Communist Party sought to promote only one voice, one ideology to be taught, and one leader to be followed. Anything that fell outside of the purview of the Communist Party had to be censored and often annihilated. During Ceaușescu's presidential years (1965–1989), massive transformations of education exercised under the influence of the Stalinist theorist Anton S. Makarenko sought to militarize schools, which became authoritarian, collective, and regimented (Perşa 1998). As early as 1967, with the establishment of the Commission on Ideology (Verdery 1991, 101), textbooks and school curricula had to receive the approval of ideology committees. The ideological turn further enhanced the State's reach through pioneer organizations, an ingenious action to strengthen the monopoly of the Communist Party over every aspect of life, including free time. Another manifestation of the ideological control was exerted in the form of numerous festivals and State-instituted holidays meant to celebrate the Party, particularly the grandiose mass event "The Song of Romania," aimed at celebrating socialist ideology and culture through songs, poems, and other creative works.

For many Romanians, ideology is a very loaded term. In describing ideology as the relation between rhetoric and social and political contexts, James Berlin (1987) purposefully chooses to define ideology in its "neutral sense" (4). I use the term "ideology" to refer specifically to the Marxist-Leninist philosophy and its uptake by the Romanian Communist Party. In Romania, the Ideology Commission was instituted in 1967, and in the following years Ceauşescu launched a more aggressive ideological control over education, reflected in his famous July speeches (July 6 and July 9, 1971). In *National Ideology under Socialism*, anthropologist Verdery (1991) refers to Ceauşescu's regime of control as "symbolic-ideological," compared to previous ones, identified as remunerative and coercive (using force) (85–6). The ideological control under Ceauşescu was not physically damaging, as was in the case of his predecessor Gheorghe Gheorghiu-Dej who took "an obsessive-preventive" approach to any adverse ideologies and actions (Presidential Commission 2006, 519). Ceauşescu's approach operated through an underground economy governed by the State, which created an informant network through the recruitment of collaborators, residents, and conspiracy hosts (Neagoe-Pleşa 2008, 11). This network represented the infrastructure for the economy of personal files, which consolidated the Party's control over people's lives.

The main purpose of Ceauşescu's July Theses (1971) and subsequent actions was to reinforce the Party's socialist realism philosophy and control of the main institutions of mass communication (e.g., "The Song of Romania") (Henţea 2011). A censorship campaign directly implicated printing houses and cultural and educational institutions. These institutions are traditionally what we might think of as brokers of literacy, except that they all functioned under the authority of one broker, the State. In September 1971, the State Council established the Council of Socialist Culture and Education (CSCE); in November 1977, CSCE's structure started to be consolidated, especially since in December of the same year, a series of press and printing committees and agencies were either demitted or restructured (e.g., the State Committee of Press and Printing—demised; Romanian Radio Television and Romanian Press Agency—restructured). In all this, the CSCE became subordinate to the Ideological Commission of the Central Committee of the Romanian Communist Party (RCP) and then to the Council of Ministers.

In 1977, CSCE's new responsibility concerned the organization of the national festival "The Song of Romania" whose main purpose was to engage the nation at all levels.[4] "The Song of Romania" was first launched from June 2–4, 1976, at the first Congress of Political Education and Socialist Culture and was meant to be "a mass manifestation of diligence, and labor, an opportunity to educate the young generation" (The Second Congress of Socialist Culture and Political Education 1982, 84). Its purpose was a reinforcement of the political-ideological education of the masses, through manifestations of so-called creative and interpretative cultural expressions. Patriotic songs and poems reflected the illusionary "happiness," the "glorious future," and the parental care of the party and its leaders, turning "The Song of Romania" into a mass masquerade where students, teachers, workers, and the entire country mobilized to bring homage to the party, and to its most "beloved" leader. This spectacle, meant to honor and glorify the Party and its leaders, activated hundreds and thousands of people in performing the Party's ideology whether they believed in it or not. Since this was the Party's initiative, specifically Ceaușescu's, to recruit people to praise the Party—a self-serving, self-orchestrated performance, its enactment was ridiculous and narcissistic in nature.

By far the most significant change with the ideological turn relates to language and discourse. The language of the Party, in addition to giving voice to the socialist ideology, aimed to erase alternative discourses. Seeking to elucidate the impact of totalitarian regimes on language and discourse, historian Jan Gross argues, "The communist rule changes language so it no longer reflects or represents reality; metaphor becomes more important than prosaic discourse, and magical words replace descriptive and logical ones" (quoted in Verdery 1991, 89).

Verdery (1991), on the other hand, does not see this alteration as a "destruction of language," but describes it as a "retooling of language *qua* means of ideological production" (89). The result of this change produces an authoritarian discourse whose goal is "to reduce words, to straitjacket them into singular intentions," impeding the growth of multiple voices or interpretations (90). This discourse, as Bakhtin describes it, comes with "its authority already fused to it" (342), and school textbooks represent a suitable space for this discourse to thrive. As Michael Apple (1988) writes, textbooks have authority to determine what "elite and legitimate culture to pass on" (81), and they certainly functioned as such in the Romanian context. Those singular meanings constituted the "official discourse," reflecting the Party's ideology and its control. Reading became highly emphasized as a means of consciousness-raising, and the spread of literature became the Party's megaphone through pamphlets, speeches, and a thriving mass production of magazines and newsletters for all school levels. Writing, on the other hand, was intended as an exclusive tool for the selected few who were appointed to represent the "hands," the "eyes," and "the voice" of the Communist Party and its ideology. However, small acts of disobedience, such as defacing a textbook, suggest that any discourse, even the authoritarian ones, engage multiple voices, albeit sometimes involuntarily. This means that people have far more agency than expected, and literacy has a powerful dialogic force that, if channeled well, can re-shape even authoritarian discourse.

Textbooks and School Curricula as Ideological Tools

The Ideological Commission's main role was to censor the content of textbooks and curricula so that these reading materials would reflect the Party's language and image. The commission paid equal attention to layout, images, and text. Each textbook was framed by precisely-chosen elements, including a front page with Nicolae Ceaușescu's image, followed by the Romanian national anthem, titled "Three colors I know in this world," the three colors representing the Romanian flag: red, yellow, and blue. Some textbooks included a famous song, called the "Union," as shown earlier. Defacing one or some of these symbols was fairly typical. I found multiple such examples in various textbooks in the archives when I was conducting research. However, since I consulted mainly copies from Central University Library in Bucharest, the frequency of these acts was reduced.

The literacy textbooks I reference here are called *Citire* (Engl. *Reading*) or *Limba română* (Engl. *The Romanian Language*). These titles misleadingly suggest a focus solely on reading. In reality, *Reading* or *Romanian* as school subjects offered training in language, writing, and literature. As such, I will use an umbrella term to account for all of these skills and will call them *literacy* textbooks. These literacy textbooks carried discursively the presence of the Party through a set of themes: nature, history, family, and the Party. Through each of these themes, the State used literacy and language to broker one's affinity for the patria. Basically, the goal was to ensure that the Romanian ethos and the Romanian nation were at the center of one's learning. In my analysis, I will only cover the *Reading* textbook for third grade, but the same recurrent themes emerged in the other literacy textbooks for fourth, sixth, and eighth grade. The third grade *Reading* textbook, published in 1987, included the following key themes:

1) *Nature-related texts* (e.g. "How Fall Starts," "Winter," "the Fir Tree," "What Happens Under the Snow").

2) *Historical texts about the ancestors of the Romanian people* (e.g. "From the Lives of the Dacians," "The Wars of Traian and Decebal," or "The Mother and the Son" (a reference to Steven the Great, an important Romanian historical figure).

3) *Family life and its role in shaping the student's consciousness* (e.g. "The Hands," "My Father," or "Grandma").

4) *The Party and implicit Party ideology*, with emphasis on work, laboring the land (e.g. "Work is Dear to Us," "The Day of the Republic," or "The Story of the Magazine: The Country's Hawks").

Each of the four themes—nature, Romanian history/ancestry, family, and the Party—emphasizes a form of affinity. It is an affinity for the patria while all other affinities are dismissed. The first theme, "nature," sets the scene for one's learning. Nature signifies a location, the ideal space where the Romanian nation lives. But readings focused on nature underline a deeper philosophical thought of Romanian writers, namely an organic, intimate connection between man and nature; nature or the geographical space becomes the cradle of a nation, a place of nurture and identity formation. The second theme focusing on history and ancestry reiterates that the Romanian patria is of noble descent (a reference here to Dacian and Roman ancestors) and an independent nation. The emphasis on independence has dual connotations. One alludes to the Romanians' efforts to unify its territories and shake off foreign rule. Another dimension relates to Ceaușescu's political strategy to remove Romania from the Russian influence, therefore referencing an ideological independence. For this reason, communism in Romania took a particular flavor as Ceaușescu added his own contribution to the Romanian ethos; in Ceaușescu's notorious speeches, Romania has always been involved in a "struggle for freedom, justice, and unity" (Mungescu 2004).[5] The third theme engages the institution of the family, which as Verdery suggests, was foundational in a socialist state inasmuch as the Party constructed its presence as a family. Family as an intimate space, a space that creates affinities between its members, has been a central trope in the Party's rhetoric. The family functions both as a way to reinforce each member's participation in the socialist patria, but also as a metonymy for the party and its role in parenting and raising ideologically minded children. Texts featuring the family also served to advance a socioeconomic class, a particular profession modeled by the parent to their child. Parents, either factory workers, drivers, or workers on a construction site or with some type of blue-collar job, are the hands and feet of the Party, building the Romanian nation both physically and metaphorically. School children, as these textbooks show, were somewhat predestined to follow their parents' socioeconomic class, and their parents' career path was scripted by larger socioeconomic and political conditions. As for the last theme, the Party and the socialist ideology permeated these textbooks all throughout. This theme seeks to engage directly with cultivating feelings for the Party and developing an emic vocabulary about the country's prosperity; in doing so, the texts highlight the Party's contribution to the formation of a culture where each member participates in anniversary events, speaks about the country's prosperity, recites, sings, and celebrates the socialist life.

To illustrate even further how these themes were reinforced by the Central Committee before they even reached the classroom, I turn to textbook revisions imposed by the Ideological Commission of the Central Committee in 1984, when a series of textbooks (first through eighth grade) were undergoing changes. These revisions were initiated in the meetings of the Ideological Commission of the Central Committee. I am relying here on meeting minutes and notes. I limit my focus to the first grade reading textbook, *The ABC*, since in the minutes and notes of the Propaganda and Agitation Department, *The ABC* received special attention, as it was called "the fundamental book of a nation." In Appendix A, I have included an overview of revisions for various grade levels, as they were reflected in the titles of the texts.

Some revisions include general changes, such as the inclusion of authors' names or changes in content to make the readings and images more age appropriate. These concerns were justified by the psychological and physiological changes in children, as the reviewers explained. For instance, it is recommended that more poems for memorization suitable for seven-year-olds should be included. Another category of changes includes specific details that reinforce the Romanian ethos through images and various socialist symbols and values. Textbook reviewers, as agents of ideological control, paid special attention to details that otherwise might have gone unnoticed:

- *On the page teaching the letter S*: the reviewers recommended: "must draw a Romanian sun, not one with Egyptian tendency."
- *In the lesson on the letter D*: there are two remarks: "the costume is "Russian-like," and "the coal miners can be replaced with teens."
  - Neither Russian nor Egyptian references were to be tolerated

since the students had to identify everything as Romanian and for Romanians. The removal of coal miners is important here since their presence can potentially be linked to one of the few reactionary events under Ceauşescu, the miners' strike of 1977.

– *in the lesson on the letter P*: it is recommended to include the symbol of bread, (in Rom., *pâine*), as a symbol of the prosperity and "high" living standards of the Romanians, another recurrent theme of the Communist Party.

– on page 9: the reviewers make specific recommendations regarding an image: "the Image 'the Festivity of Opening the New Year.'" They note that "the sky should be colored in blue, and the school courtyard should be paved with tiles."

As these examples suggest, *The ABC*, "the fundamental book of a nation" must guide one's literacy through association between letters and images, between words and concepts that tie one's affinity to the nation. The sun, teens, or images of bread must depict Romania as a prosperous nation or the land of happy childhood. In the final revisions, the reviewer lists a series of words and phrases that must be edited out since they were beyond the level of comprehension of first graders: colors with wings (Rom. *culori înaripate*); the ancestors' cradle (Rom. *vatra strămoşească*); impetuous (Rom. *năvalnic*); aspiration (Rom. *năzuinţă*); a red flag like a song (Rom. *steagul roşu ca un cântec*). All these phrases and words in Romanian have a rather archaic or poetic nuance, typically not used in colloquial speech but ideologically imbued with the Party's way of speaking, peppered with metaphors and patriotic feelings disconnected from the daily reality.

In the textbooks beyond first grade, most revisions reinforce recurrent ideological themes, constituting the "official" discourse of the party: nature and synergy between man and nature; the noble origin of the Romanian people and the historical continuity narrative; the Communist Party and love for patria; and family as the cradle of one's development. In addition to these, a fifth theme seems to emerge: the Ceauşescu theme. In several second-, third-, and seventh-grade textbooks, poems and other odes are directly addressed to either comrade Nicolae or Elena Ceauşescu, his wife, or to both. Some examples of texts dedicated to the Ceauşescu include: "The Party, Ceauşescu, Romania," "Song to Comrade Nicolae Ceauşescu," "To Comrade Elena Ceauşescu," "Nicolae Ceauşescu's Epoch," and others.

With these curricular changes, literacy becomes central in providing a cohesive textual image of the nation, through geography, the nation's place, history, political identity, and social communities such as the family. Evidently textbooks carry the ideological baggage of the dominant class, as Michael Apple (1988) suggests, however I would argue that the ideology of the dominant class also connects to ideologies of the nation or more precisely, to the intimate patria. In fact, the focus on the nation was so strong that starting in 1986 these revisions were required for implementation in other school subjects: Romanian, History, Geography, and Political Science (for more advanced grade levels) and had to be taught only in Romanian. Prior to this, education for German and Hungarian minorities was taking place in their own respective language; but with these revisions, the Romanian language became the only adequate means to express a people's affinity for the nation, the Romanian patria. German and Hungarian could easily carry the meaning of socialist ideologies, but only the Romanian language could accomplish the affinity and contribute to the cohesiveness of one patria. With the change of the language of instruction, both literacy and language were given power to regulate affinities. It is striking to see that the Communist Party had a tremendous appreciation of language and literacy and a powerful role in shaping one's learning and ethos.

While these ideologized textbooks aimed to provide models of literary expression both in form and content, writing took a somewhat secondary role. Employed in the service of the Party's ideology, writing became an exercise in imitating texts that had already been "approved" as ideologically fitted. The textbooks encouraged students to write in order to apply knowledge from these texts and to align their language and genre to the Party's ideology. In a pedagogical guide to teaching composition for fifth through eighth grade, even open composition prompts were highly prescriptive. One type of composition asked students to write a narrative with a focused theme using a set of given words. Not surprisingly, the suggested keywords are feelings for the patria, such as contentment or diligence and additional words associated with these emotions: *contentment*: street, pioneering, a bag, a militia post, meeting, gratefulness; or, *diligence*: vacation, patriotic work, lawns/sampling, [pioneer] squad, hectares, diplomas.

As someone who has learned to write this type of composition, I find it easy to predict the expected narrative: *Some pioneers find a lost bag in the street; they go to the militia post and are helped with much enthusiasm. The militia set up a meeting with the original owner of the lost bag. The owner later shows gratefulness in the local newspaper, praising such exemplary acts of humanity.* The second narrative, on diligence, would probably sound like this: *Pioneers have been rewarded with honorary diplomas for their diligent work over the summer vacation. Several pioneer squads from the neighborhood decided, out of their own initiative, to spend a good part of their summer planting saplings and maintaining school lawns in preparation for the new school year. This work was performed in addition to helping with planting hundreds of hectares in the local village. Such pioneer work demonstrates a spirit of initiation worthy to follow.*

The pedagogical approach employed for teaching reading and other subjects also applied to the teaching of writing and composition. Dictation, repetition of key socialist themes, and model-driven writing exercises helped support a philosophy promoting an authoritarian discourse. Bahktin (1981) explains that authoritarian discourse is a *priori*; it does not invite dialogism, it does not blend with other voices; it remains intact, fixed, and "fully sufficient" (342–3). In the composition exercise exemplified earlier, words were already supplied, and their fixity was established, as feelings of contentment, friendship, or diligence are always tied to the Party and its activities. Although a freestyle or open composition should allow for multiple narratives to emerge, in an authoritarian discourse, only one narrative can materialize the focus on the patria and its ideology.

Brokering Free Time with Pioneer Organizations and Pioneer Writing Genres

If reading and writing carried the ideological freight through themes and affinities for the patria and through prescribed ways of composing, literacy outside the institutional context of learning was embedded in the mundane. Writing became instrumental in recording everyday life in communist Romania. Whether students assumed roles such as the chronicler, the columnist, or the reporter in various contexts such as summer camps, patriotic activities, or festivals, they were participating in and making the socialist life through writing. This is the second strategy that the State used to broker its ideology in the "everydayness" of people's lives. In such banal contexts, students' feelings were regulated through doing patriotic work and writing and reading about patriotic work. In discussing the public sphere in Communist Romania, Gail Kligman (1990) writes that through the "everydayness" of the state power, the state seized its citizens' time, space, and modes of communication (398). Similarly, children's free time and their extracurricular activities were saturated with readings about everyday socialist life and with specific writing genres—reports, poems, and odes to the Party and its leaders—through which the Party brokered its presence. The "everydayness" of brokering was achieved through pioneer organizations whose role in regulating literacy and affinity was rather obscure precisely because they operated through routinized activities. Trainor (2008) highlights such structures when she discusses the role of schools in the formation of racial discourses and attitudes. She exposes the "infrastructure of school" as having "powerful, but largely unacknowledged, pedagogical and persuasive force" (85). Although the pioneer organizations functioned in and out of school, they created a similar infrastructure in the way they regimented students' free time, activities, reading, and writing practices.

As mentioned earlier, education reform in Romania during the Communist period modeled Makarenko's principles: authoritarian, collective, and regimented (Perşa 1998). To accomplish this type of education, in addition to formal education in schools, the State brokered its presence through the establishment and fortification of pioneer organizations. The pioneer organization, which enrolled seven- to fourteen-year-old children, allowed the Party to manage the children's breaks, vacations, and weekends. A similar structure governed two different organizations, the Country's Hawks for pre-school children, and the Union of Communist Youth (UCY), which automatically regimented all high school and college students as party members. Through these socialist organizations: the Pioneer Organization, the Country's Hawks, and the Union of Communist Youth (UCY), every member of society, including children and teens, were accounted for as members of the patria—the Pioneers, the Country's Hawks, and the UTC-ists (members of the UCY; in Romanian, Uniunea Tineretului Communist-UTC). Being a pioneer meant that one cultivates feelings of pride for being selected and ceremoniously welcomed into the ranks of the patria's family.

The socialization through magazines such as *The Daring* became the primary engine of language and literacy regimentation for these socialist organizations for children and teens. Through clubs, recitals, performances as well as hands-on patriotic work, pioneer organizations mobilized: "large numbers of learners and teachers . . . [through] elements of both compulsion and social pressure to propagate a particular doctrine" (Arnove and Graff 1987, 2). The goal was the Party's doctrine, and the means comprised all forms of social engagement: readings, activities, work in school, work outside school, etc. In one of Ceauşescu's legendary speeches at the Third National Conference of the Pioneer Organization, he tried to situate the role of pioneer organizations in connection to broader national goals: "The pioneer organizations have an important role in educating children to be creative, to work creatively, and to respect the history of the Romanian people and its majestic craftsmanship in the revolutionary transformation of society, in the spirit of the children's wishes and determination, of young adults of tomorrow to bring their contribution to the flourishing of our country" (The Third National Conference of the Pioneer Organization, 1976). This excerpt, like many other of Ceauşescu's speeches, reiterates the Party line: children and the youth should be preoccupied with the "flourishing" of the country through creativity, willpower, and transformative skills. In a subsequent examination of pioneer life and activities exemplified in school magazines, poems, and readings, we learn that the "flourishing" of the country is achieved through creative works that applauded the Party and its leaders, and most importantly, through patriotic work and advancement of the factory worker's skills and ingenuity—the ideal candidate in advancing the Party's ideology. In one of many pedagogical guides for socialist education entitled *Pioneers and Work* (1974), I found the goal of the pioneer organization clearly laid out: it must advance the doctrine of communist education: "education through work and for work of the new generation" (5). Work is a central theme here even if these guidelines refer to children.

Extracurricular activities, however, included aspects of life beyond work, such as entertainment and recreation. Interestingly, the roots of the pioneer organization are traced back to the organization called Romania's Pioneers (1945) initially known as the Scouts of Romania (established before 1914), which served a touristic purpose but gradually became a political mechanism (4). In 1948, the pioneer organization spread nationwide, and in April of 1966, it was subordinate to the Central Committee of the Communist Party. It is under Ceaușescu (who became President in 1965) that the pioneer organization became repurposed through the Party's ideologies and used to "reeducate" the "new man." With the political turn, it is not surprising that in Ceaușescu's period, the pioneer organization was refashioned to express the struggle of working-class youth for a more prosperous life, as a manual for teacher training, *The Content and Methodology of Pioneer Activity* (1978), relates.

One of the greatest accomplishments of the pioneer organization resides in the wide range of activities offered. While pioneer organizations orchestrated Party-related festivities and compulsory community labor, such as harvesting or recycling, they also started special-interest groups, called circles or clubs. On the surface, the special-interest circles appealed to the students' interests in various areas: theater, photography, archaeology, literature, expeditions, and certainly, while many focused on technology and science. Despite their appeal to children, the structure of this pioneer organization, particularly their strategic locations organized locally, regionally, and nationally—essentially served as a mechanism of collective regimentation. Through the proliferation of these circles, the State succeeded to broker its reach into the everyday life of its little citizens. This type of everyday control was less discernible than the explicit textbook manipulation and for this reason, it was less contested.

In the pioneer houses, as they were also called, literacy shaped the socialist life in an attempt to reflect a "happy" socialist pseudo-reality. In literacy-related pioneer circles—creative writing circles, the reporter's circles—but also in pioneer expeditions or summer camps, students were encouraged to write and participate in the making of the socialist life through their writing skills. Such literate activities asked students to document everyday realities, special events in a pioneer's life, or partake in writing competitions such as the *Golden Quill*. Various writing roles—the reporter, the columnist, the journalist—hoped to train pioneers in mimicking real-life work and professions. In this sense, the pioneers amplified and expanded the "voice" of the Party and its doctrine, even if they did so unaware. Of numerous venues where the pioneers' voices were provided a platform—literary circles, school magazines, creative writing circles, pioneer expeditions, pioneer camps—my analysis will engage with a few texts published in the pioneer magazine *The Daring*. *The Daring*, as a State-approved weekly magazine, was generally distributed in schools; as a broker of free time, it also sought to make socialist life fun and entertaining—while also engaging the core doctrines of the Party, in particular socialist work, the history of Romanians, and pioneer activities promoting socialist values including progress, courage, friendship in the socialist patria, etc.

Of various genres promoted in *The Daring*, I chose to focus on two—the pioneer report and the poem. Both genres are illustrative of the Party's attempt to broker its ideology and image through literate activities. The report's purpose as a typified textual strategy was to measure the socialist progress in all domains of social life: industry, agriculture, education, etc. While the report functions as the genre of everyday life, the poem is an expression of celebration and festivities, the epideictic genre, brokering the image of state and its ultimate leader, Ceaușescu. Both these genres used language to stir up feelings or one's senses; as they engage with patriotic feelings such as happiness and a spirit of initiative for the country's advancement, they regimented emotions to serve the Party's purpose. They also engaged with social bodies, particularly in the case of the poem, which demanded a performative context or a festive event.

The Pioneer's Report

The pioneer's report would generally be published in *The Daring* magazine. In the January and early February of 1980 issues, in addition to several announcements about the upcoming pioneer election, we also find the following pioneer report: "No failing student at any subject. No failing student per class" (February 28 issue of 1980, *The Daring*). Such reports were typical since in the fight against illiteracy in a well-governed socialist society, no one should fail; students had to find pleasure in reading and writing and in learning in general. The need to report only students' success shows a culture of learning where all study enthusiastically. Learning with joy was an expected duty in Communist Romania, a duty that pioneers had to honor.

In a different section of the magazine, the profile of the pioneer becomes more visible as we are introduced to the "little notebook with blue covers" and the planner of the pioneer in command, Angela Boncea. "The little notebook" and the details of everyday life illustrate the ways in which writing documented daily activities and the feelings associated with such work. Writing serves as a memory tool for all daily activities whose purpose was to build a discursive socialist citizen through the depiction of concrete details of the socialist life. Concretely, the report emphasized: 1) *socialization*, meeting people, particularly remarkable communists, reminding one that a communist identity is ultimately deeply social and collective; 2) *participation in artistic programs* as the mark of a literate, educated student who appreciates creative forms or art and contributes to promoting them; and 3) *patriotic work* always performed in the service of the country and *a sense of accountability*; all of these contribute to the profile of the little citizen. Sociability, artistic talent, and a hardworking spirit were key features of a remarkable pioneer. Quantifiable data in the form of events, people, and activities all added up in an image of the ideal socialist citizen. In this process, writing was the perfect tool to measure and report such outstanding results.

Apart from these daily activities, through which pioneers broker the image of state values, this text is also infused with *patriotic feelings*, with a particular socialist pathos. If literacy brokers in the case of refugees operate mostly to broker emotional work through personal experience (see chapter 2), here pioneers act as brokers of feelings, of collective feelings emerging from work and duty to the motherland, the patria. These feelings of "joy, pride, and responsibility"—as the report exemplifies—permeated all patriotic activities. These emotions, in fact, have been essential themes routinized through literate practices that subsequently contributed to the formation of a discursive repertoire imbued with feelings for the patria. If literacy brokers in transnational contexts recover emotional work lost in the bureaucratic processes of migration, in the case of Romania, the State as the ultimate broker sought to regiment structures of feeling through literate practices. Writing for the Party through prescribed narratives both censored and reduced one's individual expression, regimenting feelings through writing—patriotic feelings of elation and glorification of the Party—and pushed the Party's monopoly further than necessary. Similar to Kotkin's notion of learning to "speak Bolshevik," students had to learn to write the patria, and often this was accomplished through capturing feelings of happiness, peace, and prosperity. Students did not have to understand the ideological implications of their writing, nor was it expected. Mere participation and mimicry were sufficient.

The pioneer report written by the ideal pioneer, Angela, further continued with details about how patriotic life should look, smell, and feel, all of these offering a sensorial experience of the socialist life. From the report, we learn that the pioneer writer jots down a plethora of details that make it difficult for her to select and condense all this pioneer work into one short report (the actual report was quite long). Using an enthusiastic emotional tone, the report, like the school textbooks, referenced all the elements of a complex and fulfilled life: nature, the construction site, and connections to broader communities such as the local administration, the mayor or the elderly. Angela's list includes:

- *The songs of the orchestra* (a pioneer must have some skills that can be used in the service of the Party) and receiving the first prize at the country-level competition "The Song of Romania" (verifiable results).
- *Nature*: as Angela passes by a harvested wheat field, various patriotic memories unfold (the harvested field is an important mark of Romania's productive agriculture).
- *Community involvement*: Angela and the pioneers contributed to community support by helping the elderly (there is much pride in receiving letters from the elderly thanking the pioneers for their help).
- *Construction site*: the pioneers also participate in the building of the socialist country (the construction site was a recurrent leitmotif, particularly as Ceaușescu gave directives for the building of many apartments while erasing many neighborhoods throughout the entire country).
- *Advocacy for pioneer concerns*: *the Pioneer's house*: discussing with the local authorities the issue of a larger headquarters for the pioneers and the country's hawks.

All the recurrent themes and values of the socialist Party are highlighted here: nature, patriotic work in the community, patriotic performance but also the national development of patria through harvesting and the refiguring of the country's towns and villages. Yet, this report creates mental, olfactory, and tactile images that although local, join together similar experiences nationwide. It is evident that the infrastructure of schooling—established through practices, feelings, and performances—works both in and outside the actual school boundaries. It is this infrastructure that aims to sustain and maintain emotional discursive practices that glorify the patria. Every writing activity, as the pioneer report shows, solidified the structure on which the socialist ethos rests. It is a structure that prescribed ways of feeling through the use of literacy in the production of affinities for the patria.

For the most part, the regimentation of feelings through discourse failed to produce the socialist new citizen. Like the third grader who crossed out Nicolae Ceaușescu's name, most Romanians removed the political layer that oppressed them and preserved aspects of literacy that allowed their own individuality to thrive. Instead of feelings for the patria, several participants in my study spoke of feelings of derision, pity, and avoidance of the Party and its agents. Horațiu, for instance, said: "Ideological education was always considered hilarious to me and my colleagues. We avoided it as much as possible, even making jokes about it being obviously ridiculous and noneducational." Another participant, Florian, explained that he found an escape in mathematics and computer science: "I found a niche, a domain where I felt free." Similarly, Sever shares that the family was the space where one could speak freely, "I had to become a pioneer. I was a UTCist (member of the Union of the Communist Youth). But within the family, evidently, everyone spoke openly. They [the parents] trusted me that I'll keep my mouth shut, that I won't talk. And I did. With my friends, I didn't talk openly." Feelings of restraint and efforts to find freedom elsewhere suggest that the discursive spaces created by the Party were oppressive and far from the proclaimed feelings of happiness and adoration of the patria. The so-called "happy socialist life" contravened with the crude reality of people's daily lives, where citizens were desperate for food and deprived of basic human rights.

Dan, another participant, spoke of feelings of pity and a collective distrust of ideological education: "I felt sorry for the history teacher. I don't remember her name; she was trying to explain how things are getting better ('It's bad right now, but let's believe in communism'), and I honestly felt bad for her because nobody in class was paying attention to her honestly. Those classes were like, the teachers could tell that most of us didn't really care about what they were talking about. We kind of despised that." Such feelings of rejection and scorn demonstrate the Party's failure to produce any worthy emotional connections. Since these participants, especially those who were enrolled in high school before 1989, went through various stages of socialist citizenship, as pioneers and then, as UTC members, they got socialized in the pretense of the system and as a result, dissociated their feelings from the Party's agenda.

The Poem and its Role in Animating Feelings for the Patria

The poem (and recitation) represents another genre that dominated the pioneer magazine *The Daring*. If the report captured the narrative of the socialist life and feelings for the patria, the poem merged catchy refrains with performance, animating feelings for the patria through the rhetoric of the body. In *Labyrinths of Literacy*, Harvey Graff (1987) describes the typical materials used in literacy campaigns and movements as "simplified texts" and the use of a pedagogy focused on repetition and drilling (285). With its simplified form and use of recurrent themes of the Party's values, the poem as a genre perfectly befitted the Party's goals: praise to and celebration of the socialist system. In other socialist countries, the poem also served as one of the preferred genres in totalitarian regimes (Boym 2010). Rhetorically, the poem functions more effectively in straitjacketing ideas through its repeated forms, rhymes, and through the performance of the body. I view performance here, as an outer, bodily participation relatively empty of ideological content, a way of participating without necessarily internalizing the underlying philosophy.[6] In its condensed form, the poem allows strings of words to strut and repeat, even when no meaningful message is conveyed. Carrying the nation-state's ideological agenda, the poem was a preferred genre for the pioneers as they proclaimed its values and ideologies. I envision the poem as an expression of singular authorship, a poetic style that Bakhtin describes as "fully adequate to a single language and a single linguistic consciousness" (286). The poem, then, is marked by a "monologic steadfastness" since it reflects the intentions and the internal world of one single author.

The Daring, like many other magazines from this period, abounded in poems glorifying the Party. On the front cover of *The Daring* from January 24, 1980, the poem "Comrade, Friend, Parent," dedicated to Ceaușescu, is placed on the left side of the cover, next to a proud pioneer dressed exemplarily, with the adequate sartorial and joyful bodily expression of a young Party recruit. The young girl, positioned against two flags in the background (the Red Communist flag and the Romanian flag) salutes with her right hand the "glorious" future of Romania and its leader. While the poem discursively illustrates the rhetoric of the socialist Party through the title slogan "Comrade, Friend, Parent," the presence of the pioneer as well as the two flags augment the textual rhetoric with a visual representation of this performative act.

The written poem is positioned to the left side of the jubilant pioneer. The blissful image clearly dominates the text such that before reading the poem, the reader can envision a cheerful message. The poem reads:

We are coming with light of grains and flowers,
With blue skies,
With soaring, dazzling mountains.
We are coming with history written in golden letters,
With the country's flag fluttering majestically
All woven together in a beautiful bouquet,
That is called: country.
And we bring deep homage
To Comrade Nicolae Ceaușescu,
To this man of great humanity,
Comrade, Friend, Parent.

Author: Maria Cîmpean, student, from Surduc, Sălaj

Extending the visual images of the Party's ethos, the poem's text creates mental images of the Party and its leader; first, the image of the country as a *bouquet* is complemented by the visual harmony of happy colors: *blue* skies, *golden* letters, the country's flag (most likely pointing the Romanian colors: red, yellow, blue). The image of the Party is further illustrated through a series of key concepts representing socialist values: camaraderie, friendship, and family. *Comrade* points to the political identity, while *friend* denotes amiable relationships always thriving in various collectives and communities, and *parent* invokes the image of family as a necessary social cell—all pointing to the one who seemingly holds everything together, Nicolae Ceaușescu. In him, the image of the ultimate broker is crystalized, the one who controlled the Party, various social groups and collectives, as well as families. By listing these key figures in this order—Party first, collective second, and family last—it is evident that all social relations became subservient to a political identity. The collective and the family were important as they helped socialize the individual into the ideology of the Party. All these relations represent forms of affinity since they point to a political subjectivity (the Party and collective) and a personal intimate life (the family). Whether we talk about grains, flowers, or mountains, they all come together in a wonderful "bouquet" paying homage to Ceaușescu (the image of a bouquet was often used to depict harmony and unity). The Party becomes the metonymic image of Ceaușescu, and so do all other relations depicted in this poem; Ceaușescu is the friend, and he is also the parent of the nation[7]. For this reason, he emerges as the ultimate broker, as he sought to abolish all other social forms and entities. It is an image of Ceaușescu, "this man of great humanity," that must be brokered through all discursive means:

through text, image, color, and bodies. Such powerful tropes sought to harness people's affinity into one that would only glorify Ceauşescu. In this way, this affinity becomes monologic in form and structure.

To sum up, I discussed here the state's brokering in the context of children's free time. This was accomplished through specific genres: the pioneer report and the poem. Both these genres afford a more complex process of brokering. If the readings in textbooks were helpful in establishing central themes that had to be brokered—all accentuating one's affinity for the patria—brokering one's free time shifts the focus onto genres suitable for brokering one's affection. The report captures the image of the Party and its ideology through the everydayness of life and feelings associated with mundane activities. The poem, on the other hand, adds a performative dimension to brokering, seeking to engage text, image, and rhetorical bodies.

As I conclude, I return to Lenin's statement: "The illiterate person stands outside politics. First it is necessary to teach the alphabet. Without it, there are only rumors, fairy tales, prejudice, but no politics" (Arnove and Graff 1987, 7). Without literacy, crafting political subjects is quite impossible. A literacy campaign in socialist countries was ultimately a political campaign. In the case of Romania, both school literacy and free time were hijacked to develop and regulate affinity for the patria. The nation-state functioned as the ultimate broker, bridging ideological gaps in the lives of children and their institutional and noninstitutional identities. Since writing—like mass reading, the main vehicle in national campaigns of the past—has often served as a powerful ideological tool through the manipulation of feelings, texts, and images, the multiple intersections between writing and political economies need our attention. Secondary economies emerge as powerful infrastructures to support or regulate literacy in both authoritarian regimes and democratic societies because issues of power and control are a permeance in any political economy.

Chapter 5

Teachers and Shifting Ideological Positions

You will be a success.

—Adina Ghinaci, English Teacher and Artist

A discussion about the State's involvement in brokering ideology would be incomplete without discussing teachers who worked closely with textbooks and pioneer organizations. While the State's encroachment and ideological control operated through textbooks and literacy practices through specific genres, the ideological turn also manifested forcefully through extensive enrollment of the teaching staff as Party members (Documents of the Romanian Communist Party 1972). In fact, Ceaușescu specifically emphasized the role of teachers/professors in the ideological-political formation of the students. All teaching staff functioned under the guidance of the Propaganda Section of the Central Committee of the Romanian Communist Party (Documents of the Romanian Communist Party, 95). Although teachers were conceived as fundamental in curriculum restructuring—mere channels of the Party's ideology—they often held conflicting positions about their roles. In their capacity as the Party's extended tentacles, their role was reduced to transmitting the exact image of the State as the ultimate broker. In many situations, they performed as expected. In many other situations, however, they shifted positions departing from the Party's ideology and acting more like brokers, mediating between students and the Party. They exerted agency in making decisions about which ideologies they would further perpetuate and which ideologies they sifted through their own consciousness, acting outside of the Party's purview. In situations when the teacher knew the students individually and cared for their well-being—that is, in the case of particular affinities—they refrained from demanding that students perform a literate identity in adoration of the nation. Rather, they focused on the learning activity without emphasizing the socialist agenda.

Even if children were rarely targeted by the Secret police unless their parents were blacklisted or under close surveillance, they too were "catalogued" in official school records. Each class of students had its *catalog*, the US equivalent of a teacher's roll, where all teachers for that class would record grades and attendance. Each class had one and the same catalog (the exact word in Romanian); this meant that teachers were able to see students' grades or attendance in all subjects, not just in one subject area. This catalog, as its name suggests, did catalogue students. While students were listed alphabetically, at the end of the catalog, additional information about each student was included. A counselor collected specific information from the students at the beginning of each year, which was then included in the catalog. For each student, the following details was requested: name, date of birth, the parents' name(s), parents' professions, and religion. Similar to the workers in a factory who had their "labor book" and identification through various work histories and documents (Kotkin 1995, 216), children too were catalogued and identified through their parents' social and professional positions. Certainly, there were other identification documents—the student's grade book or the pioneer record book. Yet the catalog functioned as a recorder of the student's labor, a daily tool of classification based on the parents' social or economic backgrounds and religious affiliation. Through the gathered information, the catalog exerted a power of influence over the treatment given to each student. To this day, these catalogs are official school records, stored and locked in school cabinets. Besides teachers, school directors and educational inspectors have access to them. Functioning as selective tools of classification, the socioeconomic information in the catalog determined the way these students were assigned or denied roles, tasks, or privileges in the classroom and at times, beyond school. Historian Sheila Fitzpatrick (2001) explains that for Bolsheviks, class was generally considered an objective category established on the basis of hard data: economic and work-related information. However, there was also a subjective dimension of social class since many were deeply preoccupied with the "construction of a 'good' social identity" (474). Fitzpatrick (2001) explains further that it was not uncommon for people to go through different occupations, particularly as new jobs related to the Party's ideology emerged: "Certain common trajectories—born a peasant, now a worker; born a worker, now a member of the new intelligentsia—were so familiar and (from a Soviet standpoint) admirable that they needed only a minimum of explanation" (475).

Such mobile trajectories were not quite achievable for children. Children, in the context of Communist Romania, were slotted into their parents' socioeconomic class and treated accordingly. The only flexibility in this classification could have been achieved through the mediation of teachers. Teachers could function sometimes as brokers between students and the State. As discussed in chapter 4, since the State acted as the ultimate broker, it sought to re-produce its power through various other brokers, such as school teachers. Further on, I'll develop more extensively the brokering role of teachers with specific examples from Steven's life and a few other respondents. If the party's goal was to manufacture and control people's affinity for the *patria*, teachers contributed to this state project, as they were the extension of the Party into students' everyday life. Given that literacy is conceptualized as a social practice, connecting economic systems to literacy education affords a better understanding of how the State functioned as an ultimate broker and how teachers perpetuated its presence in the classroom. While the broker holds that middle position among multiple stakeholders, when a centralized power such as an authoritarian state overtakes that position, it reorganizes all social relations, identities, and interactions. It also recasts its power and control into multiple other relations: small centers of control in regional areas or organizations that mobilize citizens on behalf of the centralized power of the State, leading to the formation of local agents of control. In the case of schools and educations, teachers become such agents that orient education toward the official discourse of the Party.

Through the presence of teachers and instructors, the ultimate broker, the communist state, propagated its ideological presence on the ground. Equally important, the presence of teachers/instructors affords an exploration of fissures in these "iron-cast" models and of ways in which individuals reposition themselves in relation to oppressive systems. While hierarchical structures operating through local, regional, and national organizations and commissions consolidate the Party's control and mobilize masses of all ages, the individual often intervenes to disrupt this control. In this sense, totalitarian regimes seemed both indestructible and somewhat flexible, but always contingent on the individual's experience, history, and predispositions. In situations of flexible positioning, rather than simply implementing ideological requirements, teachers often engaged in "a process of negotiation among contested positions, ideologies and languages" (Juzwik 2004, 541). Instead of reverberating the Party's monologic rhetoric, teachers as brokers of ideologies opened spaces of dialogue.

Teachers in this case acted like literacy brokers moving on a large spectrum from inflexible monologic positions where they themselves mirrored the exact rigid discourse of the official rhetoric, from mixed mono-dialogic discourses to truly dialogic discursive positions. In this way, they operated similarly to brokers in the immigrant community discussed in chapter 2. Drawing on an interview with Steven Bonica, the owner of the *Romanian Tribune*, I explore how teachers navigated these transitions from rigid brokers of ideology to agents of dialogic mediation, acting and intervening despite the Party's ideological control. I will also include other participants' perspective and add my experience as a student as well.

When referring to the educational experience in Romania, Steven recalls those teachers who constantly ridiculed, physically mistreated him, or publicly pestered him with questions about his beliefs regardless of the class subject matter: "The others were persecuting me, they were told to give us a hard time. Why? Because we were neo-protestants. We were Evangelical Christian. We were supposed to be persecuted. We were supposed to . . . by the time we finished high school . . . we were supposed to be turned into atheists." Steven further recounts a frustrating dialogue with the biology teacher:

> Once the biology teacher asked me about the theory of evolution and when we got into the conversation she immediately asked me,
> "Do you believe in God?"
> and I said, "Ma'am we are not here to discuss my . . . "
> "No! Do you believe in God?"
> and I said, "Ma'am, I'm not going to respond . . . "
> She smacked me until blood came out of my nose. Then, I was angry, and I said, "You know what? Yes, I believe in God."

In this encounter, the biology teacher takes the position of an official inquisitor, identifying with the State's ideology, seeking to investigate and attack a student with questions and frame the student's religious views as alien to the official rhetoric. In a monologic rhetoric, the rhetoric of difference is reduced to one voice; alternative voices are cast as antagonistic, threatening the harmony of nation-state and its ideological position. Adopting the fixed ideological position of the State, this teacher censored any other form of affinity, especially the one attached to a religious identity.

Another example comes from a conversation Steven had with the math teacher. If the biology teacher used the theory of evolution to position Steven's identity and his Christian beliefs against the official atheistic ethos of the Party, the math teacher did not resort to such techniques. She openly and regularly challenged Steven about his time spent outside school. Free time, as discussed earlier, was to be brokered and brought under the purview of the Party through patriotic work, supplementary readings, and pioneer activities. For this reason, the math teacher asked questions about free time and habits outside of school. Every Monday morning, she called on Steven, always by his last name: "Bonica, come up front." To every Romanian student, this summoning meant an oral examination on an arbitrary topic. For Steven, the examination started with a question about church attendance,

> "Ok, so did you go to church yesterday?"
> "Yeah."
> "What was [happening] in church? What was new in church?"
> It was all for mocking reasons. So, the first time I fell in the trap and answered, and the second time I answered, thinking: "Okay, first time was an accident, now she was going act differently." No, I realized that she only wants to mock us, so I refused to answer.

The teachers' inquisitive approach about students' daily activities reiterates the fact that school was about enforcing "taken-for-granted practices and rituals" and about creating "emotioned frameworks" (Trainor 2008, 85). Since Steven's church attendance fell outside of the acceptable pattern of behavior and feeling, the teacher decided to expose and ridicule the student for such deviation. As expected, religious texts and ideology violated the Marxist-Leninist ideology but also the official national discourse, defining the Romanian ethos through an Eastern Orthodox faith, not a Protestant religious identification. In an earlier discussion about the rhetoric of "cataloguing" students into socioeconomic and religious molds, I explained that these categories assigned children ideological roles as little citizens in the production of socialist Romania. As an Evangelical Christian, Steven was cast against the official ideology and mocked for his beliefs. Going to church on Sunday prevented one from participating in patriotic work or other Party manifestations and, as a result, it was subject to chastisement.

Religious ideology and the rhetoric of religious affiliation have been oppositional to the Communist ideology. In the case of Communist Romania, religious identity became even more complicated as the Eastern Orthodox faith had been gradually officialized as the only acceptable religion, although other denominations were permitted to function by law. The reason why the Orthodox Church's intervention was both acceptable and desirable is justified by the fact that its purview operated within national boundaries, serving the interests of "the local Caesar" (Shafir 1978, 23–4). In other words, using the institution of the Orthodox church served the purpose of the Party. It became an identity marker, a socialist ethos. To be called a Christian, other than Christian Orthodox, literally meant a rejection of the Romanian identity.[1] It meant to be non-Romanian and to show affiliation with a religious denomination originating in the West. This contravened not only with the Communist ideology but with the Romanian state such that non-Orthodox Christians were often classified as political enemies. In *Peasants under Siege*, Kligman and Verdery (2011) explain that the new language of the Party created categories of difference that were relatively flexible since "they could be applied instrumentally to anyone at any time, thereby making everyone vulnerable" (220). While certain aspects of these categories were definitely manipulated and used arbitrarily to incriminate and deem everyone vulnerable, I suggest that these categories were malleable only when brokers intervened to strengthen or weaken them. Therefore, aspects of difference, as in Steven's case, would be enhanced or diminished depending on the broker and their ideological beliefs.

Eventually, Steven was expelled from school when his parents received the official notice that formal papers, their passports, were being processed. During this time, most Romanians did not own passports as mobility outside the country was rare. There were mainly two reasons to own a passport: to travel in the interest of the Party or to emigrate, as was the case of very few ethnic and religious minorities. Steven's family was among the fortunate ones whose papers were approved. In school, his case exposed an oppressive system where teachers functioned as brokers of ideology, turning the learning experience into a regimentation of the Communist Party's ideological system. When provoked, Steven often refused to answer and repositioned himself rhetorically to expose the irrationality of being examined based on his religion affiliation. Years later, Steven affirmed his religious identity when he established his own publishing house and the first Romanian newspaper in the Chicagoland. The Romanian newspaper, the *Romanian Tribune*, founded by Steven, placed on its front page a logo written in Latin: *Nihil Sine Deo* (Engl. *Nothing without God*). With this rhetorical assertion of his religious belief, Steven seemed to respond to an oppressive past that denied his chosen religious identification. By invoking God, through a textual logo in his newspaper, Steven attached to his newspaper a particular affiliation informed by Judeo-Christian beliefs, the very same ideology and identification that were penalized under the Communist regime. Hence, Steven's Romanian newspaper became a space where an alternative voice emerges, where Steven expressed his religious beliefs.

At the other end of the spectrum were teachers who brokered students' literacy by separating themselves from the official ideology. In their strategic positioning, they diminished the ideological force of their pedagogy, opening spaces of dialogic communication for their students. As such, Steven mentioned a second category of teachers who were particularly influential in nurturing, rather than censoring his literacy and love for books. With much excitement, Steven gave credit for his literary predisposition to his Romanian language teacher for encouraging him to pursue his passion for reading and books. He explained, "She saw that I was reading with an emphasis, acting out my reading. She gave me more poems to learn and recite. Took me to competitions" (Personal interview).

The poems mentioned by Steven engaged the same recurrent themes discussed in the previous chapter: praising the Party or possibly the great history of the Romanian people, the nature, etc. The teacher in this instance influenced Steven not only in reading but in nurturing his passion for books. In this brokering process, the teacher established a relationship with the student without emphasizing his deviation from the Party framework; rather, she fueled his love for books. Eventually, Steven contributed to the school library and due to his great investment in this process, he was appointed a student librarian. One significant aspect of this library was the mobilizing efforts of various students, Steven's in particular, to grow the school's library. The reason why Steven was able to contribute with many books relates to his passion for books but also to his entrepreneurial skills. In a context where books were very scarce and literature censorship was at its peak, Steven craftily used informal networks available to him. Since Steven's mother was an extremely talented seamstress, in his search for books, Steven appealed to his mother's clientele, particularly to bookstore managers and clerks. These women, having direct access to various books and book warehouses, were key gatekeepers in these literacy transactions. Using informal economies of literacy was typical in the Communist regime in Romania and extensively developed in other sectors—grocery stores, apparel, and others. Steven's connections became the infrastructure for attaining his literacy goals.

A similar informal path was used when Steven was approaching his departure from Romania and decided to ship all his books to the US, where he eventually set up the first Romanian library in the community. Before his departure, Steven mobilized friends and family, and these people, in their turn, mobilized more acquaintances. For instance, his uncle agreed to donate his books to Steven, and then his aunt, a postmaster, arranged most shipments to the US. without technically breaking the law. This strategic planning, in which the aunt enlisted her whole family as shipping expediters, was necessary to carry out the book shipments. Working in the post office, the aunt knew the rules and how to get by the monthly limitation of one 11-pound package per person: "She figured out the rules, and she listed all her members of the family at one shipping location, but then she talked to another postmaster friend of hers and registered others at another location. So, they were working off two or three locations. And they were shipping all the books." By recruiting people, especially family members, Steven created reliable networks and asked others to join in. Once the books made it to the US., they continued to travel with Steven to various places: Detroit, California, and Chicago. When friends and visitors went to see Steven's library, they requested books from him. Eventually, he was offered his own office space in the church that he was attending. Over the years, the library expanded, and in 2002, Steven set up the first Romanian library in Chicagoland.

This Romanian library in Chicago area, initially housed at the Romanian Heritage Center, in Niles, IL, started with Steven's personal library in Romania, and Steven's personal library was motivated by his passion for books nurtured by a teacher of the Romanian language and literature. As a broker of literacy, rather than a mere tool in the service of the Party, the teacher refused to regiment her students into the Party's ideologies. Instead, she riskily adopted a flexible position relative to the Party, her students, and the curriculum. The cost of brokering literacy in this environment was high but also highly uncertain. It all depended on circumstances and the caprice of other higher authorities. Basically, each teacher had to assume the responsibility for their actions and the ensuing consequences, which could range from mild reprimand to no reprimand, to severe penalties such as losing one's job. A teacher could intervene on behalf of a student and *selectively* report aspects that conflicted with the Party's ideology, or they could report *everything* that was required according to specified guidelines.

Besides the teachers, a series of literacy brokers established through an informal network also supported and brokered Steven's books. Among these, Steven's uncle, his aunt, and all the relatives that his aunt managed to recruit constituted a powerful network that nurtured alternative literacies. Such networks, informed by knowledge of political economies, not only evaded official regulations but had the capacity to move literacy transnationally as well. Steven's books were able to carve a way through regimes of censorships, through laws and limitations, and even when the shipping process slowed down, the books made it through. These literacy artifacts, Steven's books, were moved through the assistance of brokers and networks constituted through deep social connections. The brokers' powerful impact emerges from their potential to multiply, expand, and engage additional networks. Referring to the language of informal economies, the possibilities of "doing a *hatâr*" (doing a favor) are quite immense. One's social connection engages another's and another's and, in this manner, they create the necessary socioeconomic support for literacy to move and travel in its material form. Steven's account shows that whenever necessary, his family became remarkable brokers of literacy. They complemented the work of official brokers of literacy in school—his teachers. Some of his teachers helped while others hindered his learning.

While the brokers' strategic position allowed maneuvering official and unofficial political economies, it was often ambivalent. Dan, another participant in the study, spoke about this ambivalence when relating a story about the *same* teacher shifting her attitude toward him quite frequently: "She was very weird teacher and she sometimes praised me: 'Oh Dan, you're the greatest,' and sometimes, she would make me the worst person. She's the one who gave me a one [the lowest score]. In school I was [a] good [student], so she turned it a ten later [the highest score]. She would make fun of me in class. In one of her threats, she said: 'I'm not gonna make you UTCist,' and I'm thinking, 'Who cares?'" The ambivalence of the teacher is evidenced not only in how she arbitrarily switched praises for threats, but also in her capricious grading: from a grade of one—representing lower than an F, a failing grade—to a grade of ten (ten representing an A+). In the Romanian educational system with grades from one to ten (ten being the highest score), a grade of four is already a failing grade. A grade of one or two was never assigned, unless used as a tool to reprimand students for a particular behavior rather than a learning failure. Dan's situation was extreme in that the teacher graded him capriciously and then unpredictably changed the grade from a one to a ten by adding a zero after one. This teacher fluctuated between her authentic evaluation of Dan as a great student and her allegiance to the Party's ideology, which demanded to cast Dan as "the enemy of the state." Like Steven, Dan's religious identification of Protestant faith disqualified him from being a dignified socialist citizen. This is why the teacher asserted her authority over him, when she threatened that she would not "make" him an UTCist (a member of the Union of Communist Youth, in Romanian, Uniunea Tineretului Comunist). Other participants mentioned that they were turned UTCists without showing up at the official ceremony. In Radu's situation, which is similar to Dan's, the class teacher issued him a UTCist card without even asking him to participate in the official ceremony. In this case, the teacher brokered his passage into an ideological identity he did not believe in. As such, the teacher intervened on behalf of the student, arranged that he received a card, and informed him that he could request it if he ever needed it. She also "excused" him even from participating in the official ceremony.

These examples show that the brokering of ideology is quite complex. Each situation was contingent on several variables, and in each case, the teachers had to make choices to carry on the image of the ultimate broker or shift their positions on behalf of the student. Dan related another situation, one where the school principal "closed his eyes." Dan and another friend could have been punished because he lent his friend a Christian book, *The Burning Bush*. This friend read the book in public while he was performing a school duty. Evidently, no book concerning a different ideology was permitted on the school grounds, yet the school principal, who discovered Dan's friend reading the book, decided to "close an eye." Dan got away with only a warning and learned that breaking rules in school simply depended on the person. This account illustrates the principle of particularism that I explore at length in chapter 6. In a particularism framework, social relationships are established based on particulars between those involved—the affinity or lack thereof that forms between various people. Whether these texts were censored depended on the individual or the supervising teacher. Literacy in this political economy and its affinity power was contingent on local circumstances and the teacher-broker's decision.

In other situations, severe consequences followed when Christian books and literature surfaced in official contexts or competed with the official discourse. Reverend Popovici, pastor at the First Baptist Church in Des Plaines, IL, shared the story of his expulsion from college. In 1966, he was living with his family in Bucharest. He was a senior at the university in polytechnic studies when he decided to write a harsh review of a book that had just been translated from Russian and was directly mocking Christianity. The book, titled *The Funny Bible*, sought to disparage those who, in the age of progress, of sputniks and rockets, as Popovici relates, still believed in God. After writing the book review, Popovici presented it in church publicly. He remembers that his review was equally scathing, measuring up to the mockery of the original book. At the end of the church service, the secret police agent who had been present there all along summoned the leadership of the church and asked for the written review. But, faster than the agent was Popovici's mother, who had already snatched —and probably destroyed—it right after his presentation, erasing any trace of its presence. After this audacious action,

Popovici was expelled from school by Tuesday. Although Popovici's presentation took place in a church setting, the review attacked directly and publicly the official discourse and its ideology. As a result, it demanded immediate action, with no possibility for any mediation or intervention.

Ideological Role of Teachers in My Story

I was eleven years old when the December 1989 Revolution broke out. I remember it vividly, gunshot sounds outdoors competing with the TV broadcasting the revolutionaries live as we sheltered indoors; this was the same TV that had been broadcasting only propaganda news and scripted Party messages until *that* moment. That year we did not celebrate Christmas with the church as we did every year in the past. We were at home, praying for the safety of the people in the streets. I was born under a Communist dictatorship and with the imagination of child, I thought countries had concrete walls between them, not barbed wires or "iron curtains." Inside these walls, I knew of police surveillance as I was the daughter of clergy. Since our father was the pastor of an evangelical church, a denomination seemingly antagonistic to the Marxist Party line, my siblings and I were deemed "enemies of the state" along with other non-desirables such as intellectual elites, certain ethnic groups, any religious affiliates other than the Eastern Orthodox, and others. Our family was blacklisted, resulting in stricter surveillance of phone and all conversations, interactions, and mobility. Inside these walls, I also experienced the somewhat abstract ideological control of Communist Party through the concrete presence of teachers and schools. Schools were the ideal place to regiment children.

As a child, the first thing I learned in school was that I belonged to a non-desirable social class due to my parent's profession, my father the pastor. As a first grader, I noticed my teacher, who was otherwise a good neighbor, directing her attention to the children of doctors, of militia, and other economically or politically privileged classes. With a child's eyes, I saw preferential systems unfold before me. I learned that irrespective of my efforts to succeed in school, a pre-established ceiling had already set, and irrespective of efforts, I could only advance to a certain position. The top positions had already been secured for the children of influential political subjects. Unlike Steven's narrative, where teachers fell into two categories: those who helped and those who hindered, I experienced a third category: the non-interventionist. My elementary teacher was like that—she didn't help, nor did she hinder.

Earlier I mentioned those teachers who assumed ambiguous roles and how, at times, they would help a student while at others, they would threaten or persecute them. I have vivid memories of those who persecuted students, even years past the 1989 revolution. Yet, this third category of teachers—the non-interventionist—those who could have helped but did not, is perhaps as problematic as those who blindly followed the ideological dogma of the Romanian Communist Party.

The non-interventionist position is problematic because in unequal power dynamics, in systems of oppression, by not helping, one in fact helps the system. Brokers, as I have defined them in this book, occupy at times the volatile middle-ground. They can take flexible positions, and through their repositioning, they can offer assistance through writing or through language of empathy. In radically oppressive systems or institutions of control, this middle-ground is narrower and perhaps less stable. Teachers in Communist Romania clearly occupied this unstably ground daily. My elementary teacher, like many others, perhaps struggled in negotiating her role during that oppressive system. She was a good neighbor, and regularly visited us. It was expected that in formal settings, she would follow the polices instituted by the Party. She did not harm or persecute me. She simply followed the prescribed Party line with little intervention. What she lacked the most was the language of empathy, the language of hope.

To understand how important this was for a child born in a dictatorship, one has to imagine a world set on unmovable tracks, with little possibility for change, a prescribed identity and limited career paths. Perhaps a good way to describe this world is how writing was taught— through dictation. Even free-style compositions were a form of dictation. "Dictation is a police state . . . with grammar as the law. Dictation can ruin a child's relationship to language" explains Alice Kaplan (1993) in *French Lessons: A Memoir* (99). Dictation indeed affected my relationship with language, and like all other school activities, it prescribed a way of being. Teachers, I believe, were the only human agents who had the ability to break through these prescribed ways of being. My teachers, I imagined, could advocate for me and—even if briefly—through a language of hope, break away from mandated scripts. Most teachers did not. In fact, only seven years later, after Romania had experimented with democracy, did I receive my first words of hope from a teacher when I graduated from high school. During my high school exit exam, an examiner from a different school asked me about my career plans. While I do not recall what career plans I shared with her then, I will never forget her response: "You will be a success." From elementary through high school, it was the first time I heard such words. A language of empathy, and in this case, a language of hope was a minimal intervention that could have shaken up scripts of oppression. Few teachers did this. In my case, only one.

Teachers and Shifting Ideological Positions

To sum up, teachers functioned as brokers of ideology; based on their own personal convictions, teachers decided when and if to intervene on behalf of the student regarding curriculum, ideologies, and the pioneer organizations. In the examples offered in this chapter, their role concerned a mediation of the conflicting ideologies, particularly the Protestant Christian faith in opposition to the Party's ideology. The Christian ideology nurtured Christian literature and a religious identity that needed more mediation than other less antagonistic identity markers. Certainly, there were other ideologies that challenged the official discourse. Among these, any political involvement with other parties would place one in a rigid category of "enemies of the state." Mr. Doru, an engineer and a schoolteacher, explained that he had to become a Party member even though he did not want to. Given his family's political affiliation with the National Peasants' Party, he had no chance of assuming any respectable position of leadership unless he joined the "right" Party.

As Steven's account, Dan's, and mine show teachers as brokers operated on a wide spectrum of rhetorical and ideological positions. Facilitating or withholding the UTC-ist ID card depended on the teacher's disposition. Participation in school events, as well as participation in class activities, were all contingent on the teacher's position vis-à-vis the official ideological discourse. While some teachers reflected more closely the presence and values of the ultimate broker, others dissociated themselves from the State's grip. Teachers and other brokers moved from formal sites to informal ones and did so based on various affinities to those for whom they would advocate, creating a web of relationships between formal and informal economies. Others chose to be non-interventionist and in doing so, they identified with the ultimate broker in action and language, denying the possibility of imagined futures for their students. By following the state scripts, they became authoritarian and regimented themselves.

Chapter 6

Librarians and Scholars as Brokers of Information in Literacy Research

After you are granted permission, you pay this fee at the accountant's office and then, you can take digital photos. You can pay for 2–3 digital copies and then we close an eye.

—A Romanian Librarian

This epigraph is an excerpt from a conversation with a Romanian librarian who was instructing me on how to understand and maneuver institutional rules and regulations at a certain library while doing research in Romania. Her advice was meant to help me both follow the rules and, to some extent, also break them. In doing so, she brokered my access to the librarian's documents. Complex connections between researchers and librarians and archivists provide some insights into how institutions can manipulate access to resources and knowledge. These connections further reveal additional layers of brokering embedded in the research process of this project.

When I visited Romania in 2011, my purpose was to conduct archival research and work in Romanian libraries to document the official literacy education before 1989. It was my first time to conduct research in the Romanian system of education; prior to this visit, I had used the Romanian library system as an undergraduate student, but it was mostly to check out books that had already been required for specific courses. My entire training in research methods and methodologies took place in the US educational system. This is why the instruction provided by the librarian offered guidance on what to do, how to do it, and especially how to circumvent some official rules that were set in place. I was counseled on the procedures of obtaining digital copies of documents, which meant: writing a formal request letter to the director of the library, obtaining a signature that the request has been approved, and returning the proof of formal approval to the librarian. The soft rules, however—not recorded in print, but shared with me verbally as the epigraph shows—allowed a space of negotiation for the numbers of copies I declared I would make and the actual number of copies I made. I call this entire process of interaction with the library a process of brokering boundaries, of brokering access to information, and negotiating roles in doing literacy research. The level of brokering has been established by the type of affinity between the researchers and librarians and archivists. The closer the interaction, the higher the chance of a successful research visit.

However, despite these limitations, my research path would have been completely different—potentially impossible—five years earlier. In 2006, an important document was released to the public, the Presidential Commission Report (2006), that paved the way for more open access to censored files and documents from the Communist period. In 2007, Romania joined the European Union, and that too engendered a series of new policies concerning censorship and transparency. Therefore, before I got to the Romanian libraries and archives, much work had been done to open my access and that of many. In my research path, networks of affiliation reveal the important work of librarians/archivists as brokers as it is shaped by knowledge-making and knowledge-preserving institutions and stakeholders. Prior to starting my research, the culture of censorship in Romania has begun to change due to the brokering work of Romanian and transnational scholars. These networks of scholars, established on the virtue of academic prestige, opened access to knowledge and documents that have been closed to the public for more than half a century. These scholars and others thereby relied on the informal brokering work of librarians/archivists as brokers of knowledge, a necessary practice due to the legacies of the Communist regime. One such legacy is the culture of censorship and stratified access which facilitate the emergence of the figure of the broker in the context of research.

First, transnational research posits a series of opportunities that are attached to or framed by institutions of power and prestige. University of Illinois, a highly prestigious research institution with a vibrant Department of History and program in Eastern European Studies has welcomed many Romanian students who paved the way to various archives in Romania. The respective Romanian students and other scholars trained and provided useful information to the novice, and in turn, the archivists in Romania became familiarized with receiving students and scholars from abroad. I will elaborate on these networks of scholars later, but important to note is that the institutional affiliation and prestige, networks of access, histories of access and censorship, all contribute to whether access to certain knowledge is facilitated or restricted. Second, nation-states where the research takes place also exert their own influence. There are more opportunities for US-trained scholars to travel, have access to, and do research elsewhere, particularly in third world countries than the reverse; scholars from those regions may come to the US, but generally have limited funds and barely hold any leverage if their access is denied or limited. The case of Romanian libraries under discussion is only to some extent idiosyncratic to Romania. Institutional power and unequal access to resources are, in fact, pervasive problems in research. Transnational research elevates some of these concerns to new levels of awareness, especially political economies worldwide shape this research.

Romania's History of Censorship and Knowledge Brokers

The Presidential Commission Report (2006) is one of the first official attempts to denounce the Communist regime in Romania, particularly in terms of access to information. The report, released seventeen years after the fall of Communism, unearthed sources and information about the regime, about important political figures and institutions that helped maintain its totalitarian control in place. Among others, it revealed numerous sources from the Romanian National Archives that had been open to the public. Since the publication of the report in 2006, which was made available via open access online, it has caused much commotion; it exposed a disturbing past sealed in secret policy files, including the current post-communist politicians' deep ties to the old regime. Presided by Vladimir Tismăneanu, a Romanian-American political scientist, the commission included remarkable Romanian public intellectuals and scholars, some of whom had lived in exile in Western Europe or the US for many years, having been ostracized during the Communist regime (e.g., Virgil Ierunca, Monica Lovinescu). The purpose of the report, and implicitly of the commission, has been to unveil detailed information and sources about many aspects of Communism in Romania, particularly informants, secret police files, etc. The report represents an effort to confront a traumatic past, but it also tries to achieve more transparency about the Romanian history shrouded in much falsehood, secrecy, and even conspiracy.

While the report was published in 2006/2007, only in the last few years have the files of the Secret Police and of the Romanian Communist Party been gradually released to the public. Since 2006–2007, with the establishment of various institutions (e.g. the Institute for the Investigation of Communism's Crimes and the Memory of the Romanian Exile (IICCMER) established in 2006) aimed at investigating the Communist period, libraries such as the Library of the Academy[1] started to open their doors to researchers outside exclusivist scholarly networks. This means that when these libraries and archives began to grant access, they have done so in stages. As mentioned in chapter 4, the production of secret files in Romania was indeed an important agenda of the Communist Party, creating a written archive through which the Party exercised its control. The sorting and organizing of such files have been labor intensive while also politically driven at times. As such, in the process of archiving and organizing files before making them available to the public, some of these documents have disappeared, especially those that could have compromised current political figures. This report, among other things, shows why accessibility and information brokering have been highly problematic in Romania to this day.

Following Romania's inclusion into the European Union on January 1, 2007, new legislation[2] concerning open access to information required the administration to issue amendments to align its statutes and laws with other European states. The issue of access to information, however, is an ongoing problem. On June 18, 2012, a petition has been circulating online with the purpose of collecting support to "maintain[ing] transparency at the Romanian National Archives" (Society for Romanian Studies, Personal Communication, June 18, 2012). The email, sent by the Society for Romanian Studies, has been asking for signatures of scholars and public intellectuals from Romania and the Romanian diaspora in response to the unexpected and most likely ungrounded suspension of historian Dorin Dobrincu, the director of the Romanian National Archives since 2007. This example, where the Romanian diaspora are asked to intervene to advocate for transparency and access to information, along with other mandates from the European Union, shows that access is layered but so is the brokering process of powerful stakeholders. At times, these brokers operate locally or transnationally depending on the power agents and institutions.

The Presidential Commission Report (2006) stirred many inquiries not only about general access to information and its potential impact on people and institutions, but also posed questions about this commission's access to the resources cited in the actual report at a time when the institutions housing these materials had not been open for research. These scholars, like many others, received preferential access to these archives. Their access is a form of particularism built through intimate connections. As the Presidential Commission Report reveals, at times these scholars function as brokers of knowledge, but other times they represent structures of control that censor access to information. When they manage boundaries between the public and access to knowledge, they can become brokers of that information crucial in the research process. However, when they resort to their own positions built through long held social networks in institutions such as the Romanian National Archives, the Library of the Academy, or other political or cultural affiliations, they reinforce hierarchies of privilege and power.

In an earlier discussion of writing and composition scholars functioning as information brokers, Lunsford (2012)—drawing on Haythornthwaite's work—defines the information broker as "an individual who has contacts with more than one cluster; he or she controls the flow of information from one part of the network to another" (222). Extending Lunsford's conception of the writing researcher as an information broker and other forms of brokering discussed here, one must examine the *nature* of the networks created to understand the dynamics of interactions and the flow of information. In the case of public scholars and intellectuals in Romania, the networks are marked by selective affiliation to intellectual circles in Romania and abroad and to institutional affiliation such as the Library of the Academy as exemplified earlier. Another example of information brokers comes from the University of Illinois. As various student researchers mostly of Romanian origin began to study at US institutions, they formed a cluster that is slightly different than the one of Romanian public intellectuals. Since their education is a hybrid of Romanian and US ideologies, they created networks through interactions that merged formal institutional connections, such as reading groups or area cluster studies (Eastern European Reading group is an excellent example), with informal knowledge gathered from navigating bureaucratic labyrinths in Romania. This knowledge—concerning research sites, archives, libraries but always paths to access more effectively valuable resources—has been further shared in various ways. In 2011, the Romanian Student Club at University of Illinois invited historian Dr. Mihaela Wood, a graduate of this school, to speak about the process of doing research in Romania. In her talk and through various informal conversations, Wood (2011) brokered access to information at research institutions, archives, and libraries in Romania, facilitating the research process with specific steps and guidelines. This network, built through common research interests, has also developed based on shared ethnic or national background of researchers located at US research institutions. Younger than the previously mentioned cluster, these researchers are driven by different motives and research methodologies generally shaped by US research practices and institutions rather than Romanian intellectual traditions.

Both clusters—public intellectuals in Romania and abroad and the new wave of researchers like the one at University of Illinois—engage in research practices aware that state institutions and public service continue to *particularize* access depending on, as Mungiu-Pippidi explained, one's proximity to groups of power and influence. The interplay between particularism and universalism as philosophies of relating to state powers and institutions should be viewed on a continuum rather than in a dichotomous relationship. If particularism is often more prevalent in communal societies (Mungiu-Pippidi 2005), in the context of transnational mobility communities become more flexible and changing. Essential about particularism is the way it indexes a set of intimate connections. Particularism is in fact a manifestation of a particular affinity in an interaction or connectivity through an experience. Universalism strives for equality and, in doing so, it often creates distance and alienation. Particularism creates bridges, fills gaps, and allows for flexible approaches to rigid circumstances. One should not exclude the other, as their joined work achieves more access and transparency. This interplay of affinity and universalism can be illustrated in the example of the new wave of Romanian researchers studying in the US institutions. Although they built intimate connections based on ethnicity, they also act and develop universal practices shaped by educational institutions and disciplinary spaces.

Knowledge of how particularism and universalism work in practice requires awareness of how nation-states organize their power structures and how institutional, political, or cultural affiliations shape each other. A higher professional status for instance does not always translate in higher access, not when particularism is invoked. Wood (2011) provides such an example when in the late 1990s, she had to use her educator credentials, not her university student status, when she sought access to the Library of the Academy. Only the former identification afforded a legitimate identity that would grant her access, while the latter, the university student status at a top, research-intensive US institution was ranked lower in the scale of accessibility. However, in a different research situation, at the National Archives of Romania, Wood (2011) confessed being granted access to take digital photocopies of documents before open access was instituted because of her connections to a personal acquaintance. Such particularism represents then a form of breaking the rigidity of norms and institutions that often cannot legitimize their practices of control and surveillance. This particularism invokes local knowledge that impacts the researcher as well as the research process; it is local knowledge that a broker, such as Wood's acquaintance, develops with an understanding of institutional restrictions and the larger context of information censorship in Romania.

In the context of transnational mobility, practices based on particularism and local knowledge are sometimes transferred and recontextualized. In the case of Wood, her local experience and research activity have been repurposed when, in her talk in 2011 at the University of Illinois, she deployed that knowledge transnationally to broker access to other researchers. As such, local knowledge gained in a particular context becomes mobilized through new networks created through people's movement. Wood's experience as both educator and student in Romania became valuable resources in her new role as a graduate student and researcher in the US. Simplifying context as either global or local (Sassen 2010), or using hybrid terms such as glocalism (Sarroub 2009), prove insufficient to capture the intricacies of local knowledge. As researchers are increasingly more mobile, other contingencies, including age or affiliation with a particular cohort, influence the type and degree of access. While former intellectuals were reinstituted as legitimate public researchers and intellectuals, the new wave of Romanian researchers must strive to build their own legitimacy and social networks to gain access to various types of resources. To some extent, affiliation with a US institution may occasionally destabilize certain privileged networks formed in Romania. The cluster of new Romanian researchers formed at US institutions—and by extension affiliations with other transnational institutions—seems to disrupt both the mentality of particularism and the research practice itself. The interplay between national, transnational, and local affinities is essential in understanding access and research practices in international contexts. As the case of Romania shows, understanding the role of the state and affiliated institutions as well as a long history or censorship is crucial to untangle the role of information brokers and their interactions and impact on information access. In the following sections, I discuss how access is connected to other types of brokers, librarians and archivists but also to hierarchical institutions that regulate one's research access.

Librarians and Staff as Brokers of Knowledge and Research

The importance of librarians and archivists in doing research in Romania cannot be overstated. Examining the role of librarians as brokers of access to knowledge reveals how networks of particularism operate in practice. Generally, librarians develop identities closely shaped by the institutions where they work. Seeing themselves as guardians of books and special documents, opening and closing access depending on particular networks of power and influence, librarians, and archivists brokered long-established hierarchical structures, at the Library of the Academy and to a lesser extent, the Central University Library.

As more and more studies in Rhetoric and Composition scholarship assess the challenges and benefits of doing research transnationally (e.g., Donahue 2009; Hesford and Schell 2008; Horner, Lu, Royster and Trimbur 2011), more attention should go to understanding and negotiating disciplinary and cultural boundaries in addition to language difference (Horner, Necamp, and Donahue 2011). Just as writing research in the US has deep roots in monolinguistic ideologies and institutional histories connected to the first-year writing class at Harvard, research in Romania involves brokering practices tied to national, historical, and material conditions. Rather than conceptualizing this research site as a center-periphery binary (Canagarajah 2002), researchers need to acknowledge the internal hierarchical structures already existent in the national territory and the historical context of state and public institutions that impact research processes.

In Romania, the role of librarians and archivists as brokers of knowledge becomes clearer when reviewing a brief history of one of its most influential institutions, the Library of the Academy in Bucharest, which ties its hierarchical structure to its mission. The Library of the Academy is the most prestigious library in Romania. Established 1867, one year after the institution of the Romanian Academy Society, the Library of the Academy prides itself with the preservation of the oldest manuscripts in Romania and of texts in the Romanian language. This library's crucial role in affirming and preserving old documents, newspapers, and literature is linked to the formation and the establishment of the Romanian national identity (Anghelescu 2000; Dumitrescu 2011). Given this history of its engagement in legitimizing and affirming the Romanian national ethos through texts, it often controlled the Romanian literary and cultural scene just like the state controlled various other social spheres.

The history of the Library of the Academy essentially reveals that this is more than a research site. It is a contested space where knowledge-making has been entrusted to a limited number of elite scholars who became the spokesmen of the Romanian people. This hierarchical center of knowledge needs to be further understood in the largest context of post-communist Romania and the role of the state in regulating literacy and access to literacy. While the Romanian nation has officially and publicly declared its discontent and desired break with the Communist rule at the Revolution of December 1989, deep-established forms of institutional practice could not be instantaneously disrupted. Given Romania's forty-year history of building a nation as a "collective individual" (Verdery1996, 23), it comes as no surprise that through this representation, the Romanian citizens have been socialized into identifying their public identity with one entity: that of the state. Although often in disagreement with state policies, state employees and, in fact, Romanian citizens, learned the art of duplicity of preserving and assuming an official identity depending on circumstances (Shafir 1978, 25).[3] At the same time, the same "collective individual" learned to detach the personal from the public self, especially as the state and its destructive policies sought to invade even private spaces.

Librarians, as agents of the state, have learned to serve as tools of surveillance and control. Through their institutional affiliation from which they derive their authority, librarians function as brokers of research knowledge. This practice has been visibly incorporated in the librarian's official identity and it often goes unquestioned; this meshing of identities—sedimented in phrases such as "this is the system" suggests a reality that apparently cannot be changed as the librarians seem to embody the system. A few of these librarians' practices include enforcement of rules, refusal to disclose information, bending of rules, control over bodies, access to books and manuscripts, and ultimately control over knowledge. Contextualizing the librarians and archivists' practice provides a framework for understanding the historical conditions that had shaped these state-governed institutional identities. Yet, as the beginning account showed, librarians may shift from their assigned role as state employees to negotiate spaces of flexible identities. As such, they maneuver hierarchical institutional structures disrupting them as centers of knowledge and sites of cultural control. In this sense, librarians are similar to teachers discussed in chapter 5, especially in the way they find or create spaces of negotiation.

To understand the way librarians and archivists are involved in the research process as brokers of the research path, I offer a narrative of my own process of gaining access to the Library of the Academy. This account follows a step-by-step process about how I obtained a library permit, learned about the library's catalogs, how I requested materials, and photocopied resources for further analysis. Most importantly, this research narrative offers details about librarians' interventions and their role in facilitating, delaying, or controlling my access to sources at this institution. The librarians as brokers of knowledge in my research path influenced the types of materials that I consulted, the quantity, as well as reproduction and preservation of these materials.

Step 1: Brokering the Library Card

Before my research visit at the Romanian public libraries and the Romanian National Archives, I was actively reading scholarship pertaining to my area of specialization, including sources about Romanian history and culture during the 1980s. This work was done in preparation for the special fields examination, a necessary step in identifying major themes and potential topics of inquiry. Since I surveyed an extensive body of literature, I felt strongly equipped to further explore primary sources such as school curricula, literary school magazines, official education-related documents of the Romanian Communist Party, and additional resources. Before leaving for Romania, I consulted with several student-researchers of Romanian descent, all PhD candidates at University of Illinois, who had preceded me in this process. I also sought the counsel and expertise of Dr. Keith Hitchins, a remarkable historian and researcher.[4] In my conversations with Dr. Hitchins, I was advised on the most important libraries and archives most useful for my research interests. I also received a letter of introduction from him in case I could use it to gain more direct access.

By the time I got to Bucharest, I was confident that I had prepared well for this research trip. I started with my first research site at the Library of the Academy. Armed with two letters of introduction and the I-card from the University of Illinois, I thought obtaining a library permit would be a smooth process. A few years prior to my visit, acquiring a library permit had been difficult. In the late 1990s, the director of the Library of the Academy made decisions about issuing library permits after a thorough "interrogation;" at that time, college students were generally denied access (Wood 2011). The underlining assumption was that college students held a lower scholarly position compared to renowned scholars, published writers, and educators who were exclusively entitled to access valuable scholarship. In my case, the library permit was obtained relatively easily but not without obstacles. At first, I could not request a library permit, because I had forgotten to bring a photo ID for the library permit that was supposed to be stapled onto the card. This would have delayed my work by a day, which meant at least 8 hours of work wasted. Missing a day of research does not seem significant, except that when I arrived in Bucharest, I learned that the Library of the Academy would close within two weeks for summer break. Therefore, every hour mattered. As I arrived in Bucharest, I also learned that the staff hired to make photocopies was leaving on vacation in the following two days. Needless to say, such constraints on the research process, dealing not only with access to information but services such as photocopying or dig-itizing documents of interest, were difficult to navigate. As I sat there for ten long minutes, wondering how I could obtain a photo within the next hour before the library closed, the receptionist remained silent. Eventu-ally, she decided to help me. She instructed me in detail about what to do. She told me where I could obtain the required photo ID at a nearby photocopy facility. She advised me on where to go, what to do and what to say so as to obtain my ID within the next 15 minutes. Although not a librarian but hired staff, she had the power to open or delay my access into the library by offering (or retaining) details about institutional reg-ulations. As a broker of access, she deliberately withheld or delayed of-fering an essential piece of information necessary for obtaining a library permit in a short period of time. This illustrates a brokering strategy that implicates not only knowledge of the institution where the broker works, but also knowledge of the local context: the neighborhood, the photocopy facility with all its regulations (the type of photocopy needed, the cost, etc.) and the entire step-by-step procedure needed to fill gaps of knowledge, that I clearly had in abundance.

Step 2: Brokering access to bibliographic catalogs/materials

Shortly after this first obstacle, I was allowed to enter the reference room. Soon, I found myself surrounded by a mass of small drawers filled with hundreds of typed or handwritten reference notecards. Although the reference cards were organized alphabetically and thematically, finding sources required hours and hours of searching through hundreds of bibliographic notecards. Next, filling out information request forms re-quired substantial time, followed by another waiting period, after which the librarian on duty would bring the requested books. The level of reg-imentation and limited access manifested through a series of rules: only five books could be checked out at a time; the researcher had to sit in a designated spot in the reading room with a number attached to it, and almost all belongings had to be checked in the locker room. Another re-striction that nearly offset all my research plans concerned the in-house photocopy service, which allowed only thirty pages a day. In the first half an hour, I had already used up my photocopy allowance for the day. Cer-tainly, similar restrictions about locker rooms and assigned seating are in place at other libraries here in the US. The restrictions at Library of the Academy and Central University Library were similar to my visit at the National Archives in Chicago, where even chewing gum was on the re-stricted list. One difference, however, concerns the behavior and attitudes of the librarians. In Romania, librarians or archivists acted as guardians of knowledge as if they had been personally entrusted with keeping the public *away* from the books/documents rather than helping *gain access* to them. In the US, rules—even those restrictive such as chewing gum—are framed to represent institutional regulations rather capricious expectations of librarians/archivists. Prior to my visit to the archives in Chicago, I exchanged numerous emails with one of the archivists. When I arrived there, he came to meet me personally and walked me through all the steps and trainings. He also informed me of all the rules and regulations, but the assumption in this entire process was that I had the right to access documents, and the archivist brokered my access to various documents with an open attitude and desire to help. In Romania, all or most of these restrictions are, however, negotiable and often contingent on the availability and disposition of the staff. A fellow researcher explained that we often rely on the "kindness of the archivist," almost always being "at their mercy" (Wood 2011). Based on Wood's experience and that of many other scholars, research in Romania at these institutions is a highly subjective and contingent experience. It depends on one's personal connections but also on the broker's "kindness" and "mercy." As such, connecting with a librarian/archivist not just rationally, but also on the personal and emotional level, influenced the type of access and the extent to which a researcher received extra leeway in manipulating institutional regulations. This means that, as Sharon Crowley explains, "Elaborated experience [is] one that is connected to other experiences" (quoted in Trainor 2008, 87) and has more persuasive force than the punctuated one. In the case of librarians, the level of connectivity on multiple levels afforded a better position to influence them to be helpful despite strict regulations.

I note here two important brokering situations. In the reference room, although I asked the librarian on duty several questions, hoping to receive assistance in navigating the old bibliographic system more efficiently, I hit a wall. The reasons for her resistance could be multiple: lack of knowledge of how to guide me, distrust or disinterest in my own research topic or in me as a researcher, or unwillingness to offer more assistance. At a different library, the National Library, whose resources I only examined on one occasion given that all their deposits were blocked due to relocation, I experienced a similar resistant attitude when I asked similar questions. However, having already been acclimated to the "system" and to other librarians, I gained courage in speaking up. Tired of capricious attitudes and half-answers, at some point I boldly asked the librarian to provide more guidance on their library system. The first question about how to navigate the multitude of bibliographic entries on small notecards was received with admonition. The librarian proceeded to scold me about how I should come prepared to check up their catalogs and informed me she was not there to do my job. With respect and firmness, I turned the next five minutes into a pedagogical moment. I took my librarian through a tour of my research project, scholarship, and materials consulted, research questions, etc. My deposition worked wonders. Her attitude changed instantaneously. Suddenly, her stiffness melted entirely. Kindness, even an apologetic explanation followed as she walked me through the organization of bibliographic catalogs. Slightly embarrassed, she admitted to the limits of their system as well as the chaotic situation caused by the library's relocation. In this situation, despite my apparent illiteracy of the bibliographic system in place, I brokered my own access halfway through by using my researcher status as well as research expertise. The other half, the librarian continued the brokering process through pieces of information I was lacking. The researcher status and specialized knowledge constituted essential strategies in establishing my credentials despite some limits: some language failure in trying to explain my research in Romanian and certainly, lack of knowledge of an obsolete bibliographic system.

The second example of brokering took place at the in-house photocopy center at the Library of the Academy, whose history of hierarchical structures I have outlined earlier. Trying to adjust to the 30-page per day photocopying limit was certainly a challenge. It required that I was much more selective in examining the sources I wanted to consult. The day when I learned about this rule, I also found out the staff making these photocopies was leaving on vacation for the rest of the summer. The news was disheartening, but the only thing I could do was to rethink my entire approach. Specifically, I began to redesign my reading strategies and note-taking but also the selection criteria for what was going to be photocopied or not. My interaction with the staff responsible for photocopying started with her proclaiming all the rules: the photocopy limit, her vacation time, and the fact that I came too late for that day as she was about to leave. There were at least 30 more minutes before the official closing time. Like my interaction with the receptionist, I was baffled, wondering how I could broker my way in. As a Romanian, I had experienced in the past both the system's strict rules and the brokering of these rules, most of the times through illegal paths. Some of these strategies included bringing gifts to the librarians (or to other gatekeepers, depending on context). I never mastered such strategies, but as I connect easily with people, I used to broker my way through social ties. Rather than leaving, I engaged in conversation with her. I tried to explain my situation and the fact that I have little time to collect as much data as possible. I did not say more than that. Just like the librarian from the National Library, this library employee brokered my access to these resources, offering not only to break the rule for my first set of books, but to do it for future photocopying jobs as well: "Come first thing in the morning and I will take care of it." In the first example, the librarian met me halfway and through my research knowledge and status, access to bibliographic catalogs was brokered successfully. In the second example, the staff brokered my access to photocopies but only on her own terms: I had to come back the following day, rather than claim my right to her services that day. In following her rules, I gained more than if I had followed institutional guidelines. While I engaged in conversation, she had the sole authority under those circumstances to broker my access to more photocopies than the institutional limit. I could have certainly made a petition to higher authorities such as the Director of the Library, but this path would have been longer and probably less successful.

Although these two examples are similar, the motivation for the brokering process is different. As Wood (2011) explains, sometimes the brokering depends on the staff's "kindness" or "mercy," but sometimes it depends on intellectual persuasion that becomes a legitimate ground to broker access. The first example illustrates a more intellectual or logical argumentative process, while the second denotes an affective brokering; yet, both instances involved highly subjective interactions that yield results depending on the person. In her talk, Wood (2011) advocates strongly to "build connections, drop names," and "to navigate the personalities of librarians and archivists." Establishing connections, sharing experiences—such as what brought one to the archives—and engaging in conversations are strategies through which one builds affinity with those in positions of influence and power. Based on these affinities, librarians/archivists then use their position to soften the rules. All these affinities are built in time and through repeated conversations rather than through one-time encounters. But eventually, and most of the time, they yield good results. Rigid rules become flexible as the networking strengthens through daily encounters.

Step 3: The Study Room: Brokering Reading and Studying

One final setting where the brokering occurred is the study room. As mentioned earlier, the rules were quite strict, like those at the National Archives in Chicago: nothing but a notebook and a writing tool were allowed. I had an assigned seat and filled out by hand numerous information request forms for each book or document I requested. Since I had long lists of materials I wanted to consult, I asked at some point the main librarian in the study room if I could consult more than five books at a time. She informed me that she had already delivered more books than I was allowed to, although I do not recall having more than five books at a time. In this situation, I learned that sometimes librarians, out of their own initiative and without any prompting or persuasive strategies, would volunteer to help and broker one's access. In the study room, I was offered more "help," and advice on how to keep the books for several days than in any other location.

As I started to build a practice of consulting materials every day, with a strict schedule of seven or eight hours a day, I started to notice a slight change in the librarians' attitudes: from an impenetrable identity mimicking an official, rigid ethos to one of a broker operating between the institution and the researcher. This flexible institutional (re) positioning accounts for the failure of Romanian institutions to reclaim the legitimacy that was historically lost through their compromise with totalitarian political regimes. A distrust of formal institutions gives birth to processes of mediation and negotiations that often subvert the very system that legitimizes the identity of librarians as state-employees. An example of this negotiation and dissociation of librarians from the system comes from a situation when I had to pay a relatively high fee for making digital copies. I introduced this instance through the epigraph at the beginning of this chapter. As I was given instructions about writing a petition to the director (or assistant director) of the library, I was also told, "After you are granted permission, you pay this fee at the accountant's office, and then, you can take digital photos. You can pay for two or three digital copies, and then we *close an eye*." Basically, the librarian instructed me in how to work the system. Librarians know that generally taking only two or three digital images is rarely sufficient and most researchers need to make several digital copies. However, they offered to "close an eye" because they too acknowledge indirectly that the institution, whose representatives they are, had set an unjustifiably high price for digital copies. As a result, librarians functioned as brokers and intervened in resolving this situation. The "closing of the eye" suggests that librarian do adopt a "bird's eye perspective" on what happens in the library. They are there to watch over what happens, "the eyes" that survey and, if necessary, reinforce control over knowledge. "The closing of an eye" is in fact an interruption of the surveillance.

A more comprehensive overview of the brokering strategies I encountered in my research path is found in Table 6.1. To reflect equitably all situations with librarians and archivists, I also inserted a final category: "refuse to broker." Not all situations can or will be brokered; my experience shows that sometimes librarians or archivists decide to reinforce a rule or to delay/withhold information instead of offering to help. This happened even in situations when as a researcher, I believe I had the right to obtain particular information. I did not include brokering through other means, such as small gifts to librarians and archivists,

Table 6.1. Brokering in Research

Brokering Strategies	Brokering Situations
Brokering through local knowledge	Using a local photocopier in the neighborhood to obtain a photo ID for the library card
Brokering through the researcher's ethos (knowledge of research/research methods even if from a different system) (intellectual persuasion); co-brokering	Learning to use credentials and knowledge from the US system (knowledge of research) to build a case for credibility in the Romanian system (in spite of limited knowledge of bibliographic catalogs)
Brokering through the affective or subjective ethos of the broker	"Learning to navigate the personalities of librarians and archivists" Being at the "mercy" and "kindness" of librarians
Brokering by "closing an eye:" manipulation of institutional regulations/rules	Making digital copies: paying for a small number and receiving unofficial permission to take as many digital copies as needed
Refuse to Broker	Delaying or withholding information Reinforcing a rule

because I did not resort to these tactics. A similar practice of doing a favor ("hatâr") or paying a bribe ("bacşiş") I described in chapter 4 in the context of informal economies. Such practices sought to appease the gatekeepers and evade powerful institutions or state control. While the fall of Communism removed the structures of control, the residue of old practices remained in place for decades. Brokering strategies continued to thrive as well, and I would argue they remain stable in all contexts of power relationships.

To sum up, information brokers and network affinities built prior to and along the research path are pervasive and important in accessing sources. Created through attachments of ethnicity, nationality, institutional identity, and cultural and epistemological beliefs, these affinities take different forms and engage different networks depending on context. The presence of institutions and librarians as guardians of access of information was evident, and so was their brokering work that gradually opened my research path.

A final reflection concerns my own identity as a researcher and the affinities that granted me access. Being a trilingual researcher has been widely influential in how I conducted research. My ability to speak Romanian allowed me direct access to research materials without resorting to a translator. Both the language and the cultural understandings of hierarchies of power served as guides in interactions with librarians and archivists. Knowledge of the Romanian language and culture also create powerful affinities as they carry values, beliefs, experiences that build affective experiences. Research at the Romanian archives, despite all the obstacles, was still efficient since I can read and speak Romanian, and all documents were in Romanian. In the Romanian immigrant community, my affiliation based on ethnicity opened doors to research that are otherwise impenetrable. Certainly, the Romanian community is open to sharing stories and information both on a personal and communal level. Yet, based on my involvement in the community in everyday circumstances—going to church picnics, having dinner with a family, or volunteering to help at community events, etc.—I learned more about the community while *being in* the community with the people than just learning about them.

None of our affiliations as researchers are negligible. In certain contexts, certain aspects of our identity matter more than others. In transnational research challenges, the researcher should always become an information broker, seeing first to evaluate the type of affinities they have built and then, seeking to bridge knowledge transfer, as well as methods and methodologies. If we understand the researcher as a broker through a series of affinities, we can better understand not only motivations for research, the relationships built with informants, the access established through various paths, but also the entire research process. Affinity, while not always following a pattern of logic, is built through everyday encounters, and it always fills a space with experiences and interactions that fall outside the realm of prescriptive practices. Affinity allows for creativity to unfold, for interruptions to occur, and for new discoveries in the research path.

Conclusion

Literacy as Affinity

Theoretical and Pedagogical Possibilities

I recently attended a round table engaging community members connected to immigration in South Florida. Of the many issues discussed, educating students in diplomacy and advocacy became a central subject of conversation that elicited different responses. We heard from a lawyer, a CEO of Catholic Charities, a community member living in a migrant camp, an immigrant artist who uses podcasts and exhibits art to communicate immigrant issues, and a few others. At some point, an important question was raised: "What good does it serve to have an education? How will this impact the migrant who must walk for miles without hope that they would reach a safe harbor?" Essentially the question asked—an issue that keeps coming up in other public sphere contexts—what good is it to educate students (and ourselves)? What is the purpose of education if the lives of immigrants who face hardships are not directly or promptly affected by education? I gave this considerable thought. What direct or immediate impact does our teaching, learning, reading, writing, or research have on the life of the migrant who has to walk on foot for miles to find water or food or refuge? While I cannot offer miraculous interventions to resolve or respond to human suffering, I pose a different question: What is the alternative? The absence of education means no knowledge or, in other words, ignorance. No knowledge or limited knowledge means that decisions and actions in practice are at best speculative.

Conclusion

As a teacher-scholar, I believe that by educating ourselves and looking for answers to problems—big or small, practical or theoretical, political or economic—we do make an impact on those who are at the
margins, who need assistance in figuring out structures of power and
political economies so that they can make it in this world. This book
centers on the work of those who have been through hardships, who
connect to other humans through personal experiences, and help them
with reading and writing. These are the brokers performing *literacy as
affinity* when they intervene on behalf of others through assistance and
advocacy in and across contexts. Literacy as affinity, as I developed it
here, involves linguistic and textual repertoires meant to recapture or
compensate for what is displaced, managed, or contained in the process of transnational mobility. Literacy brokers also intervene within
the nation-state, particularly in bureaucratic contexts, to make up for
the erasure of the personal, of emotions and emotional discourse, and
affective relations. This is the reason why they matter. Brokers and the
political economies where they operate see the entire personhood, and
because they understand how political economies are set in place, they
do affinity work manifesting precisely in contexts where human dimension is most likely neglected or erased.

Literacy Brokers and the Dangers of the Social

New Literacy Studies (NLS) scholars have long advocated for and re-
searched literacy as a deeply social practice (Baynham and Masing
2001; Papen 2010). Yet, too often, the assumption is that a social context
carries similar meanings across contexts, that the social is inherently
good and conducive to writing persuasively. A reassessment of literacy
brokers that I offer in this study complicates a superficial understanding
of the social, directing attention to the relationality of brokers in assisting others with textual practices. In doing so, literacy brokers create
powerful webs of connections through a series of personal, institutional, national, or communal affinities. However, literacy brokers—when
embodied by authoritarian regimes—also manipulate interactions between people, within and across institutions, political economies, and all
the social spheres where they infiltrate. More attention should be given
to romanticized views of the social as inherently good. While literacy
brokers, as I have presented them, act for the most part for the good of
those whom they represent; they can also misrepresent, misuse, or seek
to extract benefits from the act of socializing (chapter 4 and 5 on the
Romanian state as a broker of literacy exemplify such negative effects resulting from oppressive social relations). In transnational research this is
even more important because one lacks the necessary historical context

to understand and gauge the way social relationships impact literacy and writing.

Literacy as Affinity and Political Economies

Literacy as affinity warrants further consideration in rhetoric and composition and literacy scholarship for the ways in which it deploys an emotional repertoire (personal stories, a language of empathy, personal stories, and relationality), a much-needed linguistic resource in a season when machine writing powered by artificial intelligence aims to produce efficient and quick writing outputs. Rationality and efficiency dominate our current public discourse reducing writing to a mere tool, thereby rendering nuances, experiences, and even, diverse socio-economic contexts unimportant. Yet, literacy as affinity does not merely reflect socio-political structures but rather uncovers literacy work in places of obscurity, in places of transit, and through a revelation of hidden transcripts and secondary economies. Because of this, literacy as affinity foregrounds agency. The immigrant stories in this book capture this agency either through individual brokers or co-brokering (collective brokering). Writing, then, in these spaces of ambiguity and rationality like bureaucratic contexts, invokes relationships, desire, experiences, motives, and a host of resources gathered and curated from formal and information economies. Writing for these immigrants is power.

Co-brokering. I developed the term co-brokering to identify those partnerships that immigrants build to negotiate legal papers, documentation, and application procedures, all comprising collaborative "file selves," a term introduced by Julie Chu (2010). Co-brokering operates both at small and large-scale levels. Immigrants learn to co-broker, for instance, categories of immigration, which as expected triage people based on the interests of the governing nation-state. Economic immigrants are expected to contribute to the prosperity of the welcoming country, however as economic and political conditions may shift, these immigrants' resort is to create their own systems of survival. Co-brokering functions at a small scale too, in specific situations such as compiling documents and building a case for immigration purposes. In such situations, immigrants learn "to build texts," creating hidden transcripts that mimic the official language of bureaucracy. In chapter 3, I showed that co-brokering develops among those groups who share affinities in terms of socio-economic class, but also those who are legally or racially marked as other. Although co-brokering involves partnerships between similar socio-economic groups, these partnerships are ethnically and racially unequal. While Romanian immigrants willing established partnerships developed through points of affinity, they eventually dissolved after each party completed its function.

Conclusion

These points of affinity require a complex process when ethnic relations come into the picture. Romanian immigrants become aware of their advantage through language mastery and economic power, a temporary gain until they speak and reveal their accents. As such, co-brokering did not only reveal partnerships but exposed systems of difference and inequality, and for this reason, it deserves further inquiry. I hope others will ask: What is the nature of co-brokering in other contexts? What sustains them and how does it shape literacy practices?

Bi-institutional perspective. I also discussed the bi-institutional perspective as a concept operating in discursive spaces where emotions are not permitted, how they are managed, and ways in which emotions might be recovered. Institutions have generally been criticized for their control of emotions (Trainor 2008), for promoting a writing style that is depersonalized and asocial. Whether these are educational, state-governed, economic, or political institutions, the ability to move from one setting to another and to learn various discursive practices affords a critical position as exemplified in several chapters. I also discussed the role of institutions in chapter 6 when I examined the writing scholar as a broker operating in research institutions such as libraries. Although I focus more on sedimented practices and ideologies associated with these institutions, the identity of the researcher is marked by institutional affiliation as well other affinities of ethnicity, nationality, and personal interests. Engaging discursive practices from these multiple perspectives can produce an accumulated repertoire of language experiences. With this repertoire, one can develop a discourse of empathy and experiences through which to connect with people and their own perspective.

The work of brokers and co-brokering processes becomes significant as we consider people's stories and how they tell stories about who helped them on a daily basis, not just the sponsor who remained an official "helper" (also needed) in formal papers. Attention to the daily, mundane things can lead to a neglect of the larger forces. Yet, the amazing work of brokers materializes in their knowledge of larger socio-economic and political structures and, when necessary, the co-creation of their own systems of survival. Thus, political economics revealed in these immigrant stories and the work of brokers expose those macrodiscourses without which the world would not be able to function. In the case of refugees and economic immigrants, alternative economies were necessarily considered, used, or re-purposed to serve individual ends. The field of rhetoric and composition must engage more directly with political economies, not just as abstract frames as my critique shows in chapter 3. Rather, we must conceive, use, and constantly, re-frame writing in light of socio-economic and political activity.

Conclusion

Literacy as Affinity and the Politics of the Personal

For immigrants, personal narratives matter. The story of immigration in particular mobilizes the personal in such a way as to give a sense of belonging and coherence to an experience that uproots the individual from one context and replants them in a new place. Writing about Hmong immigrants, Duffy (2007) notes that their stories of literacy development are "profoundly personal" (194). In the case of Romanian immigrants, the personal and individual experience need special attention given the historical context of this immigrant group; as explained earlier, the individual in a socialist country was expected to matter only as long as they were included in a social group and regimented as a political subject, an adherent of Marxist ideology. The context of immigration, foregrounds the personal when immigrants talk about their stories of immigration or stories of "escape." While many narratives share some similarities—some immigrants left Romania on foot into Hungary or swimming across Danube to Yugoslavia; others left through work visas or family reunification—each followed a different path. Each story is unique in the way it intersects personal motives—some religious, some economic, some political—with various social groups: family, community, immigration agencies, or workplace contexts. The personal matters also when it surpasses individual expression and serves as a vehicle for political change; such is the case of Eugen, who used personal stories to advocate for those refugees trapped between countries in refugee camps. Personal stories may constitute grounds for building empathy, particularly in contexts where institutions seek to manage and regulate emotions. Manuela's personal experience as a former alien builds a space of empathy that connects her experience to that of her clients. Although as paralegal, she can only help immigrants towards achieving legal status within the limits of the law, she can build empathy through her personal experience.

Understanding literacy as affinity by allocating more attention to personal experience may resurrect long-held debates about the place of the personal in academic discourse. The personal versus the academic argument carries long histories of scholarly dialogues (see for instance Bartholomae/Elbow debate, 1995). As this study engages the personal, specifically personal narratives and experiences, it contributes to such scholarly conversations in writing studies by showing the complexities of the personal. In my study, personal stories in the context of bureaucratic writing—which Richard A. Lanham (2003) calls "unvoiced" and "asocial" (117)—gain a rhetorical force, deeply intertwined in political and economic discourses. When brokers assist people with crafting their

Conclusion

stories of immigration and persecution, they socialize the applicant's experience. They become the audience for this story, but also co-authors, as they work with the immigrants' texts; brokers socialize the immigrant experience even if the final product is changed into an asocial legal account. Although this socializing process is rather invisible in the final textual product, the work of the brokers affects intimately day-to-day communication, a process that ultimately matters for the individual.

Another important dimension of the personal and its deployment resides in its ability to establish historical and transnational connections. This means that these immigrants' personal narratives do not present a liberal conception of the individual as professed in the Western world, which upholds the liberal philosophy that "cultivate[s] the private realm as a sphere of unfettered and authentic individual subjectivity" (Hellback 2006, 86). Rather, these immigrant personal narratives emerge in contexts in which the whole personhood has been regimented or erased in the service of a political doctrine. This historical understanding of the personal, I believe, should help us reconsider binaries such as personal/academic, emotional/rational, or personal/public, and attend to multi-layered political, socio-economic, and religious factors that implicate the personal. Understanding and approaching literacy as affinity orients us towards a communicative practice that engages the entire human experience. It binds the rational and the emotional, the personal to political economies in a symbiotic relationship rather than treat them as independent, discrete entities. Literacy as affinity is ultimately about relations. It is about relationships with one's past experiences and with larger rhetorics of nation-states that impact the human experience.

Pedagogical Applications

When considering literacy as affinity, there are multiple pedagogical possibilities, some of which I referenced in the previous section. As I reiterate that transnationalism has its double emphasis on trans- and -nation, I envision writing classes that engage with the trans- as a mark of mobility—whether it is expressed in flexibility of genres, topics, rhetorical invention, or audience. With an emphasis on the trans-, writing is dynamic, as it changes and adapts depending on context. Such changes could mean a study of genres cross-culturally or historically, a study of writing as travel, or writing from a transnational perspective. Transnationalism also puts the nation at the center and national policies that impact the teaching of writing. In a chapter devoted fully to taking up emotion as an analytical tool in the classroom, Micciche (2007) introduces the citizenship narrative assignment as a useful discursive exercise in which students not only learn about various forms of citizenship but

151

also about the emotions associated with such definitions. Although Micciche's (2007) goal in the respective chapter is to present pedagogical approaches to teaching emotions as performative and embodied acts, I find her suggestions applicable to getting students to think critically about the nation, immigrant literacy, immigrant narratives, and the intersection of writing and larger political structures.

Since literacy as affinity emerges precisely in this context of instrumental discourse, where bureaucratic structures seek to depersonalize and expedite communication, we need to pay more attention to ways in which writing in the classroom becomes a decontextualized practice, performed only in response to a course assignment. In a dialog on the issue of the instrumental nature of technical writing, Patrick Moore (2004), a supporter of instrumental discourse, suggests that instrumental discourse has been overly criticized by professors as means for capitalist venture, mainly used for "profiteering, dehumanization, domination, and expediency" (56). Writing in academic contexts continues to be taught as a practice independent from other discursive contexts. Even with the public turn in composition and the opening of our classroom towards service-learning, students continue to be taught that efficient communication is about being "objective . . . impartial, and *unemotional*"—an old piece of advice found in an outdated technical writing textbook, yet unfortunately a current belief professed even today (Miller 1979, 611, emphasis added). Immigrants, international students, and other marginalized groups know about the objectifying power of language precisely because they often must wrestle with bureaucracies more than others. As such, these experiences and exposure to various styles of "objective" discourse can prepare students to engage with and expose various forms of discursive management. Our pedagogies should reflect these multiple perspectives on writing and encourage students' participation as their views may align, examine critically, or complement US writing conventions. Too often, students continue to be taught implicitly or explicitly that academic writing conventions are generalizable to all rhetorical contexts with little consideration of other rhetorical possibilities. Whenever possible, writing pedagogy may be reframed to render relevant the experiences of students from immigration or international backgrounds. In "Class Affects, Classroom Affectations," Lindquist (2004) clearly shows how emotions management in the college writing class can also be a site for manufacturing authenticity in exchange for a good grade (197). In other words, the classroom becomes a space of artificial discourse unless it is attuned to the students' authentic selves and rhetorically situated.

If the writing classroom indeed becomes situated in specific socio-

Conclusion

economic and national contexts, then our teaching practice (and vocabulary) will change. If we consider, for instance, the learning outcomes in a first-year writing course, we must acknowledge that students will practice critical reading skills of text written in English and shaped by US institutions and policies, that the genres students are expected to become proficient in—well-supported arguments, research papers, annotated bibliographies—are largely shaped by Western rhetoric. The imagined scholarly conversations are configured by information networks, libraries, and databases that provide articles and resources in English and for an English-speaking scholarly community (possibly with a few rare exceptions). In other words, all assumptions about discourses, genres, and even identity must be acknowledged and made explicit. When Andrzejewski and Alessio (1999) discuss the learning they experienced in formal education in the US, they critique the omission as well as the bias embedded in school curricula, particularly as students are taught dominant paradigms that serve the interests of the developed countries. In a similar conversation about global citizenship, Karlberg (2010) explains the need to move away from "identity constructs based on race, nationality, ideology, religious sectarianism" as through this lens, the world becomes divided into "us" vs. "them" actions (133). He thus shows the limitations proposed by Andrzejewski and Alessio (1999) for grounding their view of global citizenship in political citizenship within the nation-state. While I understand Karlberg (2010)'s critique, the reality of immigrant narratives shows that we need to consider how nation-states frame their interests and how those interests impact the individual even as we consider global interdependence. Immigrant narratives show the intricacies of human experience and the ways in which the personal, the bureaucratic, and the national shape, control, and interact with each other. Immigrant narratives uncover notions of global citizenship as a misnomer. Global citizenship, while it is an interesting albeit abstract concept, needs to be connected to situated, rhetorically contextualized learning. People have dual or multiple citizenship depending on specific nation-states' laws and the conditions based on which the respective citizenship is acquired. Even more so, countries like the US designate specific conditions under which individuals in pursuit of US citizenship qualify, as discussed in chapter 3. Therefore, I suggest we focus more on real-world genres like the immigrant narrative, rather than invented genres or artificial constructs that neglect the reality of the people they are trying to humanize.

Additional pedagogical applications should also center on literacy brokers and how they can be studied in and integrated into the writing classroom. Others have experimented with this. Maria Jerskey (2013), for instance, relates her study of language and academic brokers—terminology derived from Lillis and Curry's (2006) analysis of brokers in academic publishing—to a campus-wide pilot program whose goal was to offer support to multilingual faculty writers. Specifically, the program was meant to "cultivate a proactive and community-based approach to an individual's text production" (Jerskey 2013, 201). Although intended as institutional support for faculty having difficulty either with the English language or with academic research expectations, the program ran into the issue of targeting particular writers; this particularism, which was equated to a form of deficiency, was rendered more visible through this program. Despite such limitations, Jerskey's (2013) experiment is a model that can expand to various situations when applied well. One additional example is dissertation boot camps and programs, such as the National Center for Faculty Development and Diversity (NCFDD), that create networks for writing and publishing, develop mentorship programs, establish writing groups, as well as teach time management and psychoemotional coaching. A literacy brokers program, as Jerskey (2013) implemented, can serve not just for multilingual faculty but also for other writing groups. I see such a program implemented in schools that are creating partnerships with schools abroad, in writing classrooms with traditional and non-traditional students, multilingual, or immigrant students, or in service-learning classes that connect academic settings to other organizations and businesses.

Finally, the impact of classroom-based literacies remains limited unless we envision them as enduring, emotioned discourses developed through everyday practices. This means that literacy in the classroom must transcend the classroom space, a move reflected in scholarship on transfer, writing for the public, or community-based research and pedagogy. My proposal here suggests that points of affinity developed by immigrants as they craft texts are persistent and resilient; each participant in this study had the ability to remember the writing in the context of immigrants across cultural contexts and after many years because it was marked by powerful emotions or connected to affinity groups. If we tap into literacy as affinity's potential to elicit those affinities in students as well, I believe we can engage the entire personhood in the learning process. And if the entire personhood is involved in the learning, it leads to sustainability and long-lasting impact.

Sharon Crowley (2006) explains that "Affective influence depends on whether the experience is elaborated or punctuated" (84). Crowley (2006) further defines elaborated experience as one that is attached to "experiences and memories" (85). With this definition, we can envision literacy as an experience that connects people to other experiences. Affinities and emotions emphasize relationality and support in developing new concepts through connections. More than understanding literacy as affinity for the individual is seeing its potential to connect the individual to other contexts of learning beyond the classroom—communities, families, geopolitical spaces of nation-states, ethnic enclaves, and so on. All these spaces are imbued with values and belief systems that shape literacy development and literacy education at any given moment. Thus, literacy as affinity provides a sustainable frame for learning and research by engaging larger communities and partnerships that reach beyond formal sites of learning. Literacy as affinity, then, is about sustainability and lifelong learning as much as it is about transforming gaps into opportunities for knowledge making.

In times of economic instability and political reorientation of nation-states toward safeguarding national sovereignty, it may prove challenging to affirm multiple forms of belonging and the transnational turn. Yet, I maintain that a transnational approach gives us a analytical lens, helping to reassess taken-for-granted epistemologies and practices. In other words, transnational research has the potential to reactivate critical inquiry in areas that remained sedimented or uninterrogated. Histories of writing, for instance, take different trajectories than those rooted in the Harvard freshman composition course of 1874 or developed dialectically with other branches of the English department at US institutions (Berlin 1987). Xiaoye You's (2010) book *Writing in the Devil's Tongue* provides a history of writing in China and, in doing so, reveals myriad ways in which writing is shaped by national and transnational conditions. Jay Jordan's (2022) analysis of cross-border education in *Grounded Literacies* also brings forth the necessity of numerous contextualizations whether they are national, academic, personal or collective, without which one cannot grasp the complexities of the learning experience.

A transnational approach that foregrounds personal stories and literacy as affinity is also needed in the current socio-economic and political landscape because, as my introduction shows, our lives have been ravished by traumatic experiences. These traumatic happenings have intensified significantly in the last few years through pandemics, wars and forced expatriation, territorial invasion and unfathomable human loss, weather devastations and more. Because literacy as affinity challenges us to rethink writing through emotions and personal experience, it becomes a necessary frame in such contexts of persistent suffering, loss, and economic or political changes.

Literacy as affinity is built on the premise of empathy. It is in fact an exercise in empathy, which is why it is nearly impossible to profess literacy as affinity while one routinely practices a discourse of individual or collective self-preservation. This book encourages one to engage the heart, and to do so persistently until we build intimate affinity with another.

Appendix A

This overview of textbook revisions highlighted in chapter 4 addresses the inclusion of specific texts with rich patriotic or ideological content (from CC of PCR, Propaganda and Agitation Section, File 37/ 1988).

Table Appendix A

Textbooks	Revisions
The *ABC* (last revised in 1970)	p. 8: Comrade Nicolae Ceaușescu and Elena Ceaușescu should be in color, from a more recent period (where pioneers and the country's hawks should appear) p. 9: the image of the opening festivity of the school: the sky should be colored in blue and the school yard should be paved
Reading, Second grade (last revised in 1979)	More poems included to be dedicated to patria and the party and Nicolae Ceaușescu: "Song to Comrade Nicolae Ceaușescu" "To comrade Elena Ceaușescu" "Romanian Voice" Revise the section "Knowledge about nature"
Reading, Third grade	Inclusion of more significant texts: "How the fall begins," "Work is dear to us," "From the lives of Dacians" "The Wars of Trajan and Decebal" "The Hands" "The Story of the 'Country's Hawks'"

Appendix A

Romanian, Fourth grade (last revised in 1979)	Similar to second grade but it should include texts concerning industry and agriculture and the new life of people in towns and villages poems for Nicolae Ceaușescu "Nicolae Ceaușescu's Epoch," "Song," "The Supreme Oath."
Romanian, Fifth grade (last revised in 1983)	Old texts: "The Spring's Guests" (V. Alecsandri), "Memories from my Boyhood" (I. Creangă), "My Country" (I. Nenițescu), "The Chicken" (I.Al. Brătescu-Voinești), "Mr. Trandafir" (M. Sadoveanu) New texts: "As a Boy I Was Roaming the Forests" (M. Eminescu), "Brother Ioane" (T. Arghezi), "Seen from the Moon" (Z. Stancu), "The Battle at the High Bridge" (N. Iorga)
Romanian, Sixth grade (last revised in 1983)	New exercises of composition included with the main literary texts and supplemental readings. Some valuable texts already included: "Our Patria" (G. Coșbuc), "Our Language" (Alexe Mateevici), "Winter" (V. Alecsandri), "Sobiesky and the Romanians" (C. Negruzzi) New texts: "Letter III" (M. Eminescu), "To my Country" (V. Voiculescu), "Song to Michael the Great"
Romanian, Seventh grade (last revised in 1975 and 1977)	Existent literary texts with rich patriotic-educational content: "The Party, Ceaușescu, Romania" (Alexandru Andrițoiu), "The Party" (N. Labiș), "History of Michael the Great" (fragment by N. Iorga), "The Country" (Z. Stancu), "The Field of Liberty" (St. O. Iosif)
Romanian, Eighth grade (last revised in 1975 and 1977)	The change will involve two textbooks: one for literary texts and one for grammar. Both the structure and the conception, as well as the content of the textbooks will be superior to the previous one in its patriotic-educative value. The purpose of this textbook is to be a synthesis of all previous work, as an end of a segment. Emphasis is on writing in various diverse situations of the school life and adult life. Study of grammar and vocabulary will be emphasized, especially the cultivation and perfection of expression in the Romanian language.

Appendix B

Table Appendix B. A Sample of the Interviews with Key Themes and Notes

Name/ Pseudonym	Background Info	Themes	Comments
1. M.C.: higher ed; transcript finished	College professional skills came through job opportunity and family reunification	- Passion for books and knowledge -A library (bought books from Romania) -Reads and writes blogs	- I need to ask for his maps/ journals? from RO - I need to look at blogs
Name/ Pseudonym	**Background Info**	**Themes**	**Comments**
2. Laura: higher ed; downward mobility; transcript finished	- College: Romanian/ French - Temporarily downward mobility (bec. of visa status) - Working as a tutor for a family (private educator) - Mobility through Canada (knowledge of French/ higher ed and Canadian system open to high skilled immigrants)	- Skill transfer: Romanian language teaching in a Romanian community in Chicago - Transfer of knowledge/ adapting it to new needs - Becomes a mediator/advocator for legal papers/ ways to stay in status, by advertising a school	- I need to ask for syllabus for the Romanian language class
Name/ Pseudonym	**Background Info**	**Themes**	**Comments**
3. Ema P.: (higher ed) transcript finished	- College: French/journalism - Purpose: pursue MA degree in French lang/ lit - Mobility through knowledge of French/ some friend's connections - Work similar to RO/teaches French	- Use of French to compensate for what she thinks is deficiency in English (felt silent; unable to communicate at the beginning) - Disciplinary alternative: journalism as a practice of freedom from imposed rules in writing	

Appendix B

Name/ Pseudonym	Background Info	Themes	Comments
4. Luci S.: downward mobility transcript finished	-College: higher education; engineer degree in RO; not used in the US. downward mobility because of English language proficiency? leaves RO with family who filed for papers for all family members; religious asylum	- Issue of downward/upward mobility (not transferable the notion of a particular social class) - Family as a source of mobility - Learning language based on reading skills acquired in RO; reread religious novels in English to learn vocabulary - Literacy intermediaries/ brokers (mentions help from church members)	Q: Has she ever considered using her previous degree in engineering here?

Name/ Pseudonym	Background Info	Themes	Comments
5. Ioan P.: transcript finished	- Green card lottery - A friend sponsored him, but then left to Europe. - Hard: no brokering	-Diversity through multiculturalism - Reads world literature: cosmopolitan -Taxi driver: writes blogs about his life as a taxi driver in Chicago ("the client of the day") - "Speaking American": we don't share the same language; "We don't have a common language, we don't have the same stuff to discuss, and I can't say I don't adhere to their way of thinking, it's simply that they talk about the same stuff, use the same words, and the same intonation."	Quotes: "[Job application process is] much more fluff. You must emphasize things that seem normal, that anyone should do." "Speaking your mind not valued: speaking your mind in a positive way, at the moment when someone is willing to listen, not when you want;" he doesn't like the fake. "people are not what they appear to be. It's an image thing; here the image is very important; people smiling in the streets. When you start talking to people, they change, their expressions. They are finished. A European way of thinking."

Name/ Pseudonym	Background Info	Themes	Comments
6. Octavian C.: transcript finished	- Leader in the Romanian community - politically involved	-"You have to forget who you were" - Downward mobility - Learning language on his own - Man brings the bread, the wife goes to school - Learning language on the job - Points to multilingualism in Romania (Hungarian, Serbian, Czech) - Writing (absent): considers himself semiliterate	

Appendix B

Name/ Pseudonym	Background Info	Themes	Comments
7. Valentin. P.: transcript finished	- Pastor	- Has extensive historical knowledge about churches and relationship to language and culture - Information about the first immigrants, his grandparents and the American way of life at the beginning of the 20th century - First Baptist Church in 1967–68 spoke only English. - Language and job church significant site for culture maintenance	- First immigrants: spoke in regional dialects rather than standard Romanian. - Some barely spoke English at all - Language and culture "refreshed" with the new immigrant wave in the 70s and 80s.

Name/ Pseudonym	Background Info	Themes	Comments
8. Steven B.: business adm; associate degree transcript finished	-Came to the US with family - Stripped of Romanian citizenship - House was seized and sealed by Communist authorities; forced to leave the country - Details about the journey, refugee camps in Italy	- Love for books- constant and inspired by a teacher (elementary or middle school) - Builds a library in RO, and then gradually has his books shipped to the US. - Builds library in Cleveland, then in Chicago. Key point: Literacy brokers (his work as a paralegal) mediates between refugees and lawyers - Becomes the spokesman and representative of the Romanian community (initiates the Romanian American network, Romanian-American publishing house, Romanian-American newspaper, *The Romanian Tribune*)	Important investigation: literacy brokers (turning a personal story into a legal document that will make one eligible for citizenship) - Investigate refugee organizations and stories/letters sent from refugee camps

Name/ Pseudonym	Background Info	Themes	Comments
9. Aron D.: unfinished ed.; self-employed transcript finished	-Escaped Communism unique narrative with various details about his escape	Storyteller - His "escape story" amazing example of a literacy event/historical event (Notes: use of present tense, introduces characters in his story, explains their role, orchestrates events, etc.) - He wants to share his story in other contexts too - Entrepreneur type - Literacy mediator? he becomes his own advocator (in court)	

Appendix B

Name/ Pseudonym	Background Info	Themes	Comments
10. Diana: higher ed; downward mobility transcript finished	- Works in an office/ administration - With college degree	- Writing her personal story: "Refusal to live in Romania" - Books as a way of investing in "interior life" in contrast with money-driven work space	

Notes

Introduction: From Warzone to Natural Disasters

1. Presidential Proclamation of March 14, 2020: https://trumpwhitehouse
.archives.gov/presidential-actions/proclamation-suspension-entry-immigrants
-nonimmigrants-certain-additional-persons-pose-risk-transmitting-coronavi
rus-2/

2. See Kate Viera, Rebecca Lorimer Leonard, Kaia Simon, Eileen Lagman, John Duffy, Juan Guerra, Ralph Cintron, etc.

3. I am referring here to labor agreements between the US and Mexico
such as the Bracero Program of 1942.

4. Graham Smart, "Writing and the Social Formation of Economy."

5. Smart, "Writing and the Social Formation of Economy."

6. Anthropologist Goody explains that writing was primarily "invested
and practiced" for economic activity. While some critics have pointed to the
original uses of writing in the temple, Goody argues that even in that setting (the
temple), writing was used for economic activity.

7. For more information about the complexities of empathy, see Ann Jurecic's (2011) discussion of the contradictory views of literary and medical hu-
manists relative to the post-humanist affect theorists. While the former sees the
potential of empathy for transformation, the latter problematizes empathy as a
source of political power.

8. After the book signing event, Horia Dicher became a participant in my

study. His book, *Earthly Manuscripts: Baroque Journal* was published in Romania in 2011 by the Niculescu Publishing House, a Romanian press. In this book, Dicher relates personal experiences from childhood to adulthood, oscillating "like an electron," as he explains, between his Romania and the Atlantic shore.

9. At the Romanian National Archives, I examined the files from the Archival Fund of the Central Committee of the Romanian Communist Party: Chancellery: file 76/1979; Propaganda and Agitation: files 2/1975, 1/1977, 1/1977, 35/1982, 21/1984, 13/1985, 1/1989; Gabanyi Collection: files 15/1974, 110/1981–1984, 150/1987, 221/1987.

10. A sample of my grounded coding is included in Appendix B.

11. A further, in-depth exploration of my choice of this term "broker" has been discussed and explained in chapter 1, the section titled "Definitions and Implications of Literacy Brokers and Co-brokering"

12. I refer to languages of nation-states and institutions in the same way that John Duffy uses the term rhetorics to denote "languages of governments, schools, media"—general frames of language and discourse wherein the individual operates. The plural form of rhetorics is used to suggest more than "a single, coherent, all-unifying 'rhetoric'" (Duffy 2007, 15).

13. MFN was an economic agreement given by the US to a particular state. The benefits emerging from this special status included special trade rates, with Romania exporting goods of almost one billion dollars worth and importing about $300 million of American goods (Gwertzman 1986).

14. The history of immigration shows a clear and complex interconnectedness of ethnicity and race as categories of difference, often considered innate. The history of immigration also shows the use of these categories as basis for exclusion: the 1857 *Dred Scott* Supreme Court decision barring people of African descent from citizenship; the Immigration Act of 1882 excluding Chinese immigrants; or the discriminatory quota system of 1924 based on national origin.

Chapter 1. The Transnational Turn in Literacy Studies

Epigraph: Minnix 2017, 76.

1. There has been an increased number of studies or recent edited collections focused on transnational work. See for instance *Mobility Work in Composition*, edited by Bruce Horner, Megan Faver Hartline, Ashanka Kumari, and Laura Sceniak Matravers, a collection that proposes the mobility paradigm as the norm. The collection also summarizes recent work on mobility.

2. The change of name from Immigration and Naturalization Service (INS) to Citizenship and Immigration Services (CIS) occurred in 2003 with the new restructuring of various offices and departments. Currently, the Department of Homeland Security (DHS)—established formally with the enactment of the Homeland Security Act in November 2002—includes three refashioned

divisions: the CIS or USCIS, US Immigration and Customs Enforcement (ICE), and US Customs and Border Protection (CBP). Some of these units were formally included under INS.

3. I mention both studies on affect and on emotions, but my work is focused on emotions, not affect. Because I do not examine bodies in action and the affect built in this movement, I do not rely on studies on affect. At times, these studies include emotions, which is why I referenced them here.

Chapter 2. Literacy Brokers in the Community

1. Generally, US historians and social scientists call this period late socialism. I follow the example of scholars in Writing Studies (e.g., Prendergast 2008) in using as much as possible the language of the participants in the study, who with no exception, refer to this period as the Communist regime.

2. I'm in debt to Kate Vieira for this term and her valuable feedback.

3. I distinguish here between initial sampling and theoretical sampling in accordance with grounded theory (Charmaz 2006). Theoretical sampling is informed by ongoing data analysis and emergent themes.

4. All the primary documents used in this chapter are part of special collection, the Gabanyi collection found at the National Archives in Bucharest, Romania. Anneli Ute Gabanyi, a Romanian of German heritage, was a researcher and head of the Romanian Research Department. Regarding her role as a researcher, Gabanyi explained "the researchers wrote the so-called Situation Reports and Backgrounds Reports in English. These reports were read and quoted by academics, governments, and major newspaper editors worldwide." (Anneli Ute Gabanyi pers. comm., October 20, 2022)

5. Archival documents from Radio Free Europe attest the United States often pressured Romania to release a number of Jewish people, German minorities, and religiously-persecuted groups, in exchange for a renewal of Most Favored Nation status (Gwertzman 1986).

6. I understand the use of qualifications similar to Sally Engle Merry's (2011) discussion of indicators in human rights rhetoric. Engle describes indicators as mechanisms of control where the governance is shifted from the nation-state to the individual. Similarly, qualifications are taken as "the rule of law," and rarely is there an investigation about the process involved into producing such categories and their intended goals.

7. The Romanian word is "subințeles," which basically means a meaning that is hidden underneath. It is not the same as double meaning. In the "underneath" meaning, there is that sense of covert, hidden meaning which is not captured by "double meaning."

Chapter 3. Economies of Writing

1. The terminology that I reference here (economies of writing) is derived

from scholarship that I surveyed which includes: political economies employed in the 2016 *CCC* special issue with a focus on neoliberal policies and labor conditions (e.g., Abraham, Scott, Soliday and Trainor); economies of writing referenced in the 2017 edited collection *Economies of Writing: Reevaluations in Rhetoric and Composition* where authors interrogate the capitalist frame as "monolith" and aim to unsettle economic governmentalities; and, economic frames explored in Edwards' comprehensive evaluation of our field's deployment and exploration of economic terminology and economic scholarship. Additional articles that I cited throughout the book and this chapter use either one of the above listed terminology.

2. A version of this chapter was previously published as an article in *CCC*, vol. 73(3), in 2022.

3. Hidden transcripts will be discussed later in the chapter. Its core definition comes from J. Scott in *Domination*, where he explains hidden transcript as a "behind the scenes" practice, a "critique of power spoken behind the back of the dominant" (xii).

4. In "Diverse Economies," Gibson-Graham introduce a diverse economy framework by referring to transactions, labor, and enterprises. Some of these activities are placed under market or alternative market; some are capitalist or alternative capitalist, while other involve pay, alternative pay, or no payment at all. (See Figure 1: A diverse economy on p. 616).

5. For more information on neoliberal markets, see Giroux's "Neoliberalism and the Demise of Democracy." A brief definition posits that neoliberalism organizes all economic, social and political matters on market, profit-driven principles. Transnational corporations control the power of capital, and the government—previously invested in the public good, social responsibility, etc.—is now concerned with the empowerment of transnational enterprises (e.g. the World Trade Organization (WTO), the International Monetary Fund (IMF), etc.).

6. In *Cosmologies of Credit*, Julie Chu calls the "file self" the collection of forms and official papers, the "bureaucratic paper trail" that bound people's socioeconomic and political lives (p. 62).

7. In his article theorizing "alternative economies," Healy (2020) identifies some limitations with the term "alternative," namely that it is inherently positioned against a mainstream, normative economy. The implication derived from this is that alternative economic frames will remain volatile and as Healy explains, "weak." While I use occasionally the term "alternative" to acknowledge the scholarship that has influenced my work and cite it accordingly, the most adequate term for my study is "informal economies" that develop in conjunction with dominant, official economic frames. My ethnographic data shows this interplay between informal and formal worlds, between unofficial and official discursive practices.

8. In my use of the term "agency," I rely on Cooper's work who conceptualizes agency as not necessarily an expression of a conscious agent. Rather, Cooper sees agency as emerging from an interplay of "emotions, intentions, actions, meanings, memories, dispositions, and narratives" (430). For Cooper, knowledge derived from one's lived experience shapes the rhetor's action whether consciously or not.

9. Different than *emotional*, I use *emotioned* as defined by Jennifer Trainor (2008) to point to the "related dynamics of lived affective experiences, emotional regulation taking place through institutional and cultural practices, and language" (85).

Chapter 4. Iron-Cast Literacies and the Role of the Authoritarian State as a Literacy Broker

Epigraph: Arnove and Graff 1987, 7.

1. I use the Party in singular to refer to the Romanian Communist Party (RCP) and since there was only one functional Party, I will only occasionally refer to it as the RCP.

2. Both translations are a good rendition of the Romanian term, *patria*. Yet, I wish to emphasize that "fatherland" connotes a patriarchal ancestry and lineage, which represented mainly the rhetoric of the Communist Party and its attempt to establish the legitimacy of the Romanian nation. I also use *patria* to establish the semantic connection between *patria* and "patriotic" work.

3. In proposing this strategy focused on history, context, and problem, Gilyard is citing the work of Bernard Bell (Gilyard 2023, 23).

4. In official documents of the Central Committee, the Propaganda and Agitation Section, the plenary meeting minutes offer specific details about how to organize the festival, and how to involve workers, students, and all citizens in this mass festival.

5. In *Comrades No More*, De Nevers (2003) explains that under Ceaușescu, socialism was only "nominally" present, highly centralized, but rather than collective, it was a "one-man dictatorship" (243). Verdery (1991) takes a more sophisticated approach to why, in Romania, socialism merged with nationalism. After an overview of explanations proposed by various scholars, Verdery suggests that in addition to subtracting Romania from a Russian monopoly that has always been somewhat resented in Romania, even under Gheorghiu-Dej, the discourse of the nation has always been a home discourse, deeply ingrained in the Romanian ethos (125).

6. I take this position based on what my participants expressed about these practices. Mr. Doru, for instance, explained, "There were meetings, and you had to say something there, to 'kiss their a—.' You had to praise the leaders and so forth. I was a member and I participated. I can't deny that."

7. When I first introduced "patria," I provided two possible translations:

motherland or fatherland. Grammatically, motherland would be a fitting translation for patria because they are both feminine gender nouns. However, semantically and thematically, fatherland works best at times because Ceaușescu often positioned himself as the father or parent of the nation.

Chapter 5. Teachers and Shifting Ideological Positions

1. For a more detailed discussion about the role of Orthodoxy in the formation of national identity, see Verdery (1991), Boia (2001a), but also Hitchins' (2003) *The Identity of Romania*.

Chapter 6. Librarians and Scholars as Brokers of Information in Literacy Research

1. The Library of the Academy has a long-standing tradition for guarding cultural texts and manuscripts, and in doing so, has been elitist and exclusionary in its practices.

2. While there have been many changes concerning the National Archives of Romania, after January 2007, there is an urgent need to archive related legislation in Romania (Law 14/1996- the Archives Law) especially as it relates to facilitating access to documents, simplifying procedures, and as explained on the National Archives website, "confining abuse due to the personal subjectivity of the public workers and institutional dysfunctionalities." (http://www.arhive lenationale.ro/images/custom/image/Pdf-uri/Proectul_Legii_Arhivelor.pdf)

3. In reference to Communism in Romania, Lucian Boia argues that doublethink and doubletalk are some of most problematic legacies of Communism (2001b, 140).

4. Dr. Hitchins was one of the first American scholars to have conducted research in Romania during the Cold War period, and his scholarship has been highly recognized nationally and internationally.

References

Ahmed, Sara. 2004. *The Cultural Politics of Emotion.* Routledge, New York: Routledge.

Andrzejewski, Julie, and John Alessio. 1999. "Education for Global Citizenship and Social Responsibility." *Progressive Perspectives* 1(2): 2–19. Accessed from University of Vermont, College of Education and Social Services, John Dewey Project on Progressive Education.

Anghelescu, Hermina GB. 2000. *Public Libraries in Modern and Contemporary Romania: Legacy of French Patterns and Soviet Influences, 1830–1990.* Ph.D. Dissertation. The University of Texas at Austin, ProQuest Dissertations and Theses.

Apple, Michael W. 1988. *Teachers and Texts: A Political Economy of Class and Gender Relations in Education.* New York: Routledge.

Arnove, Robert F., and Harvey J. Graff, eds. 1987. *National Literacy Campaigns: Historical and Comparative Perspectives.* New York: Science+Business Media.

Bakhtin, M.M. 1981. *The Dialogic Imagination: Four Essays by M. M. Bakhtin.* Edited by Michael Holquist. Translated by Caryl Emerson and Michael Holquist. Austin: University of Texas Press.

Bartholomae, David. 1995. "Writing with Teachers: A Conversation with Peter Elbow." *College Composition and Communication* 46(1): 62–71.

Bauman, Zygmunt. 1998. *Globalization: The Human Consequences.* New York: Columbia University Press.

References

Baynham, Mike. 1993. "Code Switching and Mode Switching: Community Interpreters and Mediators of Literacy." In *Cross-Cultural Approaches to Literacy*, edited by Brian Street, 294–314. Cambridge: Cambridge University Press.

Baynham, Mike, and Helen Lobanga Masing. 2001. "Mediation and Mediators in Multilingual Literacy Events." In *Multilingual Literacies: Reading and Writing Different Worlds*, edited by Marilyn Martin-Jones and Kathryn E. Jones, 189–208. Amsterdam: John Benjamins.

Berlin, James. 1987. *Rhetoric and Reality: Writing Instruction in American Colleges, 1900–1985.* Carbondale: Southern Illinois University Press.

Bertaux, Daniel. 1981. *Biography and Society: The Life History Approach to the Social Sciences.* Beverly Hills: Sage Publications, Inc.

Bertaux, Daniel, and Martin Kohli. 1984. "The Life Story Approach: A Continental View." *Annual Review of Sociology, 10,* 215–37.

Blommaert, Jan. 2010. *The Sociolinguistics of Globalization.* Cambridge: Cambridge University Press.

Boia, Lucian. 2001a. *History and Myth in Romanian Consciousness.* Translated by James Christian Brown. Budapest: Central European University Press.

Boia, Lucian. 2001b. *Romania: Borderland of Europe.* London: Reaktion Books.

Boler, Megan. 1999. *Feeling Power: Emotions and Education.* London: Routledge.

Boym, Svetlana. 2010. *Another Freedom: The Alternative History of an Idea.* Chicago: University of Chicago Press.

Brandt, Deborah. 1995. "Accumulating Literacy: Writing and Learning to Write in the Twentieth Century." *College English* 57(6): 649–68.

Brandt, Deborah. 1998. "Sponsors of Literacy." *College Composition and Communication* 49(2):165–85.

Brandt, Deborah. 2001. *Literacy in American Lives.* New York: Cambridge University Press.

Brandt, Deborah, and Katie Clinton. 2002. "Limits of the Local: Expanding Perspectives on Literacy as a Social Practice." *Journal of Literacy Research* 34(3): 337–56. https://doi.org/10.1207/s15548430jlr3403_4

Brandt, Deborah. 2005. "Writing for a Living: Literacy and the Knowledge Economy." *Written Communication* 22(2): 166–97.

Briggs, Laura, McCormick, Gladys, and J.T. Way. 2008. "Transnationalism: A Category of Analysis." *American Quarterly* 60(3): 625–48.

Burke, Kenneth. 1950. *A Rhetoric of Motives.* Berkeley: University of California Press.

Canagarajah, Suresh A. 2002. *A Geopolitics of Academic Writing.* Pittsburgh: University of Pittsburgh Press.

Canagarajah, Suresh A. 2006. "The Place of World Englishes in Composition: Pluralization Continued." *College Composition and Communication* 57(4), 586–619.

References

Cintron, Ralph. 1993. "Wearing a Pith Helmet at a Sly Angle: Or, Can Writing Researchers do Ethnography in a Postmodern Era?" *Written Communication* 10(3), 371–412.

Charmaz, Kathy C. 2006. *Constructing Ground Theory: A Practical Guide through Qualitative Analysis.* London: SAGE.

Chu, Julie. 2010. *Cosmologies of Credit: Transnational Mobility and the Politics of Destination in China.* Duke University Press.

Crawford, Ilene Whitney. 2010. "Growing Routes: Rhetoric as the Study and Practice of Movement." In *Rhetorica in Motion: Feminist Rhetorical Methods and Methodologies,* edited by Eileen E. Schell and K. J. Rawson, 71–85. Pittsburgh: University of Pittsburgh Press.

Crowley, Sharon. 2006. *Toward a Civil Discourse: Rhetoric and Fundamentalism.* Pittsburgh: University of Pittsburgh Press.

Cushman, Ellen. 1998. *The Struggle and the Tools: Oral and Literate Strategies in an Inner City Community.* Albany: State University of New York Press.

De Nevers, Renée. 2003. *Comrades No More: The Seeds of Change in Eastern Europe.* Cambridge: The MIT Press.

Dicher, Horia. 2011. *Earthy Manuscripts: Baroque Journal.* Bucharest, Romania: Niculescu Press.

Documents of the Romanian Communist Party. 1972. *The Development and the Perfecting of Teaching/Instruction.* Bucuresti, Romania: Politica Press.

Donahue, Christiane. 2009. ""Internationalization" and Composition Studies: Reorienting the Discourse." *College Composition and Communication* 61(2): 212–43.

Duffy, John M. 2007. *Writing from These Roots: Literacy in a Hmong-American Community.* Honolulu: University of Hawai'i Press.

Dumitrescu, Iulian. 2011. "Saxons from Communist Romania, Sold to Germany." *Ziare,* April 19, 2011. Accessed March 20, 2022. https://ziare.com/europa/germania/sasii-din-romania-comunista-vanduti-germaniei-1089215

Edwards, Mike. 2014. "Economies of Writing, without the Economics: Some Implications of Composition's Economic Discourse as Represented in *JAC* 32.3–4." *Rhetoric Review:* 33(3): 244–61.

Elbow, Peter. 1995. "Being a Writer vs. Being an Academic: A Conflict in Goals." *College Composition and Communication* 46(1): 72–83.

Fitzpatrick, Sheila. 2001. "Making a Self for the Times: Impersonation and Imposture in 20th Century Russia." *Kritika: Explorations in Russian and Eurasian History* 2(3): 469–87.

Follis, Karolina S. 2012. *Building Fortress Europe: The Polish-Ukrainian Fontier.* Philadelphia: University of Pennsylvania Press.

Foner, Nancy and George M. Fredrickson. 2004. "Immigration, Race, and Ethnicity in the United States: Social Constructions and Social Relations in Historical and Contemporary Perspective." In *Not Just Black and White:*

References

Historical and Contemporary Perspectives on Immigration, Race, and Ethnicity in the United States, edited by Nancy Foner and George M. Fredrickson, 1–22. Russell Sage Foundation.

Frost, Alanna. 2011. "Literacy Stewardship: Dakelh Women Composing Culture." *College Composition and Communication* 63(1): 54–74.

Galiş, George. 2013. "A Look Back . . . the Arrival in the U.S." In *Philadelphia: An Open Door for You, 40thAnniversary*, edited by Florin T. Cîmpean and Ilie U. Tomuța, 28–32. Niles: Center Focus Publishing.

Gibson-Graham, J.K. 1996/2006. *The End of Capitalism (As We Knew It): A Feminist Critique of Political Economy*. Minneapolis: University of Minnesota Press.

Gibson-Graham, J.K. 2008. "Diverse Economies: Performative Practices for Other Worlds." *Progress in Human Geography* 32(5): 613–32.

Gilmore, Hannah. 2022. "Pushing Anti-Immigrant Agendas: An Analysis of US Refugees Policy." *The Internationalist* VII(II): 42–53.

Gilyard, Keith. 2023. "On the Sematic Borders of White Nationalism." In *Writing on the Wall: Writing Education and Resistance to Isolationism*, edited by David S. Martins, Brooke S. Schreiber, and Xiaoye You, 19–30. Utah State University Press.

Giroux, Henry A. 2004. "Neoliberalism and the Demise of Democracy: Resurrecting Hope in Dark Times." *Dissent Voice*. Accessed November 2022. http://dissidentvoice.org/Aug04/Giroux0807.htm.

Goody, Jack. 1986. *The Logic of Writing and the Organization of Society*. Cambridge, England: Cambridge University Press.

Graff, Harvey. 1987. *The Labyrinths of Literacy: Reflections on Literacy Past and Present*. Pittsburgh: University of Pittsburgh Press.

Guerra, Juan C. 1998. *Close to Home: Oral and Literate Practices in a Transnational Mexicano Community*. Teachers College Press.

Gwertzman, Bernard. 1986. "Rumania to Allow More Than 1,000 to Emigrate." *The New York Times*, June 3, 1986. Gabanyi Collection: File 220/1986–1987. National Archives of Romania, Bucharest, Romania.

Hardt, Michael. 1999. "Affective Labor." *Boundary* 26(2): 89–100.

Hawisher, Gail E., Selfe, Cindy. L, Guo, Yi-Huey, and Lu Liu. 2006. "Globalization and Agency: Designing and Redesigning the Literacies of Cyberspace." *College English* 68(6): 619–36.

Healy, Stephen. 2020. "Alternative Economies." In *International Encyclopedia of Human Geography* 2nd edition, edited by Audrey Kobayashi, 111–17. https://doi.org/10.1016/B978-0-08-102295-5.10049-6.

Heclo, Hugh. 2008. *On Thinking Institutionally*. Boulder: Oxford University Press.

Hellback, Jochen. 2006. *Revolution in my Mind: Writing a Diary under Stalin*. Cambridge: Harvard University Press.

Henţea, Călin. 2011. ""The Song of Romania," Literary Group "The Flame," and the Group "You:" Propagandistic Potpourri, the Illusion of Freedom,

References

and the "Lizard" Student. *Historia*, Issue 112, 41–4. (Translated from Romanian)

Hesford, Wendy S. 2006. "Global Turns and Cautions in Rhetoric and Composition Studies." *PMLA* 121(3): 787–801.

Hesford, Wendy S. and Eileen E. Schell. 2008. "Introduction: Configurations of Transnationality: Locating Feminist Rhetorics." *College English* 70(5): 461–70.

Himmelweit, Susan. 2002. "Making Visible the Hidden Economy: The Case for Gender-Impact Analysis of Economic Policy." *Feminist Economics* 8(1): 49–70.

Hitchins, Keith. 2003. *The Identity of Romania*. Bucharest: Encyclopaedic Pub. House.

Horner, Bruce, Lu, Min-Zhan, Royster, Jacqueline Jones, and John Trimbur. 2011. "Language Difference in Writing: Toward a Translingual Approach." *College English* 73(3): 303–21.

Horner, Bruce, NeCamp, Samantha, and Christiane Donahue. 2011. "Toward a Multilingual Composition Scholarship: From English-Only to a Translingual Norm." *College Composition and Communication* 63(2): 269–300.

Horner, Bruce and Christiane Donahue. 2022. "Introduction: Teaching and Studying Transnational Composition." In *Teaching and Studying Transnational Composition*, edited by Christiane Donahue and Bruce Horner, 8–26. Modern Language Association of America.

Hurezeanu, Emil. 1987. "The Calvary of Leaving the Country Definitively." Radio Free Europe, July 2, 1987. Gabanyi Collection, file 150/1987. Romanian National Archives, Bucharest, Romania.

Ironmonger, Duncan. 1996. "Counting Outputs, Capital Inputs and Caring Labor: Estimating Gross Household Output." *Feminist Economics* 2(3): 37–64.

Jacobs, Dale and Laura Micciche, eds. 2003. *A Way to Move: Rhetorics of Emotion and Composition Studies*. Portsmouth, NH: Heinemann.

Jerskey, Maria. 2013. "Literacy Brokers in the Contact Zone, Year 1: The Crowded Safe House." In *Literacy as Translingual Practice: Between Communities and Classrooms*, edited by Suresh Canagarajah, 197–206. New York: Routledge.

Jones, Tamara. 1983. "Desperate Romanians Wait for US Permission to Immigrate." B-Wire, November 25, 1983. Gabanyi Collection: File 216/1983–84. National Archives of Romania, Bucharest, Romania.

Jordan, Jay. 2022. *Grounded Literacies in a Transnational WAC/ WID Ecology: A Korean-US Study*. The WAC Clearinghouse; University Press of Colorado. https://doi.org/10.37514/INT-B.2022.1503

Jurecic, Ann. 2011. "Empathy and the Critic." *College English* 74(1): 10–27.

Juzwik, Mary. 2004. "Towards an Ethics of Answerability: Reconsidering Di-

References

alogism in Sociocultural Literacy." *College Composition and Communication* 55(3): 536–67.

Kalman, Judy. 1999. *Writing on the Plaza: Mediated Literacy Practice among Scribes and Clients in Mexico City*. Cresskill: Hampton Press.

Karlberg, Michael. 2010. "Education for Interdependence: The University and the Global Citizen." *The Global Studies Journal* 3(1): 129–38.

Kearney, M. 1995. "The Local and the Global: The Anthropology of Globalization and Transnationalism." *Annual Review of Anthropology* 24: 547–65.

Kell, Catherine. 2011. "Inequalities and Crossings." *International Journal of Educational Development* 31: 606–13

Kell, Catherine. 2017. "Traveling Texts, Translocal/Transnational Literacies, and Transcontextual Analysis." In *The Routledge Handbook of Migration and Language*, edited by Suresh Canagarajah, 413–30. New York: Routledge.

Kligman, Gail. 1990. "Reclaiming the Public: A Reflection on Creating Civil Society in Romania." *East European Politics and Societies* 4: 393–438.

Kligman, Gail, and Katherine Verdery. 2011. *Peasants under Siege: The Collectivization of Romanian Agriculture, 1949–1962*. Princeton: Princeton University Press.

Kotkin, Stephen. 1995. *Magnetic Mountain: Stalinism as a Civilization*. Berkeley and Los Angeles: University of California Press.

Lagman, Eileen. 2018. "Literacy Remains: Loss and Affects in Transnational Literacies." *College English* 81(1): 27–49.

Lanham, Richard A. 2003. *Analyzing Prose*. 2nd ed. London/New York: Continuum.

Lillis, Theresa and Mary Jane Curry. 2006. "Professional Academic Writing by Multilingual Writers: Interactions with Literacy Brokers in the Production of English-medium Texts." *Written Communication* 23(1): 3–35.

Lindquist, Julie. 2004. "Class Affects, Classroom Affectations: Working through the Paradoxes of Strategic Empathy." *College English* 67(2): 187–209.

Lunsford, Karen. 2012. "Conducting Writing Research Internationally." In *Writing Studies Research in Practice: Methods and Methodologies,* edited by Lee Nichoson and Mary P. Sheridan, 220–30. Carbondale: Southern Illinois University Press.

Lorimer Leonard, Rebecca. 2015. "Writing through Bureaucracy: Migrant Correspondence and Managed Mobility." *Written Communication* 32(1): 87–113.

Lorimer Leonard, Rebecca. 2017. *Writing on the Move*. Pittsburgh, PA: University of Pittsburgh Press.

Lutz, Catherine A. 1990. "Engendered Emotion: Gender, Power, and the Rhetoric of Emotional Control in American Discourse." In *Languages and the Politics of Emotion*, edited by Catherine A. Lutz and Lila Abu-Lughod, 69–91. Cambridge: Cambridge University Press.

References

Martinez, Charles R., McClure, Heather H., and J. Mark Eddy. 2009. "Language Brokering Contexts and Behavioral and Emotional Adjustment among Latino Parents and Adolescents." *The Journal of Early Adolescence* 29(1): 71–98.

Martins, David S. 2023. "Writing Education across Borders, an Anti-isolationist Project." In *Writing on the Wall: Writing Education and Resistance to Isolationism*, edited by David S. Martins, Brooke S. Schreiber, and Xiaoye You, 3–18. Denver: Utah State University Press.

Massey, Doreen. 1993. "Power-Geometry and a Progressive Sense of Place." In *Mapping the Futures: Local Cultures, Global Change*, edited by Jon Bird, Barry Curtis, Tim Putnam, George Robertson, and Lisa Tickner, 59–69. London: Routledge.

Matsuda, Paul Kei. 2010. "The Myth of Linguistic Homogeneity in US College Composition." In *Cross-language Relations in Composition,* edited by Bruce Horner, Min-Zhan Lu, and Paul Kei Matsuda, 11–17. Carbondale and Edwardsville: Southern Illinois University Press.

Merry Engle, Sally. 2011. "Measuring the World: Indicators, Human rights, and Global Governance." *Current Anthropology* 52(3): S83–S95.

Micciche, Laura R. 2002. "More than a Feeling: Disappointment and WPA Work." *College English* 64(4): 432–58.

Micciche, Laura R. 2007. *Doing Emotion: Rhetoric, Writing, Teaching.* Portsmouth, NH: Heinemann.

Mihuţ, Ligia A. 2014. "Literacy Brokers and the Emotional Work of Mediation." *Literacy in Composition Studies* 2(1): 57–79.

Miller, Carolyn R. 1979. "A Humanistic Rationale for Technical Writing." *College English* 40(6): 610–17.

Miller, Holly Ventura, Ripepi, Melissa, Ernestes, Amy M., and Anthony A. Peguero. 2020. "Immigration Policy and Justice in the Era of Covid-19." *American Journal of Criminal Justice* 45(4): 793–809.

Minnix, Christopher. 2017. "'Global Scumbags': Composition's Global Turn in a Time of Fake News, Globalist Conspiracy, and Nationalistic Literacy." *Literacy in Composition Studies* 5(2): 63–83.

Moore, Patrick. 2004. "Myths about the Instrumental Discourse: A Response to Robert R. Johnson." In *Teaching Technical communication: Critical Issues for the Classroom,* edited by James M. Dubinsky, 45–61. Boston: Bedford/ St. Martin's.

Morales, Alejandra, Yakushko, Okasana F., and Antonio J. Castro, A. 2012. "Language Brokering among Mexican Immigrant Families in the Midwest: A Multiple Case Study." *The Counseling Psychologist* 40(4): 520–53.

Mungescu, Mirela Luminiţa. 2004. "Memory in Romanian History: Textbooks in the 1990s." In *Balkan Identities: Nation and Memory,* edited by Maria Todorova, 339–54. New York: New York University Press.

References

Mungiu-Pippidi, Alina. 2005. "Deconstructing Balkan Particularism: The Ambiguous Social Capital of Southeastern Europe." *Southeast European and Black Sea Studies* 5(1): 49–68.

Neagoe-Pleşa, Elis. 2008. "1968-the Year of the Secret Service's Reformation." *CNSAS (National Council for the Study of the Secret Service Archives) Notebooks* 1: 9–22.

Nordquist, Brice. 2017. *Literacy and Mobility: Complexity, Uncertainty, and Agency at the Nexus of High School and College*. New York: Routledge.

Orellana, Marjorie Faulstich, Meza, Maria, and Kate Pietsch. 2002. "Mexican Immigrant Networks and Home School Connections." *Practicing Anthropology* 24(3): 4–8.

Papen, Uta. 2010. "Literacy Mediators, Scribes or Brokers? The Central Role of Others in Accomplishing Reading and Writing." *Langage et Société* 133(3): 63–82.

Perry, Kristen H. 2009. "Genres, Contexts and Literacy Practices: Literacy Brokering among Sudanese Refugee Families." *Reading Research Quarterly* 44(3): 256–76.

Perşa, Adriana. 1998. "Ce se Urmărea prin Reforma Învăţământului." (Engl. "What was Sought In the Education Reform."). In Anul 1948: Instituţionalizarea Comunismului (Engl. *The Year 1948*: The Institutionalization of Communism), edited by Romulus Rusan, 481–82. Sighet, Romania: Civic Academy Foundation.

Popescu, Ion Longin. 2010. "Acad. Florin Constantiniu—"Clasa Politică decembristă Este cea mai Incompetentă, cea mai Lacomă si cea mai Arogantă din Istoria României." (Engl. Academician Florin Constantiniu-"The post-December Political Class is the Most Incompetent, the Greediest and the Most Arrogant in the History of Romania." *Formula As*. http://arhiva.formula-as.ro/2009/896/spectator-38/acad-florin-constantiniu-clasa-politicapostdecembrista-este-cea-mai-incompetenta-cea-mai-laco ma-si-cea-mai-aroganta-din-istoria-romaniei-11878.

Porter, Maureen, and Kathia Monard. 2001. "*Ayni* in the Global Village: Building Relationships of Reciprocity through International Service-Learning." *Michigan Journal of Community Service-Learning* 8: 5–17.

Prendergast, Catherine. 2008. *Buying into English: Language and Investment in the New Capitalist World*. Pittsburgh: University of Pittsburgh Press.

Presidential Commission for the Analysis of the Communist Dictatorship in Romania. 2006. *Final Report*. Bucharest: Office of the President. https://www.wilsoncenter.org/sites/default/files/media/documents/article/RAPORT%20FINAL_%20CADCR.pdf

"Reagan Extends MFN to Romania, Hungary, and China." 1986. B-Wire, June 4, 1986. Gabanyi Collection: File 220/1986–1987. National Archives of Romania, Bucharest, Romania.

References

Sarroub, Loukia K. 2009. "Glocalism in Literacy and Marriage in Transnational Lives." *Critical Inquiry in Language Studies* 6: 63–80.

Sassen, Saskia. 2010. "The Global Inside the National: A Research Agenda for Sociology." *Sociopedia.isa* 1:3–10.

Scott, James C. 1990. *Domination and the arts of resistance: Hidden transcripts.* New Haven: Yale University Press.

Scott, James C. 1998. *Seeing like a State: How Certain Schemes to Improve the Human Condition Have Failed.* New Haven: Yale University Press.

Scott, Tony. 2016a. "Animated by the Entrepreneurial Spirit: Austerity, Dispossession, and Composition's Last Living Act." In *Composition in the Age of Austerity*, edited by Nancy Welch and Tony Scott, 205–19. University Press of Colorado/ Utah State University Press.

Scott, Tony. 2016b. "Subverting Crisis in the Political Economy of Composition." *College Composition and Communication 68*(1): 10–37.

Second Congress of Socialist Culture and Political Education. 1982, June 24–25. Bucharest: Politica Press.

Simon, Kaia. 2019. "Translating a Path to College: Literate Resonances of Migrant Child Language Brokering." *College Composition and Communication* 71(1): 60–85.

Smart, Graham. 2008. "Writing and the Social Formation of Economy." In *Handbook of Research on Writing: History, Society, School, Individual, Text*, edited by Charles Bazerman, 103–12. Mahwah: Lawrence Erlbaum.

Shafir, Michael. 1978. "Political Culture, Intellectual Dissent and Intellectual Consent. The Case of Rumania." Research Paper No. 30. The Hebrew University of Jerusalem. The Soviet and East European Research Centre.

Symposium for the Study of Writing and Teaching Writing: Transnational Literacies. July 22–26 2013. University of Massachusetts, Amherst.

Tilinca, Mihaela E. 2006. *Academic Literacy and the Construction of Symbolic Power: A Study of one Academic Community.* Lancaster University: Dissertation.

Trainor, Jennifer Seibel. 2008. "The Emotioned Power of Racism: An Ethnographic Portrait of an All-White High School." *College Composition and Communication* 60(1): 82–112.

Trimbur, John. 2006. "Linguistic Memory and the Politics of US English." *College English* 68(6): 575–88.

Tse, Lucy. 1996. "Language Brokering in Linguistic Minority Communities: The Case of Chinese- and Vietnamese-American students." *The Bilingual Research Journal* 20(3/4): 485–98.

United States. Congress. House of Representatives. Committee on Foreign Affairs. 1987. "United States-Romania Relations and Most-Favored-Nation (MFN) Status for Romania." Washington DC: Government Printing Office. (House of Representatives Report 77–858) (Y 4.F76/1: R66/2)

United States. Dept. of Homeland Security. US Immigration and Citizenship

References

Services. "Our History." Accessed 2013, June 10, 2013. http://www.uscis.gov/about-us/our-history

United States. Dept. of Homeland Security. U.S. Immigration and Citizenship Services. n.d. "Green Card." Accessed May 2011 http://www.uscis.gov/greencard

United States. Dept. of Justice. n.d. "About the Office." Last modified June 17, 2024. http://www.justice.gov/eoir/orginfo.htm

"US Official Says Trade Favor Improved Romanian Emigration." 1987, June 24. A-Wire. Gabanyi Collection: File 150/ 1987. National Archives of Romania, Bucharest, Romania.

"US Praised and Warned on Human Rights Policy in Romania." 1984, January 10. Radio Free Europe, File 216/1983–1984. National Archives of Romania, Bucharest, Romania.

Verdery, Katherine. 1991. *National Ideology under Socialism: Identity and Cultural Politics in Ceaușescu's Romania.* Berkley and Los Angeles: University of California Press.

Verdery, Katherine. 1996. *What was Socialism and What Comes Next?* Princeton: Princeton University Press.

Vieira, Kate. 2016. *American by Paper: How Documents Matter in Immigrant Literacy.* Minnesota University Press.

Vieira, Kate. 2019. "What Happens When Texts Fly." *College English* 82(1): 77–95.

Webber, Martha. 2012. "Literacy Intermediaries and the "Voices of Women" South African National Quilt project." *Reflections* 11(2): 68–90.

Welch, Nancy, and Tony Scott. 2016. "Introduction: Composition in the Age of Austerity." In *Composition in the Age of Austerity,* edited by Nancy Welch and Tony Scott, 3–17. Boulder: Utah State University Press.

Wood, Mihaela. 2011. "Sport Histories and other Histories in the Romanian Archives." University of Illinois at Urbana-Champaign, Romanian Student Club. Presentation.

Worsham, Lynn. 1998. "Going Postal: Pedagogic Violence and the Schooling of Emotion." *Journal of Advanced Composition* 18(2): 213–45.

You, Xiaoye. 2010. *Writing in the Devil's Tongue: A History of English Composition in China.* Carbondale, IL: Southern Illinois University Press.

Zolberg, Aristide R. 1999. "Matters of State: Theorizing Immigration Policy." In *The Handbook of International Migration: the American Experience,* edited by Charles Hirschman, Philip Kasinitz, and Josh DeWind, 71–93. New York: Russell Sage Foundation.

Index

Note: Page numbers in **bold** indicate tables in the text, and references following "n" refer notes.

Index

Index

Index

Gross, J., 100

Grounded Literacies (Jordan), 155

grounded theory, 6, 19; coding categories, 13; constructivist approach to, 12–13; initial sampling *vs.* theoretical sampling, 165n3

hatâr, 97

Healy, S., 71–72, 166n7

Heclo, H., 39

Hesford, W., 20, 27

hidden transcripts, 21, 66–67, 75–78, 166n3. *See also* Scott, J.

Hitchins, K., 138, 168n4

Hmong immigrants, 150

Horner, B., 27, 91

human rights, 13–14, 40–43, 57–60. *See also* advocacy; personal stories

Hurezeanu, E., 42

identity, national, 6, 43, 96, 136. *See also* religious identity

Ideological Commission of the Central Committee, 103

ideology, everyday life, 106–15; socialist, 94, 99–101, 103

IICCMER. *See* Investigation of Communism's Crimes and the Memory of the Romanian Exile

illiteracy, 21, 94, 109

immigrant literacy, 7, 13–14, 17–18, 28–29, 35–37; non-traditional sites of education, 36; transnational approach, 27–28, 35

immigrant narratives: personal experience, 150–51, 153; stereotypes, 4–5

immigrants/immigration, 3–7, 11–18, 38, 60, 164n14; archival research, 11–14; community, 14–19;

48–51; categories, 81–86; citizenship, 13–14; economic immigrants, 67, 81–86; ethnicity, 18–19; forms (*see* immigration forms); heroic narrative of, 3–4; legal papers, 38–40; mobility and stoppages, 25–29; narratives of literacy, 150–51; political refugees, 38–40, 43–44; typological narratives of, 4; undocumented, 20; vulnerability of, 4

Immigration and Nationality Act (INA) of 1952, 42

Immigration and Naturalization Service (INS), 38–39, 48, 57–58, 164n2

immigration file, 11, 36, 38, **47**, 72, 79, 82

immigration forms, 20, 60; discursive space of, 61; filling out, 10

informal economies, 66–77, 93, 98–99, 115, 122, 124, 128, 166n7; co-brokering, 66, 80, 87; formal paths to, 67; formal *vs.*, 69–70; local, 75; and socioeconomic profiles, 95–98. *See also* political economies

INS. *See* Immigration and Naturalization Service

Interchurch Refugee Ministries, 48

Interfaith, 45

International Rescue Committee, 57

Investigation of Communism's Crimes and the Memory of the Romanian Exile (IICCMER), 132

Jerskey, M., 153–54

Jones, T., 62

Jordan, J., 155

Jurecic, A., 10

Index

Index

literacy education, 28–29, 93
literacy learning, 30, 50
loisir, theory of, 92
Lunsford, K., 133

Makarenko, A. S., 98–99, 107
market-driven economy, 66
marriage, 82–86; circumstantial,
    81–82, 83; documentation for,
    82–85; performance of, 85;
    transactions of, 83–85; Vieira's
    study on, 85–86
Martins, D., 91
Merry, S. E., 165n6
MFN. *See* Most Favored Nation
Micciche, L. R., 33, 60, 151, 152
middleman, 6–7, 9. *See also* brokers
minorities: Jewish, German, Hungar-
    ian, 41–43; 165n5
Minnix, C., 23, 27
mobility, 3, 23–24, 28–29; paradox
    of, 25; stoppages, 25–29
Monard, K., 71. *See also* Porter, M.
Moore, P., 152
Most Favored Nation (MFN), 14, 44,
    58, 164n13; impact on emigra-
    tion, 41–42; trade agreements,
    41–42
Mungiu-Pippidi, A., 134

National Archives of Romania,
    131, 132, 133, 134, 138, 164n9,
    165n4, 168n2
National Center for Faculty Develop-
    ment and Diversity (NCFDD),
    154
National Ideology under Socialism (Verd-
    ery), 99
nationalism, 27; nationalist discourse,
    91
National Library, 140, 141
National Literacy Campaigns, 94

National Peasants' Party, 128
National State Archives, 12
nation-states: control of mobility,
    23–24, 27–29; discourses, 39–40;
    Romania–US relations, 40–42
NCFDD. *See* National Center for Fac-
    ulty Development and Diversity
Nelson, J., 8–9
neoliberal market: cheap labor, 67,
    71; disposal labor, 74; Work and
    Travel program, 67, 73, 75, 80,
    81, 86
New Literacy Studies (NLS), 26, 147
non-interventionist teachers, 126–27
non-profit organizations, 17, 48; ad-
    vocacy, 38; sponsorship, 57
Nordquist, B., 25

On Institutional Thinking (Heclo), 39
Orthodox Church, 43, 121

particularism, 125, 133, 134–36
Party. *See* Romanian Communist
    Party
passports, 44, 59–60; emigration
    approvals, 121
patria, 90–93, 96, 98, 101–7, 110–12,
    118, 167n2; animating feelings
    for, poems role in, 113–15
Peasants under Siege (Kligman and
    Verdery), 121
pedagogy: emotion in classroom,
    152–53; immigrant literacies,
    153–54; writing instruction and
    affinity, 152–54
Perry, K. H., 29
personal, stories, 57–60; the personal,
    150–51; narratives, 11; stories of
    escape, 7, 11; literacy histories,
    11–13
personal spaces, 69
Philadelphia: An Open Door for You, 4

Index

Index

taxi drivers, 60, 79–80, 84

teachers, 116–28; ambivalence, 124–25; as brokers, 22, 116–17, 119–24; ideological role of, 126–28; inquisitive approach, 120; non-interventionist, 126–27; as Party members, 116–17; persecuting students, 119–20; shifting positions, 117, 119; supporting students, 122–24

textbooks, 99–101, 105, 111, 116; as ideological tools, 101–6; manipulation of, 91; revisions, 103–4, **157–58**

textual brokering, 60–64

Tismăneanu, V., 131

Trainor, J., 34, 90, 106, 167n9

transnationalism, 42, 62, 151; bi-institutional perspective, 39

transnational research, 19, 20, 130, 131, 147–48, 155

Union of Communist Youth (UCY), 107, 124–25

United Nations Convention Relating to the Status of Refugees, 42

universalism, 134–35

University of Illinois, 133–35, 138

unofficial sites, 66, 70

USCIS. *See* US Immigration and Citizenship Services

US Customs and Border Protection (CBP), 165n2

US Department of Justice, 57

US Department of State Work and Travel program, 67

US Immigration and Citizenship Services (USCIS), 31, 42

US Immigration and Customs Enforcement (ICE), 164n2

Verdery, K., 74, 100, 102, 121, 74; *National Ideology under Socialism*, 99; *Peasants under Siege*, 121; secondary economies, 97; socialism, 167n5

Vieira, K., 26, 28, 76, 83, 85–86, 165n2

visa impositions, 63, 72–75; overstayed their visa, 75; remote control, 73

Vizenor, G., 77

Wood, M., 133, 134–35, 140, 142

Work and Travel program, 67, 73, 75, 80, 81, 86

World Council of Churches, 45, 48, 57

Worsham, L., 33

Writing in the Devil's Tongue (Xiaoye You), 155

Writing on the Move (Leonard), 25, 74

You, X., 155

Zilber, H., 98